Vauban and the French Mili
Under Louis XIV

Vauban and the French Military Under Louis XIV

An Illustrated History of Fortifications and Strategies

JEAN-DENIS G. G. LEPAGE

McFarland & Company, Inc., Publishers
Jefferson, North Carolina, and London

Acknowledgments: I would like to express my gratitude for the friendly and helpful collaboration of Jeannette à Stuling, Anne Chauvel, Eltjo Jakobus De Lang and Ben Marcato, Nicole and Robert Fresse, Jan van Groningen à Stuling, Wim Wiese, Michèle Clermont, Véronique Janty, Christiane "Kiki" and Ludovic Morandeau, and Jean-Pierre Rorive. — Jean-Denis Gilbert Georges Lepage, Groningen, Fall 2009

LIBRARY OF CONGRESS CATALOGUING-IN-PUBLICATION DATA

Lepage, Jean-Denis.
Vauban and the French military under Louis XIV : an illustrated history of fortifications and strategies / Jean-Denis G.G. Lepage.
p.   cm.
Includes bibliographical references and index.

ISBN 978-0-7864-4401-4
softcover : 50# alkaline paper ∞

1. Vauban, Sébastien Le Prestre de, 1633–1707.   2. Vauban, Sébastien Le Prestre de, 1633–1707 — Influence.   3. Marshalls — France — Biography. 4. Military engineers — France — Biography.   5. France — History, Military — 1643–1715.   6. Fortification — France — History — 17th century.   7. France. Armée — Biography.   8. France — History — Louis XIV, 1643–1715.   I. Title.

DC130.V3L46 2010   623'.194409032 — dc22   2009034538

British Library cataloguing data are available

On the cover: Port Louis (Morbihan) Salient of Demi-Lune Richelieu (photograph by Simone and Bernard Lepage)

Manufactured in the United States of America

McFarland & Company, Inc., Publishers
Box 611, Jefferson, North Carolina 28640
www.mcfarlandpub.com

To my parents, Simone and Bernard Lepage,
for their love and encouragement,
and their guidance during childhood
that often included holiday visits to castles, forts,
historical and military sites and battlefields.

Table of Contents

Acknowledgments   iv

Introduction   1

1. The Reign of Louis XIV and Vauban's Life and Career . . . 5

Vauban's Personality   5

Youth (1633–1651)   7

The Rebellious Frondeur (1651–1653)   8

Captain Vauban (1653–1659)   9

King's Engineer (1659–1667)   9

War of Devolution (1667–1668)   11

Four Years of Peace (1668–1672)   14

Dutch War (1672–1678)   15

Commissioner General of
    Fortifications (1678–1688)   18

Nine Years' War (1688–1697)   21

War of the Spanish Succession
    (1702–1714)   24

Marshal Vauban's Last Combats
    (1700–1707)   26

Louis XIV's Death (1714)   28

2. Artillery and Engineering Corps 30

Artillery   30

Matchlock Musket   38

Engineering Corps   39

3. Siege Warfare 42

Siege Warfare Advocated by Vauban   42

Advantages and Disadvantages of
    Vauban's Method   54

Sieges Directed by Vauban   57

4. Vauban's Bastioned Fortifications 59

Italian Bastioned Fortifications   59

Vauban's Predecessors   65

Vauban's Three "Systems"   72

Bastioned Front   78

Bastion   78

Curtain   86

Ditch   90

Gatehouse   92

Outworks   98

Covered Way and Place of Arms   106

Advance Works   110

Detached Works   115

Flooding   122

Entrenched Camp   123

Military Buildings   124

Design of Fortifications   134

Construction of Fortifications   135

The Relief Maps Collection   139

5. France Fortified by Vauban 141

Northeast Frontier	143	Roussillon	218
Ardennes and Lorraine	170	Western Pyrenees	229
Alsace	180	Defenses of Bordeaux	234
Franche-Comté	188	Defenses of the Pertuis	240
Dauphiné and Savoy	193	Bretagne (Brittany) and Normandy	255
Mediterranean Coast	206		

6. Vauban's *Oisivetés* 274

Agriculture and Inland Navigation	274	Politics and Organization of the State	278
Colonies	275	Fiscal Considerations	279
Religion	277	List of Vauban's Written Works	280

Conclusion 282

Vauban's Legacy in France	282	Vauban's Influence Abroad	284

Bibliography   287

Index   289

Introduction

It was the great philosopher Voltaire (1694–1778) who gave to the seventeenth century the name that it retains to this day: the Century of Louis XIV. This designation is not just a tribute to a favorite king, it is a factual description of an age during which France became the most powerful and most brilliant country in Europe. The reign of Louis XIV (1643–1715) was the longest in French history, and represents the highlight of the Capetian-Bourbon dynasty. It was the era in which the secular state of France finally won its independence from ecclesiastical supervision and interference. It marked the triumph of absolutism, a political theory holding that all power should be vested in one supreme ruler in order to keep national cohesion and unity. "A king," proclaimed Louis XIV with his customary lack of modesty, "is superior to all other men, occupying, so to speak, the place of God." It was also the epoch of Baroque art, a heroic attempt to transcend the contradiction between order and motion. Having usurped the place of Spain in the leadership of political matters, France surmounted Italy in the artistic and cultural domains. Science was dominated by names such as René Descartes and Blaise Pascal, but it was in art that the brightness of the reign was the most remarkable. Louis XIV subsidized and housed writers, artists and scientists, who in return were encouraged to glorify him. All the immense energies and talents of the age were harnessed and shaped by the power of Louis XIV's state into a magnificent spectacle. Literature was marked by poets such as La Fontaine and Boileau, theater and drama by Corneille, Racine and Molière. The period featured moralists and chroniclers such as La Bruyère, Saint-Simon and Madame de Sévigné as well as theoreticians and orators like Fénelon, Boileau and Bossuet. Music was enhanced by the works of Lully, Charpentier, Delalande and Couperin. Painting was dominated by Le Brun, Van der Meulen, Poussin, Claude Gellée (called le Lorrain), Philippe de Champaigne, and both Le Nain brothers, Georges de La Tour and Watteau. Illustrious names in sculpture were Le Bernin, Coysevox and Girardon.

This artistic brightness, financed by a policy of state patronage, was not limited to France but also drew attention from the whole of Europe. This tendency continued into the following century, and French cultural prestige was at its peak in the eighteenth century. Civilian and military architecture, stimulated by Louis XIV's personal interest in construction, developed the French classical style, combining clearness, order, splendor, grandiosity and majesty, and imposed itself as the main reference. The French style dominated the whole continent in construction of palaces, gardens, public buildings and fortifications. During this period in Paris were built part of the Louvre, the Salpêtrière, the Hôtel des Invalides, the Place des Victoires, the Place Royale and, of course, Versailles castle. This period also saw the triumph of Vauban's French classical bastioned fortification.

The necessity to fortify France with a belt of strongholds had been felt as early as the reign of François I (1515–1547). The chivalrous king devoted all his energy to the struggle against his most dangerous enemy, Carlos V, who was king of Spain; emperor of Germany; ruler of Austria, southern Italy, Burgundy, Franche-Comté, and the Netherlands; and owner of a rich colonial empire, especially in South America. It was said then that "the sun never went down on King Carlos V's possessions." Without real national coherence, the construction of fortresses continued under the reigns of King Henri IV (1589–1610) and his son Louis XIII (1610–1643). One would wait, however, until Louis XIV's reign to see the establishment of a barrier of fortifications to defend the country and mark the limits of France. These fortified frontiers, badly wanted by the king and his ministers of war, Le Tellier and Louvois, were designed and built by numerous military architects and engineers, the best-known of them being Vauban. Marshal Sébastien Le Preste de Vauban is indeed the one who most strongly marked the western European landscape with his art. Vauban is the one name that immediately springs to mind when seventeenth century fortifications are mentioned. Vauban was one of the men of genius of Louis XIV's reign, genuinely inventive, versatile, filled with reformist ideas, whose work embraced many aspects of French national life. He built a formidable ring of fortresses to protect the national frontiers, and his career culminated in the publication of a remarkable book which advocated the abolition of fiscal privileges and the introduction of a uniform system of taxation. If the name Vauban is very popular in France (partly because of a disrespectful song by Léo Ferré), celebrated in the names of streets, squares, avenues and grammar schools, the reality of his work is not always very well known, and sometimes reduced to clichés. His dominant reputation gives rise to factual errors. Italian sixteenth century bastions and eighteenth century fortifications are commonly attributed to him with the vague and convenient reference, "Vauban's style."

The purpose of this book is to set forth a clear picture of Vauban as a skilled man of war, a loyal servant of his king, a great military strategist, a conqueror, and a designer of fortifications, but also as a humanist and a peace-loving man, a tireless worker, an economist without equal, and an eminent political and pre–Encyclopedic thinker. The author endeavors to give the tireless gentleman of Morvan a face, and to place as close to the reader as possible his exceptional personality and colorful character within the backdrop of Louis XIV's reign. The aim is also to illustrate and describe Louis XIV's bastioned fortifications, to sum up Vauban's works and to highlight what remains today.

In spite of regrettable destruction and unskillful restorations, Vauban, commissioner-general of fortification and marshal of France, has left indelible marks. A large part of his work is preserved today, evidence of his handiwork still standing on the borders of France. Thanks to the relentless work of local and regional associations as well as a properly led cultural policy at both national and regional levels, the heritage left by Vauban is still alive: Neuf-Brisach, Briançon, Besançon, Saint-Martin-de-Ré, Montlouis and many other places are admirable showpieces. With a bit of concentration and a little imagination it is still possible for a visitor today to feel what it must have been like to man Vauban's defenses in these places.

The Century of Louis XIV was one of the most fascinating periods of French history and Vauban's fortifications, more than three hundred years old, still possess an undeniable beauty. Fortifications communicate a real aesthetic emotion, sometimes a sort of excitement, a feeling difficult to communicate to others. This is probably caused by the ingeniousness and balance of their conception, by the quality of their execution, by the solidity of their masses, by the sobriety of their shapes and by their majestic proportions. Built with the ancient Roman trilogy in mind, *firmitas* (solidity), *utilitas* (functionality) and *venustas* (beauty), they radiate an impression of quiet strength through the strictness of their harmonious geometry. Their rigorous efficiency is tempered by star and triangular shapes which harmonize with the obliques of walls and glacis. However, it would be all too easy to be blinded by romanticism and militaristic indulgence. Ruins of walls overgrown with vegetation, terraces with superb views, green citadels in the middle of modern busy towns, majestic fortresses, peaceful bastions reflecting their warm colors in the calm waters of moats, and isolated forts in steep and spectacular mountains cost fortunes at a time when most of the population suffered deep misery and extreme poverty. One should not forget that Louis XIV's fortifications were built at the price of hard work done by generations of humble and exploited people. Let us keep in mind that these places of prestige, which manifested the Sun King's glory and France's grandeur, have also been in their time besieged cities crushed by artillery, looted and burned by a ruthless soldiery, places of suffering, fear, violence, war and death.

CHAPTER 1

The Reign of Louis XIV
and Vauban's Life and Career

Vauban's Personality

There are few artistic renderings of Vauban made during his lifetime. There are so many differences among the numerous works of art made after his death that we cannot really get a precise picture of him. Paintings, drawings and sculptures (e.g. by Rigaud, Desrochers, Bridan, Guyot or Larivière) represent Vauban as a middle-aged man of average height, rather muscular and vigorous with a scar on his left cheek caused by a wound from the siege of Douai in 1667. But beyond the heroic portrait rendered in classical style, it is possible to get an idea of Vauban's personality through his writings, his letters, and his achievements and through contemporary witnesses.

On the whole, Vauban appears to have been a sympathetic and interesting person. A dynamic, vigorous and otherwise healthy man, he suffered all his life from asthma and bronchitis. His tireless vitality and his prodigious activity amazed his peers. He brought a sense of duty to the point of selflessness. Vauban was indeed entirely devoted to Louis XIV, whom he identified with France. The absolute and sacred power of the king was the only thing that he never questioned. He gave up his private life to his duty and, until his last breath, served with total loyalty and unselfishness. He showed his superiors a respectful but not servile devotedness, but he never fawned and never hesitated to express his ideas, criticism and anger with plain speech and sometimes with stubbornness. As a man of action he felt more at ease on the battlefield, in a muddy trench or on a construction site than at Louis XIV's sophisticated court of Versailles. With his collaborators and subordinates, he was demanding and severe but at the same benevolent and grateful. He was not afraid to listen and adopt other people's ideas if they were good. One of his great strengths was to be able to choose good collaborators. He was capable of making right decisions quickly, and carried them out rapidly. He was not reluctant to deal with secondary details but always kept the big picture in mind and a remarkable clearness of mind on conception and execution.

His eight serious wounds testify to his audacity, gallantry and physical courage in war. Even when he had become a senior officer, Vauban took many risks by commanding on the front line. Repeatedly Louis XIV and Louvois forbade him to enter the siege trenches. As a commanding officer he always tried to spare the blood of his soldiers and the lives of civilians. Vauban was a man-at-arms who did not like violence. He wrote: "The father of war is greed, its mother is ambition and its relatives are all passions which lead us to evil." Vauban owed his astonishing career and tremendous destiny to his exceptional talent and skill, it is true, but also to his phenomenal luck. Given the tradition and standards of the time, and given his social background, he was destined to be an officer who would probably have reached the rank of colonel. His fortune came from being the right man at the right time, whose talent was recognized by powerful persons, and who attracted their attention in favorable circumstances. His competence, honesty, huge knowledge and experience were successively recognized and rewarded by d'Arcenay, Mazarin, Clerville, La Ferté-Senectère, Condé, Louvois and ultimately by Louis XIV himself. Although he knew that his advancement was the result of his own merit and although he was fully aware of his personal value, Vauban remained for a large part of his life a modest, quiet, sensitive and simple man. As he grew older, however, he became pretentious, more ambitious, less patient, more authoritarian and more vain. He frequently gave his opinion on subjects outside of his own field of competence and got frustrated and angry when no attention was paid to his remarks, and no concern was given to his proposals. He wrote more and more about such matters as religion, politics and taxes, and irritated his superiors and the king himself. The end of his life was marked by bitterness, sadness and disappointment.

In his numerous writings Vauban appears as an intelligent man, caring for people and curious about the world around him. His work is dominated by rectitude, efficiency and reason. His actions seem to reveal a man of heart, proud but tolerant, courageous and charitable towards humble, poor and miserable people. He once wrote: "Fortune made me be born one of the poorest French gentleman, but as a reward it gave me a sincere heart." Originating from the low country nobility, he knew what relative financial want was and therefore was an excellent and thrifty— almost bourgeois— manager of his personal patrimony. When he died he left in inheritance the estates and manors of Bazoches, Pierre-Perthuis, Vauban, Neuffontaines, Domecy and Epiry. Of course, Vauban's social standing and wealth give rise to several questions: Was he really such a "good guy"? How did the privileged landlord Vauban treat his own peasants and servants? Was he as generous in the practice of daily life as he was when putting humanist theories on paper? As no study exists about his own private behavior, these questions remain unanswered.

Sébastien Le Prestre de Vauban (1633–1707)

According to his contemporaries, Vauban seemed to his intimates to be a joyful companion, fond of life and keen on pleasures, though not in excess. He did not dislike the company of women and admitted to having many mistresses and a few illegitimate children. This was not shocking, neither for the manners nor for the morality of his century.

Vauban's signature (letter written to Monsieur de Caligny on March 9, 1698)

At a time when patronage triumphed, Vauban was tightly attached to Louvois's lobbying clan and strongly defended his family's interest. But he only helped friends and relatives in the strict measure of their merit. Vauban was a close friend to Marshal Nicolas Catinat, and he kept friendly relationships with his son-in-law Mesgrigny, drama writer Jean Racine, archbishop and writer Fénelon, and director of fortifications Le Peletier de Souzy.

Youth (1633–1651)

Sébastien Le Prestre de Vauban was born on May 1 or 4, 1633, and baptized on May 15 at Saint-Léger-de-Fourcheret, a small village situated southeast of Avalon in the Morvan Mountains (north Burgundy). His family, originating from the lesser rural nobility, took its name from the domain of Vauban, situated in the village of Bazoches-du-Morvand, which was purchased in 1555 by Sébastien's great-grandfather, Emery Le Prestre. His father, squire Albin Le Prestre, and his mother, lady Edmée de Carmignolle, had inherited the domain of Vauban at Bazoches. Very little is known about the early years of the future marshal of France. He certainly received his first education from his parents, especially his grandfather, and from the village priest. After years as a country boy, the young Sébastien was placed in the Carmes College in Semur-en-Auxois, where he was taught how a gentleman would behave in society, reading and writing, a bit of French history, some superficial Latin and a smattering of mathematics.

At the time of Vauban's birth, western Europe was putting an end to a century of religious and civil wars. The unity of Christianity was forever broken. Northern Europe had become Protestant, England was Anglican, and middle and southern Europe had remained Catholic. The formative years of the young Sébastien Le Prestre were spent in a very troubled France, at the end of the reign of Louis XIII and during the minority of Louis XIV.

The future *Roi-Soleil* (Sun-King) was born at Saint-Germain near Paris on September 5, 1638, and was only five years old when his father's death made him king in May 1643. The birth of Louis XIV ruined the ambitions of Gaston of Orléans (Louis XIII's brother) to become king of France. Louis's mother, Queen Anne of Austria, assumed the regency while Mazarin, recommended by Cardinal Richelieu (who had died in 1642), was appointed prime minister. From 1635 on, France took an active part in the Thirty Years' War in Germany. Richelieu's aim was to bring down the power of Austria and to conquer natural borders to the kingdom. The Thirty Years' War was a gruesome conflict, marked by the defeat of Corbie and by the victories of Rocroi, Arras, Lens and Perpignan. It came to an end in October 1648. The Treaty of Westphalia was signed at Münster with the emperor of

Germany, Ferdinand II, and with Sweden. By the treaty, France obtained parts of the province of Alsace (without Strasburg) and the three bishopric cities of Verdun, Toul and Metz. However, war between Spain and France continued until 1659.

In 1648, the first troubles of the "Fronde" revolt began. The parliament and the people of Paris, exasperated by the hardships of Mazarin's policy, entered into rebellion. The situation got rapidly worse, barricades were raised in the streets of the capital and, on the night of January 5 to 6, 1649, Mazarin, the queen-regent, and the young monarch were forced to flee and take refuge in the castle of Saint-Germain-en-Laye. For four years Louis XIV was obliged to roam about his kingdom with a few loyal troops. Louis XIV would never forget these tragic events and this explains why he disliked Paris and the parisians, and why he later decided to demolish the capital's fortifications and install the royal court at Versailles and not in Paris. The Fronde evolved from a rebellion into a civil war exacerbated by the rancor and appetites of the princes of the realm. Some of them, blinded by ambition, did not hesitate to compromise with the Spanish enemy.

The Rebellious Frondeur (1651–1653)

In 1651, Vauban, aged seventeen, enlisted as a cadet in Captain Charles-Antoine Coningham d'Arcenay's company, which belonged to the Prince of Condé's regiment. Vauban, who was all his life to be a loyal servant of Louis XIV, yet began his military career as a rebellious Frondeur. It must be said that the young Le Prestre joined the rebellion more by accident than by conviction. In the Fronde army, Vauban, who had a little knowledge of fortification, already manifested a predilection for the work of military engineering. He took part in the early 1650s in the design of the defenses of the town of Clermont-en-Argonne in Lorraine, and distinguished himself during the siege of Saint-Menehould. His gallantry was rewarded by the rank of cavalry master. Vauban then saw action in different operations during which he was wounded several times.

In 1652, the Parisian rebels were beaten after the intervention of Turenne's royal troops. The cardinal of Retz, the principal chief of the Fronde revolt, was arrested, and Louis XIV triumphantly made his entry in Paris and firmly imposed his authority. The Fronde was defeated. Mazarin was re-installed as prime minister and became more or less the young Louis's stepfather. It was rumored in court that the cardinal had secretly married Louis XIII's widow. In any case, he dominated the youthful king, kept him on a short leash and continued his education. Working from the lessons of the Fronde, Cardinal Mazarin outlined the main orientation of the future reign: the king would have no prime minister; he would contain the Parliament; he would keep the high nobility from political affairs; he would make the monarchy an absolute and personal authority; he would rule himself and would demand submission from all his subjects. Thanks largely to the work of Mazarin, Louis XIV had a stable platform from which to launch his plans for a stronger France and his own glory based on absolute monarchy.

In spring 1653, Vauban was captured by a royal patrol, but still mounted on his horse and with his loaded pistol in hand he negotiated the conditions of his surrender. Mazarin, to whom the anecdote was told, was amused and summoned Vauban. It did not take long for the cunning cardinal to convince the young and brave rebel to enter service in the army of the legitimate king.

Captain Vauban (1653–1659)

When Vauban returned to legitimacy under the king's banner, the Fronde was defeated, but war with Spain continued. Vauban was placed under the command of *Maréchal de Camp* (Major General) and later General Commissioner of Fortifications Louis-Nicolas de Clerville (1610–1677). Clerville started his career as chevalier (knight) in the galleys of the order of the Hospitallers of Saint John of Jerusalem (since 1530 also known as Order of Malta). He took part in the Thirty Years' War in Germany as officer in the Noailles Regiment, and graduated as a military engineer in 1643. He participated in various military actions in Greece and Italy, and faithfully supported Louis XIV during the Fronde. Under Clerville, Vauban participated in the siege of Saint-Menehould, which he knew well, having taken it two years before. After the surrender of the town in September 1653, he attracted the attention of chevalier Louis-Nicolas de Clerville, who charged him with the repair of the fortifications which had been damaged during the fighting. In spring 1654, the young and talented Vauban was appointed as Clerville's assistant during the siege of Stenay on the river Meuse and, though wounded, participated in the siege of Clermont-en-Argonne, which he had himself fortified. After the operation, he was charged with the demolition of the defenses. In May 1655, aged twenty-two, he was promoted to the rank of king's ordinary engineer and took part in the sieges of Landrécies, Condé-sur-l'Escaut and Saint-Gillain, near Mons in Belgium. Again he was commissioned to repair the damage. The following year, Vauban was wounded during the siege of Valenciennes and taken prisoner by Spanish troops. Thanks to Mazarin's intervention, he was rapidly liberated and soon distinguished himself again by defending the stronghold of Saint-Gillain. During this operation he was noticed by Marshal de La Ferté-Senectère, who rewarded him with the rank of captain at the head of a company in his regiment. Only five years after the beginning of his military life, Vauban had achieved an astonishing position. He had become king's engineer, captain of a company and had won his chiefs' respect and esteem.

With heavy casualties, La Ferté's regiment took possession of Montmédy, where Vauban was wounded again. Hardly healed, he went back into action and had shared in the victorious sieges of Mardyk and Dunkirk. In June 1658, Spanish forces commanded by the prince of Condé were defeated by Turenne at the battle of the Dunes, while Marshal de La Ferté (and Vauban) seized Gravelines, Ypres and Audenarde. This series of French victories in Flanders hastened the conclusion of the war with Spain, which had lasted a quarter of a century. The Peace of the Pyrenees was signed on November 7, 1659. France obtained the border provinces of Roussillon, Cerdagne and Artois and the duchy of Bar as well as the fortified cities of Philippeville, Marienburg, Montmédy and Thionville. After hard negotiations, the prince de Condé was pardoned and re-established in his rank and possessions. Louis XIV married the infanta Maria-Theresa (Philippe IV of Spain's daughter) and began to rule personally after Mazarin's death in March 1661. Louis XIV was then twenty-four years of age, and for the next 54 years, devoted himself single-mindedly to the task of ruling France.

King's Engineer (1659–1667)

France was then at last at peace and the young and proud king made use of this situation to increase his authority. Keenly aware of the importance of his royal role, the hard-

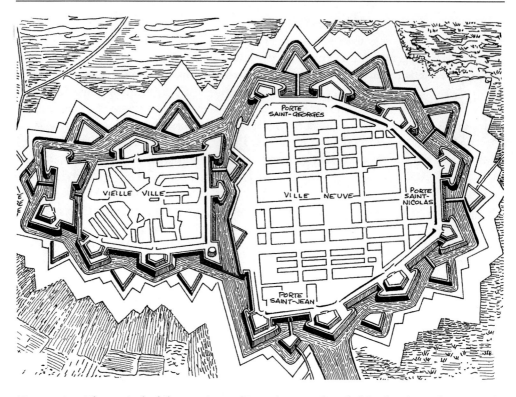

Nancy 1645. The capital of the province of Lorraine was founded in the eleventh century by Duke Gérard of Alsace. The duke built a castle in the marshes along the river Meurthe. In the fourteenth century, the city was enclosed by a stone wall, towers and gates. The town extension was created by Duke Charles III between 1588 and 1620. The Italian architect Girolamo Citoni established streets and squares according to a draught-board structure and his colleague, engineer Stabili, built fortifications consisting of eight bastions with orillons and cavaliers, a citadel and a wet ditch with seven demi-lunes. The town was occupied by the French in 1633 and severely damaged during the Thirty Years' War. Louis XIV occupied Lorraine and agreed to give the city back to Duke Charles IV provided that the fortifications be destroyed; this task was executed by Vauban. Nancy became permanently French, after the death of the ex-king of Poland and duke of Lorraine Stanislas Leszcinski in 1776.

working and zealous Louis XIV devoted himself to his kingly function with ceremonies and rituals which he himself devised. The young king, who until then had led a frivolous life, became an absolute monarch who exercised the functions of government by divine right and who was thus the originator and infallible interpreter of divine, natural, and human law. The notion of princely absolutism had been developed by the Italian political writer Niccolò Machiavelli (1469–1527), and several other thinkers such as the philosopher Jean Bodin (1530–1596), and Jacques Benigne Bossuet (1627–1704), bishop of Meaux, the most celebrated theologian in the age of Louis XIV. The Sun-King followed these precepts to the letter. His will was supreme; he was above the law; the life of his subjects belonged to him; he represented God on earth; nobody had the right to criticize his actions; and whoever was born as a subject had to obey without asking. Bossuet wrote: "The royal throne is not the throne of a man but the throne of God Himself. The King's majesty is an adequate expression of God's majesty." Like many historical sayings, the one almost universally attributed to Louis XIV, "l'état c'est moi" (I am the state), was probably never uttered by him, but he acted as though he had actually said it.

For Vauban, after eight years of action came a period of maturation. He was garrisoned at Nancy in Lorraine and had time to think about improving siege methods, how to defend strongholds and where the best and strongest frontiers for France were. In the beginning of 1660, he obtained a short leave and returned home to his native Morvan, where a marriage had been arranged with Jeanne d'Osnay, the baron of Epiry's daughter. Jeanne d'Osnay and Vauban eventually had three children: one boy who died early and two daughters (Charlotte and Jeanne-Françoise). The honeymoon was short and right after his marriage, Vauban was requested to return to Nancy with a new mission: the dismantling of the city defenses. This demolition job kept him busy in the years 1661 and 1662.

After the less-than-glorious demolition of Nancy's defenses, Vauban's career reached an important turn. He had succeeded in attracting Louis XIV's attention, and the king entrusted him with a secret mission concerning the city of Marsal in Lorraine. Satisfied with Vauban's service, Louis XIV offered him command of a company (which brought substantial income) in the prestigious regiment of Picardie. Meanwhile, in 1665, Louis XIV's jealousy and Colbert's hatred brought the disgrace and banishment of the greedy general-superintendent of finance, Nicolas Fouquet. Fouquet's fall marked the end of the private state which could defy the king's authority within the realm. His successor, Jean-Baptiste Colbert, eventually joined the work of financial-controller to the functions of superintendent of buildings, State-Secretary to the Maison du Roi and head of the French navy. Colbert was a tireless and competent worker who gave a new enthusiasm to all branches of national activities. Thanks to Colbert and Louvois, and to several other administrators drawn from the bourgeoisie, France became a great modern state, the most advanced in Europe, and Louis XIV could embark on a policy of conquest.

On Colbert's advice, Louis XIV entrusted Vauban with the renovation of the fortifications of the town of Brisach in Alsace. During the work, Vauban was involved in a misappropriation of funds scandal. This was a complicated affair, which until today remains totally unclear, and which embarrasses many French historians (at least those eager to present Vauban as an unstained idol). Was Vauban duped by dishonest entrepreneurs and manipulated and unfairly treated by the bursar of Alsace, Charles Colbert (the cousin of Minister Jean-Baptiste Colbert)? Was he guilty of illegal personal enrichment by deliberately asking exaggerated prices? Had Vauban's success attracted jealousy? What interest was actually at stake? Did inter-service rivalry between the Colbert clan and the Louvois lobby play a role? Anyway, Vauban had powerful enemies, it is certain, but he fortunately also benefited from strong support and cover. Eventually, his innocence was recognized in 1671, but all documents related to his role in this scandal were destroyed by fire on order of Louis XIV, a strange fact which only makes the "Brisach affair" more shadowy.

From 1664 to 1666, Louis XIV employed Vauban on different special diplomatic missions in Germany and in the Netherlands in order to prepare for the next war.

War of Devolution (1667–1668)

The Peace of the Pyrenees had left France with a considerable residue of unsatisfied or controversial claims to territory and influence, notably in the Netherlands and the Rhine-

Citadel of Lille. The Lille citadel was the symbol of Louis XIV's authority and Vauban's genius and was his first major design. With its regular pentagonal shape, five bastions, moats and outworks, the citadel of Lille was directly inspired by the citadel of Antwerp built by Paciotto in 1560. It was constructed between 1667 and 1671 by Simon Vollant, and constituted a military city on the side of the civilian town. Vauban was governor of Lille and lived in the citadel for nearly thirty years.

Besançon citadel entrance

land. Feeling himself to be the heir of Charlemagne, Louis XIV dreamed of providing France with what he called a "natural frontier," meaning the acquisition of the province of Alsace and most of the other territories on the left bank of the Rhine, including Franche-Comté, the Rhenish Palatinate, the Spanish Low Countries (today Belgium) and the southern part of the Dutch Republic (today The Netherlands). If this scheme worked, the king would be able to establish an undisputed hegemony of France in Europe. The pretext for the so-called "War of Devolution" was provoked by Louis XIV's claim to the rights of his wife on a part of the Spanish Low Countries. The French forces directed by the king himself and commanded by Turenne invaded Flanders on May 24, 1667.

Vauban, in presence of the king and his whole court, attracted a good deal of attention, which considerably increased his popularity. He conquered Tournai, Douai and the very important place, Lille. As a reward, Vauban was admitted as a lieutenant to the illustrious Gardes-Françaises Regiment, the best unit of the Maison du Roi, and given a yearly pension of 24,000 livres. Louis XIV took possession of Franche-Comté in February 1668 and, over two months, Vauban resided at Besançon in order to construct a new citadel. By that time, the Republic of the United Provinces (today the kingdom of The Netherlands) concluded the Triple Alliance in The Hague with England and Sweden. Louis XIV was obliged to accept the Peace of Aix-la-Chapelle in May 1668. France had to give back Franche-Comté but was allowed to keep the territories conquered in Spanish Flanders, with twelve important fortified cities—Charleroi, Binche, Ath, Tournai, Douai, Audenarde, Courtrai and Lille being the most important. Louis XIV ordered the fortifications of these new border towns to be improved at once. This was an important moment in Vauban's life. Until then he had the reputation of a good soldier and a city-conqueror, and now, in Lille, he was given the opportunity to demonstrate his value as a builder of fortifications.

Officially, the construction of the new citadel of Lille should have been designed by the commissaire-général des fortifications (general-commissioner of fortifications), Chevalier de Clerville, who had held this position since 1658. But thanks to Louvois's intrigues and pressures, Louis XIV gave preference to Vauban's design. The talented and loyal Clerville, whom Louvois did not like, was then supplanted by his ambitious pupil and dismissed from favor. The embittered and disappointed Clerville had to step aside. He was entrusted with minor work such as digging the Canal of the Midi, and the design of the citadel of Marseille. In 1671, he was appointed governor of the remote island of Oleron, and was allowed to keep the official title of commissaire-général until his death in 1677, but from 1667 onward, the work was carried out by Vauban. The reconstruction of Lille began in 1667 and four years later the "queen of citadels" was completed. Vauban, aged thirty-five, was given the flattering title of governor of Lille citadel. After Clerville's eviction, Vauban had reached an exceptional position: he was in charge of all fortresses under Louvois's War Department, which included all the work along the northern border, on the right bank of the Rhine, in the Alps and in the Roussillon.

Four Years of Peace (1668–1672)

The Aix-la-Chapelle treaty left Louis XIV unsatisfied and for four years the king and the war lobby (Louvois, Condé and Turenne) carefully prepared the next war against Holland. The army was modernized, reinforced and increased in size, while Louis XIV and his diplomats cunningly established a large network of alliances all over Europe. Peacetime did not mean rest for Vauban. On the contrary, during this period of preparation, he played a military and diplomatic role. Having been acquitted in the painful and unpleasant scandal of Brisach, and supported by Louvois, he was then working on the fortifications of Ath, Audenarde, Charleroi and Dunkirk. At Dunkirk, Vauban — a country gentleman by birth and origin — discovered another element: the sea. With passion he began the construction of the place. On Louvois's command, Vauban was sent on an inspection journey. In the mid-

Briançon

Templar Castle Collioure

dle of the winter of 1668, Vauban accomplished an incredible trip. During this long, tiresome and complicated journey, which would be followed by many others, he traveled in the Alps (Pignerol, Briançon and Grenoble), then went to Valence, Antibes and Toulon, continuing all the way down south to Perpignan, Collioure and Villefranche-de-Conflent. In every halting place he inspected, studied the defenses and made new designs. Back in Lille in the spring of 1669, he went again to inspect the cities in the province of Artois : Douai, Bapaume, Saint-Venant, Béthunes. He carried on directing the works in Lille, Dunkirk and Ath and traveled again to Pignerol in the Alps. There he was ordered to rush back north when Louis XIV wanted to visit the fortifications on the Belgian frontier. In July 1670, Louvois sent Vauban to Savoy on a diplomatic mission: to rally the duke against Holland. To wheedle and persuade the duke of Louis XIV's goodwill, Vauban made designs for the fortification of La Verruca, Vercelli and Turin. At the end of September 1670, Vauban was back in Lille and continued the works on the northern border. In the spring of 1671, Louis XIV came again to the region to see for himself the advancement of the expensive works. The royal inspection was accompanied by sumptuous feasts at Dunkirk, Tournai and Ath. Once the triumphant king and his court were gone, Vauban wrote, on Louvois's request, *Mémoire pour servir d'instruction à la conduite des sièges*, a treaty about siege warfare.

Dutch War (1672–1678)

This conflict was desired by both Colbert and Louis XIV. The main objective was to bring down the formidable economical strength of the Republic of the United Provinces,

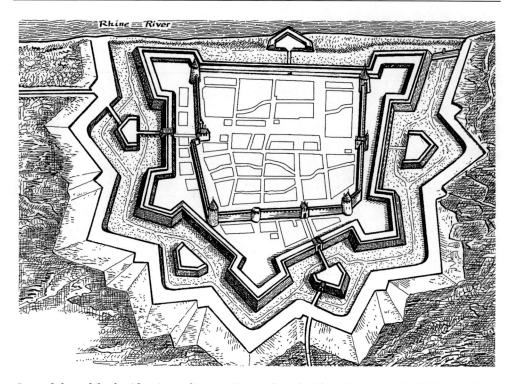

Groundplan of the fortifications of Orsoy. Situated on the Rhine River north of Cologne, Orsoy was one of the cities taken by Vauban and Louis XIV during the victorious opening phase of the War of Holland. The bastioned fortifications of the town, designed by the Italian engineer Giovanni Pasqualini, dated from the second half of the sixteenth century.

which stood in the way of Colbert's commercial development based on self-rule and protectionism, called *colbertism*. Louis XIV also wanted to avenge the Aix-la-Chapelle humiliation, to eradicate Dutch Protestantism and to silence the impertinent news-sheet writers from Amsterdam. Tolerant Calvinism, commercial mercantilism, political liberalism and the insolent bourgeoisie of this small but rich land irritated the Catholic absolute king.

The French forces were reorganized and brought to a strength of 100,000 well-equipped soldiers, led by the king himself, and commanded by Condé and Turenne. The French penetrated in Belgium, crossed the Rhine in April 1672, broke into Dutch territories and seized the cities of Arnhem, Deventer, Zutphen and Utrecht, whose cathedral was given back to the Catholics. Vauban, in the presence of the king, took Orsoy and Doesburg. Simultaneously, the north of the Republic was invaded by Louis XIV's allies, the archbishop of Cologne and the bishop of Münster, while the English fleet attacked the North Sea coasts. However, the well-prepared invasion did not turn out to be a decisive victory. Admiral Michiel De Ruyter defeated the British squadron at Sole Bay, the German prelates were stranded before Groningen and, in the south, the main French attack was stopped by vast and hastily created floods in the region of Amsterdam. Louis XIV, although in a very strong position, made the mistake of refusing the peace offered by the Dutch. The young Stadhouder Willem III of Orange-Nassau (1650–1702), who would become king of England and Louis XIV's most eager enemy, came to power in 1673. Willem set the situation to rights by negotiating the neutrality of England and by raising a coalition against France, regrouping the Ger-

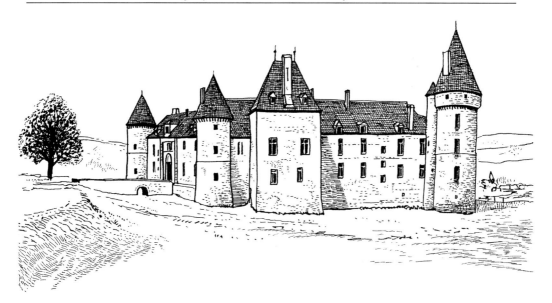

Bazoches (Nièvre), Vauban's castle. Vauban's castle Bazoches, located in the department of Nièvre in the ancient province of Burgundy, was built at the end of the twelfth century on the site of an old Roman post on the road between Sens and Autun. The castle belonged successively to the lords of Bazoches, Chastellux and Montmorillon. Vauban purchased it in 1675 and transformed the old medieval fortress into a comfortable residence for his family and his colleagues. However Vauban seldom dwelt in his pleasant castle and spent most of his life in Lille and on the road to inspect fortifications, make surveys, and take or defend towns in King Louis XIV's service.

man Empire, Austria, Spain and Lorraine. Overnight, the failures and the coalition raised against the French combined to ruin the original plans of Louis XIV. He was now committed to a long and international war.

In 1674, Vauban was commissioned to fortify the island of Ré in the Atlantic Ocean, which was dangerously exposed to Dutch sea raiders. On his way, he briefly resided in Paris, took a look at the evolution of Versailles castle and visited his cousin, Paul Le Prestre, who directed the construction of the Hôtel des Invalides. In recognition of his service, Vauban was promoted to the rank of infantry brigadier then *maréchal de camp* (major general). In 1675, he sold several of his offices and received a substantial bonus from the king which enabled him to purchase the medieval castle of Bazoches in his native Morvan.

Meanwhile the European war continued. With the involvement of the Germans, military operations shifted to the Rhine region. The French troops invaded Franche-Comté and Vauban made fortification designs for Besançon, Dole and Joux Castle. Turenne launched an offensive in Alsace. After the victory of Turckheim, Turenne was killed at Salzbach. Having lost their best strategist and commanding officer, the French troops were brought to a halt and soon forced to retreat. In this complicated and difficult predicament, Vauban disapproved of adventurous and useless conquests. Nevertheless, on Louis XIV's order, he conquered Maastricht in June 1673, using a new systematic method of siege warfare. He participated in the seizure of Valenciennes, Cambrai, Liège, Huy, Bouchain, Bergues, Saint-Omer, Ghent and Ypres between 1674 and 1678. After six years of indecisive fighting, the belligerents, exhausted and confronting crucial financial difficulties, were obliged to negotiate. The Treaty of Nimegue, signed on July 17, 1678, represented the summit of Louis XIV's success and did reaffirm the superiority of the French Bourbons over the declining Spanish Habsburgs. The main loser was Spain. France won respect by its victories, made itself the arbiter of the destiny of Europe and managed to strengthen the vulnerable northern, northeastern and southeastern frontiers. The Duchy of Lorraine was restored to Duke Charles V but without Nancy and Longwy. These two towns as well as Franche-Comté, Cambrésis and many important fortresses in Artois, Flanders and Hainaut (Valenciennes, Peronne, Bouchain, Bavai and Maubeuge for instance) were yielded to France. The possession of these Spanish places provided a more defensible border composed of a homogenic line of strongholds. The Spanish fortifications, mostly constructed on a sixteenth century Italian model, were old-fashioned and badly maintained. They were at once modernized or reshaped by Vauban. This new defensive organization of the border (to a certain extent prefiguring the 1930s Maginot Line) was called "Pré Carré" and would be, from then on, Vauban's main task and principal mission until the end of his life.

Commissioner General of Fortifications (1678–1688)

After the Treaty of Nimegue, Louis XIV's reign reached the zenith of its fame. The king kept his army on a war footing and began a very dangerous and adventurous policy of so-called *réunions à la Couronne*; these "reunions with the Crown" simply meant illegal aggression, arbitrary annexation of cities and territories based on political pressure, ruthless intimidation, and high-handed interpretation or exploitation of vagueness in former treaties. "Chambers of Reunion" were especially appointed French law courts whose task it was to establish by means of casuistry and sophistry the historical French titles of sovereignty to the contested territories.

After the death of Chevalier de Clerville, Vauban was officially appointed to the rank of commissaire-général of fortifications in January 1678. As usual, these ten years of armed peace were marked by intense activities for Vauban. In 1679, he went on inspection tour in Franche-Comté, Provence and Roussillon, where he created the fortress of Montlouis. In 1780, he was appointed governor of Douai, which multiplied his journeys and inspection tours. In September 1681, Strasburg was annexed by brutal force and Vauban was charged with reinforcing the defenses. Then he traveled to Italy and along the Mediterranean coast, where he made designs for Antibes and Toulon. In 1683, the year of Colbert's death, Vauban went to Paris and Bretagne, where he worked on the fortifications of Belle-Isle-en-Mer, Port-Louis, Lorient and Brest.

The following year, without any declaration of war, Louis XIV brutally invaded the Duchy of Luxembourg. The siege of Luxembourg city was commanded by Marshall de Créqui and led by Vauban. Spain declared war on France but had to accept the "réunion" of Luxembourg by the truce of Ratisbonne, concluded in 1684. After having repaired and reworked the fortifications of Luxembourg, Vauban was required to go to Versailles. This time Louis XIV entrusted him with a civilian project: the construction of an 80 km. aqueduct intended to divert the water of the river Eure to supply the gardens and fountains of Versailles castle; this monumental, outsized and sumptuary project would never be completed because of difficulties encountered on the site and due to lack of funds, as another war was planned.

Sentry-box at Montlouis

About 1684, after the death of Queen Maria-Thesera, Louis XIV secretly married the over-devout Madame Françoise d'Aubigné, Marquise de Maintenon (1635–1719), the ex-nanny of the royal children. A striking change took place in the character of the king. Louis, who had not merely tasted but feasted upon the pleasures of love, war and power, turned his attention towards religion, and at that time religious issues aroused violently partisan feelings. Probably under the influence of his new wife and his Jesuit confessor, Father La Chaise, the King, now a "dévot," wanted more and more to involve himself in religious matters. After complicated moves, he managed to suppress the Jansenists (men and women of severe morals named after the Flemish bishop Jansen, who taught a doctrine akin to that of the Calvinist Protestants, that Christians could be saved only if they were predestined to eternal happiness by being in receipt of a holy grace from on high) and closed their convent of Port Royal. Next, believing that the religion of his subjects could be none other than his own, the king took severe measures against the French Protestant community. By persuasion, intimidation and violence (going as far as torture and murder), Louis XIV tried to eradicate the adherents of the Reformed Religion (called Protestants or Huguenots and Parpaillots in southern France). The most odious instrument of conversion was the "*dragonnades*": ruthless Dragoons were deliberately billeted on the richest and most influential Huguenot households with orders to make themselves as unpleasant as they could be in order to obtain forced conversions. Finally, Louis revoked the Edict of Nantes, signed in 1598 by his grandfather Henri IV to put an end to the Religious Wars. The revocation was ordered at Fontainebleau on October 18, 1685. The French Huguenots were forced to convert to Catholicism, while recalcitrants were persecuted, imprisoned or sent away as gal-

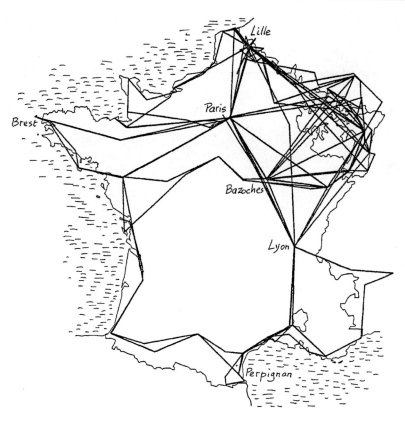

Vauban's inspection journeys between 1678 and 1688 (according to historian Anne Blanchard)

ley slaves. The revocation, enforced with the greatest brutality, was enormously popular among Roman Catholic Frenchmen, as the status of the Protestants was considered by a majority of them to be an excrescence on the unity of the realm. Actually, the revocation was a fanatical absurdity, a crime against religious freedom, and a political blunder with far-reaching consequences both on internal and foreign matters. Religiously, it was a failure. Protestantism was not extirpated from the realm, all forced conversions were a façade only, and clandestine congregations, still very numerous, continued to worship secretly all over France. In economic terms, a massive immigration of French Protestants deprived France of officers, rich merchants and capital holders, skillful craftsmen, scholars, artists and intellectuals. It is estimated that 200,000 persecuted Huguenots, barred from freedom of worship and education, helped by friends at home and sympathizers abroad, managed to escape. They left France, found refuge, and settled in Holland, England and Prussian Brandenburg, the same powers that were now solidly lined up against further French aggression. Politically, the revocation raised bitter hostility in Protestant northern Europe, and religious intolerance tarnished the glory and grandeur of France. The persecution of the Huguenots alienated France's last sympathizers among the Protestant princes of Germany. Eventually some Huguenots rebelled and took up arms against the royal forces. The resentful minorities which remained, notably in the Cevennes Mountains, were to be a running sore for the French kingdom in the later years of Louis XIV's reign.

    Vauban was one of the first, and one of the few, to firmly condemn, criticize and oppose this tragic and absurd decision. Motivated by practical reasons but also by elementary human decency and religious tolerance, he courageously wrote and published in 1689 *Mémoire pour le rappel des Huguenots (Dissertation for the Recall of the Protestants)*. Vauban's daring dissertation pleading to revoke the revocation was actually a very risky move as he directly challenged a royal decision, an action that could have cost him his situation, possibly his head. Because Vauban was indispensible, a clash was avoided, and the affair was discreetly solved. The author was firmly warned to mind his own business and the dissertation was forbidden and thus remained unheard. Though deeply disappointed by this disastrous event and embittered by the failure of his attempt, Vauban, who after all was a loyal soldier and above all a man of duty, swallowed his disappointment, stepped back into the rank and continued his task. Business as usual.

Vauban then inspected the island of Ré, and fortified the Gironde estuary, and the harbors of Sète, Cherbourg, Granville, Dieppe and Saint-Malo. He participated, together with engineer Pierre-Paul Riquet, in the construction of the Canal du Midi, the Garonne-Aude canal which enabled communication between the Atlantic Ocean and the Mediterranean Sea. Though ill and suffering from bronchitis, Vauban visited the province of Alsace, and re-adapted the fortifications of Belfort, Montroyal and Landau. He reluctantly created the stronghold of Fort-Louis-du-Rhin, because he was convinced that too many fortresses only cost time and money and scattered troops. In this period, he pleaded to abandon pikes and muskets and to replace this old weaponry with modern flintlocks with bayonets. He elaborated what has later been called his "second system" of fortification. The Huguenot affair was forgotten and apparently forgiven as Vauban was promoted to the rank of general-lieutenant in August 1688.

During this time, Louis XIV's religious intolerance and aggressive policy gave rise to resentment, grudges, protestations and anger all over Europe.

Nine Years' War (1688–1697)

Louis XIV's brutal annexations, unscrupulous violations of treaties and armed provocations had raised powerful potential enemies against him. Louis XIV demanded permanent guarantees that no one would challenge the territories he had annexed during the "reunions." At the same time, the revocation of the Edict of Nantes had raised indignation in Protestant Calvinist and Lutheran northern Europe. Another European war became inevitable. The League of Augsburg was formed in 1686. It regrouped the emperor of Germany, several German principalities (among them Brandenburg and Bavaria), Spain, Sweden and Savoy. The coalition's aim was the strict application and respect of the Treaty of Nimegue. In October 1688, Louis XIV launched what he believed would be a short war. Hostilities began with a sudden French offensive on the right bank of the Rhine. Vauban conquered Mannheim and Philipsburg, where he experimented for the first time with the artillery technique known as "ricochet fire." The French aggression was accompanied by looting on a large scale, slaughter, systematic devastation of the Palatinate and destruction of the ancient cities of Worms, Speyer, Mannheim and Heidelberg. The Heidelberg castle, beautiful even in ruins, stands to the present day as an eloquent witness of wanton destruction. The aim of this criminal and senseless devastation was the creation of an empty and inhospitable zone facing French fortresses along the Rhine. War crimes and atrocities of

Fort de la Conchée (Saint-Malo)

this kind were not new, but this time the orders were given by General Mélac with the backing of Louis XIV himself. Far from cowing the Germans, the French's savage devastations united Europe against Louis XIV and gave rise to a desire for retaliation and a deep and durable hatred against France.

Then Louis XIV made another foolish and adventurous move. He offered refuge to King James II of England, who had just been overthrown by a revolution. To help James II regain his throne, Louis XIV prepared to invade and conquer the British Isles. England and the Republic of the United-Provinces reacted by joining the Augsburg coalition. The short and victorious campaign envisioned by Louis XIV degenerated into another long European conflict. In the Alps, the duke of Savoy took Embrun and Gap. At sea, the French fleet was defeated at the naval battle of La Hougue, which saved Britain from invasion. During this difficult and indecisive war, Vauban suddenly became very ill. Between December 1689 and February 1691, he had to stop all activities. After a long year of sick leave at his home in the castle of Bazoches, he came back to service. He besieged and conquered Mons and Namur in Belgium. He inspected the Alps frontier and reinforced Grenoble, fort Barraux, Pignerol, Briançon, Embrun, Château-Queyras, Seyne-les-Alpes, and Sisteron and created the fortress of Montdauphin.

In 1693, Louis XIV elevated him to the prestigious Order of Saint-Louis. After a brief journey to the court of Versailles, Vauban went back to war and conquered Charleroi. The following year, he fortified Brest and Saint-Malo and reinforced the coastal defenses along the shores of Bretagne and Normandy because the pressure of the Anglo-Dutch navy was especially strong on this front. According to the tradition and standard of the time, an engineer was not considered a commanding officer, but exceptionally—owing to his reputation and his special relationship with the king—Vauban was given command of an army in the spring of 1694. At the head of his troops, he succeeded in repulsing an English landing at Camaret-sur-mer (June 18, 1694), therefore preventing the capture of the important

Artillery tower at Colmars-les-Alpes

port of Brest. The following year, he continued his inspection missions on the northern border. In May 1697, under the command of his friend Marshall Catinat, Vauban besieged and conquered Ath, which he knew very well, having himself fortified the place some thirty years earlier.

The war exhausted the resources of France and the internal situation was disastrous. Poor harvests, bad vintages, heavy taxes to finance the king's sumptuous life and war efforts dragged the population into misery and led to famine and trouble. Moreover Louis XIV lost his brilliant general, François-Henri de Montmorency, Duke of Luxembourg, who died in 1695. After nine years of an indecisive war, all the belligerents were ruined and exhausted. Peace was badly needed by all parties. Negotiations were followed by the Treaty of Ryswick in September 1698. The treaty was a serious humiliation for Louis XIV. France was allowed to keep the fortified places along the 1678 borders but had to restore the "reunions" of the period 1679–1689, except Strasburg and Sarrelouis. Louis XIV had to accept economic concessions and was forced to recognize his arch-enemy, Prince Willem of Orange, now called William III, as legitimate king of England. The treaty showed that the period of French magnificence, prestige and hegemony was over. Inside the kingdom, the French population, overburdened by taxes and crushed by financial and economic difficulties, lost trust in and admiration for the Sun-King.

Between 1698 and 1701, Europe enjoyed a short period of peace. Vauban, then aged over sixty, was still a busy man who continued a life of writing, traveling, inspecting and building. The fortified town of Brisach having been restored to the Germans, Louis XIV decided to build a new fortress on the French side of the Rhine. Neuf-Brisach, entirely preserved today, marks the apogee of Vauban's career and the peak of French bastioned fortification. For his competent writings on the most varied subjects, Vauban was awarded a membership in the prestigious Royal Academy of Science in 1699.

War of the Spanish Succession (1702–1714)

After the Treaty of Ryswick, the coalition of Augsburg was disbanded, but a new period of tension opened. This time the issue was the Spanish succession. King Charles II of Spain had died without a male heir. Austria and France had candidates for the throne. The patrimony was enormous. It consisted of the Spanish Empire, then comprising not only the kingdom of Spain itself, but also Spanish Netherlands (modern Belgium), a great part of Italy (Milan, Tuscany, Naples, Sicily and Sardinia), the Spanish Main (part of the West Indies, Mexico, and Latin America, except Brazil, which belonged to Portugal) and the Canary and Philippines islands, in all a handsome portion of the inhabited globe. Before his death, Charles II had refused to make a compromise or a partition and had designated as his successor the duke of Anjou, Louis XIV's grandson, who became Philippe V, king of Spain. The possibility of Franco-Spanish power broke the precarious European political stability. This led to a renewed coalition including England, the German Empire, Brandenburg, Sweden, Savoy, Portugal and the Dutch United-Provinces. The new dynastic European war began in 1702. With the inevitability of sunset, it marked the twilight of Louis XIV's reign.

The conflict started with initial Franco-Spanish victories at Friedlingen and Hochstadt in 1703, but soon things went badly wrong. The war proved long and terrible. For France, it was marked by serious reverses. Landau in Germany and Gibraltar in southern Spain

Concarneau (Brittany)

Fort de Savoie (Colmars-les-Alpes)

were taken. In the Cévennes in mountainous central France, French Huguenots (known as Camisards) entered into armed rebellion and held back several royal armies. The close collaboration between Prince Eugen of Savoy-Carignan and John Churchill, duke of Marlborough, was one of the chief reasons for the allied victories, notably the battle of Blenheim (1704), obliging French troops to evacuate Germany. The new king of Spain, Philippe V, was temporarily driven from Madrid by an Anglo-Austrian offensive. French armies lost Belgian territories after the defeat of Ramillies (1706). After the lost battle of Turin, the French were forced to retreat in the Alps. Louis XIV's armies pulled themselves together, won the battle of Malplaquet (1709) and succeeded in avoiding an invasion of France by holding fast in Vauban's Pré Carré and by winning the battle of Denain (July 1712). This ultimate victory avoided the invasion of France just in time and allowed Louis XIV to sue for an honorable peace. The anti–French coalition, tired of this endless and exhausting war, agreed to make peace. Negotiations between the belligerents led to different treaties signed in 1713 and 1714. The Peace of Utrecht was particularly profitable to England, which became the first maritime and commercial power. Philippe V was confirmed as king of Spain and kept the South American colonies, but all possessions in Italy and Belgium were lost and passed under Austrian domination. Louis XIV had to forget his dreams of domination. France had to yield a part of its North American colonies to England, notably Terre-Neuve (Newfoundland), Hudson Bay and Acadia in Canada. He was also forced to restore several Belgian towns, bringing the northern frontier back to what it was in 1697. The Treaty of Utrecht was an important moment at the beginning of the eighteenth century in the distribution of European political power. It brought a new and better balance among the three great states. Neither France nor England nor Austria could impose its hegemony on the continent. The United-Provinces lost a part of their economic power. Spain entered a period of lasting and profound economic and political decay. The duke of Savoy became king of Sicily. Prussia was founded as a kingdom and occupied ever since a preponderant place in Germany. Russia began to open herself politically and economically to the West.

Marshal Vauban's Last Combats (1700–1707)

Vauban, when approaching the age of seventy, was still a busy man, traveling on inspection tours and designing fortress projects. However from 1700 on, his health deteriorated and he resided often in Paris in a house which he had hired near the Tuileries palace. Gathering his experiences and reflections, he wrote a lot, not only on military matters, but also on subjects such as peace, forest exploitation, agriculture and taxes. At the outbreak of the Spanish Succession War, he went back to service in the field and organized the defenses of the northern frontier. In January 1703, Louis XIV rewarded his old and loyal servant by elevating him to the post of marshal of France. But this distinctive promotion came very late, and it was purely honorific; Vauban was no longer in active service. The king then asked him to write studies about military architecture, army -organization and siege warfare. Nevertheless Vauban came back to work for Louis XIV and led his last victorious siege: the fortified city of Vieux-Brisach was taken by the elderly Vauban in September 1703. The following year Vauban was decorated in the Saint-Esprit chivalric order, but ill and exhausted, he was dismissed and put aside. The marshal plunged into mourning after his wife's death and was feeling old, useless and worried about the bad turn of the war. After the disaster of Ramillies in May 1706, the duke of Marlborough took possession of Louvain, Brussels, Antwerp, Ghent, Brugge and Audenarde, and he besieged Ostende and marched into northern France with the objective of taking Dunkirk. In the middle of the debacle, Louis XIV called again upon Vauban's service. The old and sick marshal succeeded in stopping the panic of fleeing troops, regrouped the army, and organized a vast entrenched camp around Calais, Dunkirk, Gravelines, Bergues and Furnes which stopped Marlborough's offensive. After this ultimate military campaign, Vauban was very ill and obtained leave. By that time he was snubbed and ignored by a new generation of ministers. His influence at court had sharply declined, not only because he was old and ill, but also because of his growing interest in social reform and equitable taxation. Indeed, at the end of 1706 he came back to Paris, put his writings in order, what he called his *Oisivetés* ("idle thoughts," see Part 6) and decided to publish a book about taxes called *Projet de Dixme Royale*. The book was condemned and banned, the author was watched, and suspected of political subversion by the royal police. Very ill, half-disgraced, bitter and disappointed, Vauban was dying. Having heard of the marshal's desperate situation, Louis XIV, in a last gesture of gratitude, sent his best doctors, but it was too late. Marshal of France Sébastien Le Prestre Marquis de Vauban, died on March 30, 1707, at 10 a.m. in his residence in Rue Saint-Vincent (today Rue Saint Roch) near the Tuileries in Paris.

The disgraced Vauban died in the middle of the War of Spanish Succession, at a moment when the enemies of France were threatening to invade the kingdom. His body was hastily transported to his native Morvan, and buried on April 16 in the Saint-Sebastian chapel in the church of Bazoches without any official ceremony. The Academy of Sci-

Map of French provinces. Dates indicate the year when the provinces were united to the French crown. Dotted areas show Louis XIV's annexations: Artois, Flanders, Metz, Verdun and Toul, Alsace, Franche-Comté and Roussillon. The province Lorraine became French in 1766. The island Corsica was purchased from Genoa in 1768. The Comtat-Venaissin (the region around Avignon) remained a pontifical possession until 1791. The Duchy of Savoy and the county of Nice were united with France after a referendum in 1860.

ences protested against such ingratitude and organized a solemn celebration, where the talented writer Bernard Le Bovier de Fontenelle pronounced a famous, historic funeral oration: "*C'était un Romain qu'il sembloit que notre siècle eût dérobé aux plus heureux temps de la République*" (he was a Roman, which our era, it seems, had taken from the happiest time of the Republic). According to the fashion of the time and on the order of Napoléon I, Vauban's heart was cut out in May 1804 and rests now in an urn at Turenne's side in the Invalides Church in Paris. By imperial decree of December 7, 1867, by Napoléon III, the marshal's birthplace, the village of Saint-Léger-de-Fourcheret, has been renamed Saint-Léger-Vauban.

Louis XIV's Death (1714)

In the early 1700s, Louis XIV, king of France and Navarre, the incarnation of absolute monarchy, was a bitter and lonely man. Bad luck had plagued the king and his heirs: he had lost his sons, his brothers and his grandsons. The king was despised by his own people and hated by all European nations. During his later years, Louis XIV's popularity declined hugely as a result of successive devaluations of the currency, heavy taxation burdening the French, various shortages of essential commodities and the disastrous war. It must however be pointed out that, by the end of Louis XIV's reign, France was not in decline. The French colonies in America (notably the huge Louisiana Territory) and Asia were firmly established. French fashions in everything from dress and manners remained an over-

Villefranche de Conflent

whelming influence throughout Europe. French was spoken by all European elite and ruling classes, it was adopted as the common cultural and diplomatic language, and this was to remain so for two and a half centuries. Louis XIV's grandson was confirmed as king of Spain, and most of France's territorial aims west of the Rhine were satisfied; but all this had been achieved with long and hard wars.

The Sun-King had reached the end of his long course. On the eve of his death, the sick king confessed that he had loved war too much, and remorse and regret seemed to be uppermost in his mind. The moral courage with which he saw the end draw near was free of the ostentation of the rest of his life. Louis XIV died on September 1, 1715, at 8:15 a.m. at the age of seventy-seven. His reign had lasted too long and only a few faithful mourned him. When hearing of Louis's death, Prince Eugen of Savoy wrote in his memoirs: "The formidable oak is uprooted and lays now flat upon the ground." The Sun-King's heir was his great-grandson, Louis XV, who was only five. To him, before dying, Louis XIV said: "Try to keep the peace with your neighbors; Avoid my example in this respect and do not imitate my extravagance." After a regency by Duke Philippe of Orléans (Louis XIV's nephew), Louis XV reigned from 1743 to 1774.

CHAPTER 2

Artillery and Engineering Corps

Artillery

It seems that gunpowder became known to Western Europe about 1245. In the following centuries, some unknown experimenters applied the explosive force to the task of propelling a missile. The techniques of gunnery developed very slowly. Early guns were wildly inaccurate, heavy and time-consuming to load. The first efficient guns appeared on the battlefield in the fourteenth century (Crécy in 1346) but artillery remained a minor

Field and fortress gun. The field gun (left) was mounted on a carriage with two big wheels. The naval or fortress truck carriage (right) was made of elm, chosen for its ability to absorb shocks and its resistance to splintering when struck by enemy shot. The carriage was rigidly held by through-bolts and the wheels were in two halves, with the wood grain opposed. The trunnions rested on metal stripes to avoid wood damage.

arm for a long time. A certain amount of technical improvement took place during the two following centuries. The major step was the improvement of powder quality. The mixture was improved by developing a technique known as *corning*, in which the three ingredients (sulfur, charcoal and potassium nitrate, also known as saltpeter) were mixed wet, dried into a cake and then crumbled and sieved to produce a granular *corned powder*, giving rapid combustion and a more powerful result. It became possible to safely stockpile and transport it, and to charge stronger guns with more active propellant. The consequence was that projectiles had an increased velocity and a greater destructive strength. Gradually cannons were forged in once piece in bronze (copper alloyed with tin), and the gases produced by burning gunpowder generated enough pressure to propel a bullet, but not enough to destroy the barrel of a firearm. Guns rested on wheeled carriages and fired solid spherical iron shots. Owing to this progress, artillery began to gain domination, particularly in siege warfare. Constantinople, for example, was taken by the Turks in 1453 owing to heavy guns. After a slow evolution, artillery and small firearms became decisive weapons which changed the art of war and caused the appearance of new methods of fortification. The French artillery was created during Charles VIII's reign (1422–1461), organized under Louis XI's reign (1461–1483) by the brothers Bureau, and improved under Henri IV (1589–1610). Under Louis XIV, artillerymen were still individuals from the infantry regrouped in temporary units for a campaign under the command of a senior officer called the grand master of artillery. They were considered specialists rather than fighting soldiers. The reform-minded Louis XIV and Louvois, assisted by General-Inspector Pierre Surirey de Saint-Rémy, the Duke of Luxembourg and Vauban, made artillery an efficient military arm. This achieve-

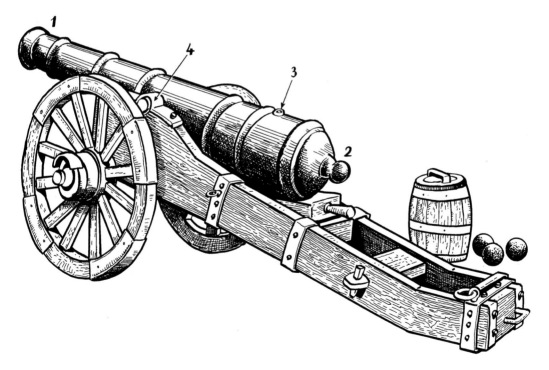

View of a gun mounted on a field carriage. The parts include (1) muzzle ; (2) breech; (3) vent; (4) trunnion.

ment was soon copied by other European powers. The King's Fusiliers Regiment was created in 1671 to protect gunners and also to serve and repair guns. Following this example other regiments were formed: the Royal-Bombardier in 1684, specialized in mortars and heavy siege guns, the Royal-Artillerie in 1694, and the Cannoniers des Côtes de l'Océan (coastal artillery unit) in 1702.

Artillery crews had to be courageous, cool and collected, well-drilled and highly disciplined. Everyone can imagine the chance taken by transporting and operating dangerous material like gunpowder, as well as firing primitive and not always reliable guns. Tragic accidents were common. Already dangerous in practice, the guns were even more so in the confusion and stress of battle.

Heavy guns, ammunition and siege equipment were not easily transported. They made enormous demands on both man and horse-power. An average field gun needed between six or eight horses or oxen to be drawn; thirty horses were required for 33 pounders. Artillery convoys were slow and, given the large numbers of wagons transporting associated supplies, stretched for many kilometers. They could only cover an average distance of 20 km. a day. For this reason, when possible, transport on waterways was preferred to traveling on bad roads. Louis XIV's artillery was numerous but rather poor in quality. Real improvements would happen only in the second half of the eighteenth century when profound reforms were undertaken by Lieutenant-Général Jean-Baptiste Vacquette de Gribeauval (1715–1789).

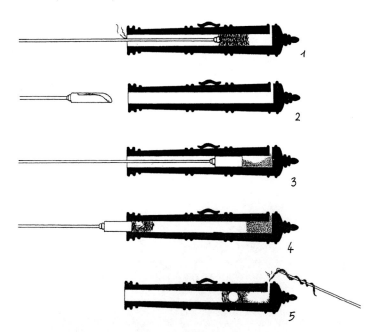

Louis XIV's artillery was divided into two main categories: field artillery and siege artillery.

Field artillery, also called close-support artillery, played a modest role in open field battle. Because of their poor range, guns had to be placed before the infantry and were therefore very exposed, vulnerable to being overrun and captured.

Siege artillery was a decisive weapon against fortifications in siege warfare.

Muzzle loading. The gun is shown here in cutaway.
(1) The gun is cleaned with a wet sponge after each shot is fired.
(2) The propelling charge is poured into the barrel with a long-hafted ladle.
(3) The propelling charge is pushed down to the chamber with a ramrod.
(4) The cannonball (wrapped in wad) is driven into the bore with a wooden rammer.
(5) The gun is now loaded; the propelling charge is ignited by a lintstock (a smoldering match attached to a stock) brought to the vent (touch hole).

European artillery in the seventeenth century was composed of two sorts of guns, produced in a great number of calibers and weights: cannons and mortars.

CANNON

In 1666 a reform brought a standardization of French cannon calibers. The nation had 4-, 8-, 12-, 24-, and 33-pounders, but many other sorts were interspersed among those main types. French artillery grew in size as captured equipment was absorbed. Since Louis XI's reign, guns had been fitted with two trunnions which allowed guns to rest on carriages. Two wheeled-carriages made transport easier and aiming more accurate. The fortress artillery was mostly mounted on navy-type carriages, a heavy duty truck moved by four small wheels. Indeed, as long as the gunners could access the gun muzzle to load it, mobility on a ship or on a rampart was less important than movement on the field. Carriages were painted dark red and metal parts were painted black.

Artillery pieces were mostly grouped in batteries. A battery was a group of guns of the same type firing in a common direction and aiming at the same target. Battery guns were mostly placed on a wooden platform made of thick planks resting on beams to avoid sinking in mud, loose ground or sand.

French artillery pieces cast during Louis XIV's reign were sometimes fine examples of decorative art. On a scroll near the muzzle was the name of the gun; below a motto was carved, then the grand master of artillery's coat of arms. Handles could be shaped in the form of dolphins. Louis XIV's personal insignia, the sun, with the motto "Nec Pluribus

Fortress gun and accessories. The items include (1) sponge (for cleaning gun); (2) ladle (to load explosive charge); (3) ramrod (to ram shot, wad and powder); (4) powder keg; (5) shots; (6) coin or wedge made of wood (to elevate or lower barrel); (7) handspike (to move the gun sideways); (8) lintstock (to ignite the charge).

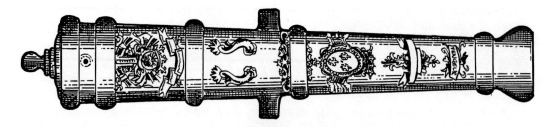

Decorated gun (seen from above)

Ammunition. (1) Simple solid shot made of plain metal. (2) Two-chained shots. (3) Grapeshot (an early form of anti-personnel shrapnel).

Impar," the royal coat of arms on a bed of trophies and the name of the manufacturer could also be carved. A gun could also be a gift. After the capture of the German cities of Mannheim and Frankenthal in 1688, Louis XIV offered Vauban four cannons of his choice from the enemy's arsenal.

Until the second half of the nineteenth century, guns were smooth-bored and muzzle-loading. Early experiments with breech-loaders were not very successful. Muzzle loading was a rather dangerous and time-consuming procedure. The successive steps were carefully carried out on a gun commander's order, who himself obeyed the battery commander. The propelling gunpowder (carried in kegs) was poured into the barrel with a lantern or ladle (long-hafted spoon) and pushed down with a ramrod; then a gunner drove the cannonball into the bore with a wooden rammer; the projectile was wrapped in a wad (old cloths, paper, mud, grass or hay) to avoid gas dispersion and to keep the round shot from rolling out; the piece was then ready to shoot and set back into firing position. When the gun was loaded, it had to be aimed at the target. Until the late nineteenth century, land service guns were used in the direct fire mode, that was the person who set the gun could see the target at which he was required to shoot. He aimed by manually moving the gun to the right or to the left with heavy handspikes and vertically by adjusting one or more wooden wedges (called coins) under the breech. Aiming was done by direct sight or with the help of instruments such as a quadrant, a pendular level or a marlinspike, but accuracy, especially in case of a moving target, was poor. The propelling charge was ignited with a lintstock, which brought a flashing flame through a narrow ignition-hole (called a vent) pierced in the upper side of the gun; the gunpowder charge exploded and expulsed the shot with flames, awful loud noise and violence so great that the gun moved briskly backwards. This sudden movement was called recoil and made re-aiming necessary after each round had been fired. Firing also produced bad-smelling clouds of smoke which soon hung thickly over batteries and obscured gunners' view on windless days. Right after every shot, the barrel was scraped with a spiral or worm (a sort of large corkscrew fixed on a staff) to remove fouling and swabbed out with a wet sponge attached to a wooden staff in order to extinguish all burning residues of wad.

Because of the slowness of loading, aiming and cleaning, the rate of fire of a muzzle-loading gun was rather low: ten to twenty shots per hour depending upon the caliber of both gun and crew. After this, the gun began to overheat; one had to cool down the barrel with water or with wet sheepskins or simply stop firing. Otherwise, the gun could develop cracks and even explode, with disastrous consequences for the crew. Range (the distance between the gun and its target) depended on the quantity of the propelling charge, the weight of the cannonball and the type of the gun. However range never exceeded one kilometer and to breach a stone fortification wall, close range fire of 50 meters (or even less if possible) was required. Cannons shot in grazing angles of 5 to 15 degrees. Firing was done in various fashions: direct or frontal, crossed, plunging, enfilading or flanking. Ricochet fire was created by Vauban and used for the first time at the siege of Philipsburg in 1688. This enfilade technique of *rico-*

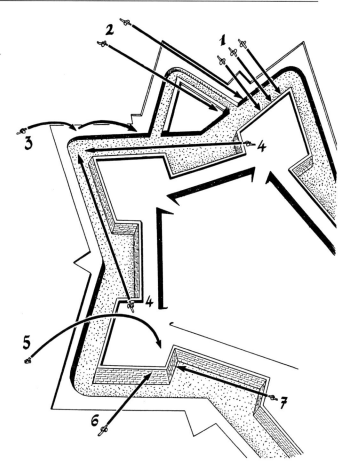

Various firing angles. These include (1) close range or breach-fire; (2) enfilade fire; (3) ricochet fire; (4) crossed or flanking fire; (5) mortar plunging or curved fire; (6) oblique fire; (7) flanking fire.

chet fire consisted of loading the gun with a small quantity of powder, which gave the cannonball a bounce and rebounce effect in order to hit more targets, the shot ricocheting across the ground like a flat pebble skipping across a pond.

Cannons fired heavy, solid, round iron balls. From the end of the Middle Ages until the second half of the nineteenth century, the caliber of the gun was given by the weight of the round, indicated in *livres*, an old French measure roughly equal to a pound (about half a kilogram). Cannonballs could destroy medieval crenellations, castle-gates, towers and masonry walls. One, single well-aimed projectile could kill a whole row of soldiers. One shot could sometimes launch two balls chained together or a ball with blades or spikes to tear away masts, sails, and rigging of ships. Iron cannonballs could also be heated and brought to redness on a grill or in a furnace; this dangerous method, first recorded in Poland about 1579, was more useful against ships and property than against soldiers. Hails of bullets, nails or stones were fired to kill or wound exposed enemies. Grapeshot or langridge (ancestors of shrapnel) consisted of a canister that sprayed the enemy with small metal balls as soon it left the muzzle. Usually used for short-range work, at 200 meters or less, these anti-personnel projectiles had a devastating effect against a troop of unprotected infantrymen or a cavalry formation.

MORTAR

A mortar was (and still is) a specific kind of gun whose projectile is fired with a high-curved trajectory, between 45 and 75 degrees, called plunging fire. Able to lob projectiles over high walls and to reach concealed objec-

Loading a mortar

tives or targets protected behind fortifications, mortars were particularly useful in siege warfare. They were characterized by a short, fat bore and two big trunnions. They rested on massive, timber-framed carriages, without wheels to withstand the shock of firing. The recoil force was passed directly to the ground by means of the carriage. Mortars were heavy and transported on wagons. The caliber was given not by the weight of projectiles but by the diameter of the muzzle. Louis XIV's mortars were 6, 12, and 18 inches. The rate of fire was low, less than five shots every hour. Precision was haphazard because laying was done without directly aiming at the target. The gunners calculated the approximate elevation angle with a quadrant. Mortar batteries were often used as terror

Mortar with projectiles. Below left: explosive bomb. Below right: carcass (incendiary bomb).

Cross-section and view of mortar

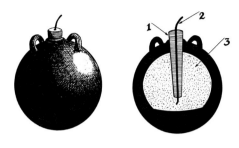

View and cross-section of bomb. (1) Fuse; (2) match; (3) powder.

Mortar on mount

weapons, fired at random in a besieged town. The range was adjusted by altering the elevation but also depended on the quantity of propelling powder charge and the type of projectile used. Certain heavy mortars could fire exceptionally to a maximum of three kilometers.

Projectiles fired by mortars were of two kinds: bomb and carcass. The bomb was a heavy, hollow, spherical, metal ball filled with powder and lit by a fuse. Its explosion projected lethal splinters in a large area and the burst caused heavy destruction. The carcass was an oval metal frame containing incendiary materials wrapped in a thick canvas envelope. The mixture was difficult to extinguish and set ablaze wooden houses and buildings. A *pierrier* was a mortar loaded with stones, metal balls, gravel or metal scraps. These projectiles were deadly for exposed personnel. To avoid damaging the bore, Vauban advocated putting this kind of primitive shrapnel in a wicker hamper. He recognized the various advantages of bombs,

Flag of the Royal Artillery regiment. The cross was white. The upper left and lower right squares were red. The upper right and lower left squares were green. The reign of Louis XIV also saw the introduction of the military uniform. This bearer's tunic was dark blue, with a black hat, and red breeches and waistcoat.

carcasses and shrapnel, but also recommended to limit their use in order to spare innocent lives among the population of besieged cities.

Matchlock Musket

Until the beginning of the eighteenth century when the flintlock musket appeared and was issued to troops, the main infantry weapon was the matchlock musket. This was used both on the battlefield and in defense, and its range was of importance for the design of bastioned fortifications. The musket was composed of a metal barrel and a wooden shoulder-stock, which extended along and under the barrel, and which at the same time supported the barrel and kept the butt steady while aiming and firing. To set off the gun, fine gunpowder was piled over a shallow pan around the touch hole (a small vent pierced on the right side of the barrel). There was a mechanical lock (serpentine), consisting of an arm which could be worked by yet another lever (trigger) under the butt. On the top end of the serpentine there was a clamp and in the clamp a piece of match (a cord impregnated with saltpeter or some other flammable substance) was placed. As a refinement, there was a moveable cover over the pan to prevent the powder blowing away in the wind. If it rained, that was just too bad, and all firing ceased. Loading the matchlock musket took some time. First the musketeer inserted and rammed in the barrel a charge of powder, the bullet, and wad (to prevent the ball rolling out), and poured fine powder into the pan. Then the slow-burning match was blown until glowing and fixed to the clamp. Now the weapon could be aimed and fired. The musketeer opened the pan cover, aimed, and pressed the trigger and this action swung the arm forward, pressed the glowing match into the powder in the pan, which ignited, flashed through the hole and exploded the powder charge in the barrel. This explosion propelled the bullet with violence out of the muzzle, resulting in a strong backward movement (a recoil absorbed by the shoulder and arms of the firer), loud noise, and a discharge of smoke. The matchlock musket weighed about 10 kg. and the musketeer usually had to support it on a forked stand. There was, however, a handgun lighter than the musket called *caliver* or *bastard musket*, which was fired without a gunrest. In addition the matchlock musket suffered from two other main faults: the necessity for keeping the match alight and the danger of explosion. After every shot the musketeer had to clean the barrel

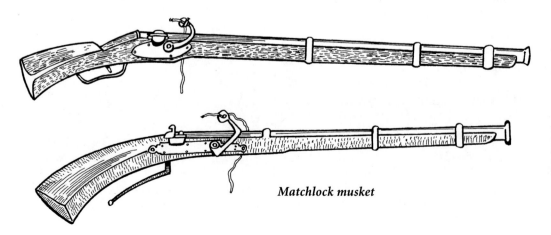

Matchlock musket

of fouling and sparks, and blow the vent and pan clear of unburnt powder. As can be imagined, the rate of fire was slow, possibly one shot per minute. Range, too, was rather poor and the inherent inaccuracy of the weapon was worsened by the clouds of smoke. Some kind of drill was thus necessary as a line of musketeers had to fire together in a volley. If they fired independently, no one would be able to see through the smoke; there had to be time for it to clear. The men were thus taught to load and fire according to a very precise series of movements (called postures), the object being that by practicing the sequences over and over they would become steadily more expert. In spite of its numerous disadvantages, the primitive musket was the weapon of the future. It was the first efficient small arm — a weapon carried and operated by the individual fighting man, and the ancestor to the modern rifle. Its bullet could easily kill an opponent, even wearing body armor, from a safe distance; and the soldier could keep his eye on the target while shooting.

Engineering Corps

The Engineering Corps was (and still is) charged with designing, building and maintaining fortifications. The corps's mission was also to collaborate closely with artillery and to establish temporary siege works. For centuries, engineers were civilian architects, master builders or artists (such as Albrecht Dürer, Michelangelo or Leonardo da Vinci) who earned money by contributing their research, experience and skill

Musketeer, c. 1685. This soldier of Louis XIV's infantry wears a uniform and a broad-brimmed hat. The uniform was blue or red for the elite troops and mainly grayish-white for the others. Except for its distinctive color, the uniform was curiously similar to civilian clothing. The man is armed with a sword and matchlock musket, and carries a leather bag containing spare bullets, a powder-flask and, slung over the shoulder, a broad leather belt from which were suspended on cords a number (usually twelve) of small wooden capsules containing pre-measured powder charges. Each of them held a bullet and the correct amount of powder for firing one shot. This bandolier was popularly called "The Twelve Apostles."

to military authorities. The first organization of what would become the *Génie* (French Engineering Corps) was created during François I's reign. The conception and execution of permanent defensive works were entrusted to civilian architects or to infantry or artillery officers who were placed under the command of the director of the fortifications. During Henri IV's reign, Maximilien de Béthunes, baron of Rosny and duke of Sully, further organized the administration of the department by clearly defining the assignment and geographical limits of the corps. This task was continued by Richelieu at the time of Louis XIII. In 1659, under Louis XIV's reign, Mazarin created the office of *commissaire général des fortifications*, commissioner general of the fortifications, and the engineering service progressively began to get specialized and militarized. The engineer became the technologist in the military world, practicing a black art which the "real" soldier could not aspire to, but without which the war could not be fought: bridges to be built, defenses constructed, fortifications mined, etc. These activities all required special skills. Engineers had to have knowledge of mathematics, geometry, architecture and construction techniques. At the same time, they were fighting men, ready to take an active part in the battle when the need arose; they thus had to have a good understanding of strategy, tactics, artillery, and military matters at large. In short, they needed to combine general engineering knowledge with a sound military education.

Engineer

In practice they were experienced men who had participated in sieges and worked on construction. Further theoretical education was done by reading numerous books and manuals, mostly translated Italian works and a few French theoretical treaties such as those of Jean Errard, Antoine De Ville and Blaise De Pagan. Engineers also studied and drew maps, constructed scale models and copied experienced colleagues' illustrations, designs and notes. When their education was complete and successfully tested at war, candidates obtained a brevet of *ingénieur ordinaire du roy* (king's ordinary engineer). Ar-

Sapper

tillerymen and engineers began to come into their own largely through the exertions of Vauban, who made use of them in siege warfare, which became the principal feature of seventeenth century warfare. Vauban can justly be regarded as the actual founder of the *Génie* in 1669. He recruited a permanent brigade of specialized officers, established rules and instructions for tasks and the organization of work, and set up an administration to handle pay, advancement and pensions. An ordinary engineer was posted in every important fortified place. These local engineers were supervised by a provincial director engineer, and the structure was directed at the national level by the commissioner general of the fortifications. For siege warfare, Vauban created companies of pioneers who specialized in digging trenches, and sappers—miners using underground explosives. In spite of Vauban's efforts, the Engineering Corps and Artillery remained in the same arm until the French Revolution in 1789. Only then was the Génie given an autonomous existence.

Though considered specialists rather than fighting soldiers, engineering officers, pioneers and sappers were particularly exposed to defenders' fire during a siege. Obviously their task was of utmost difficulty and very dangerous. Those men risked their lives at any moment and casualties were particularly high. To reduce the number of wounded and dead among them, Vauban thought the problems over and designed a better, safer and systematic method of attacking fortifications.

CHAPTER 3

Siege Warfare

Siege Warfare Advocated by Vauban

Siege warfare played an important role during Louis XIV's reign. The European kings' game was power, their board the map of the continent. Poliorcetics became the preeminent military science, and engineers played as essential a part in designing concepting and building fortifications as in conducting sieges. Louis XIV's armies were numerous but slow and unwieldy. They did not venture into hostile land with strongholds or fortresses whose garrisons could cut their supply-lines. Strategy was dominated by caution and most risks were calculated in advance. Louis XIV and his strategists preferred controllable and codified siege warfare rather than hazarding a bloody and uncertain battle in the open field. In the previous century's Religious Wars, the aim was to exterminate the enemy in order to save his soul and prevent his heresy from spreading. By the time of Louis XIV, the aim of war was a calculated exercise of power over the chessboard of Europe. Towns were pawns, captured, only to be exchanged at the conference table for some distant colonies, repossessed from a token garrison, possibly dismantled and eventually rebuilt according to strategic circumstances. Late seventeenth century warfare was for the rulers a formal game as orderly as the well-regulated gardens which surrounded their classical palaces. Louis XIV loved a good siege, the bigger the better. He was often present with his whole court, including the Princes du Sang (his own family and sons) and the ladies and damsels. Twenty of Vauban's 53 main sieges were attended by the king himself. A siege was a prestigious event, ending in a glorious victory to his armies, and Louis XIV — although a mere spectator — would graciously accept the credit for all Vauban's hard work. Warfare became a series of sieges, punctuated by battles only when some combination of maneuvering skill, confidence, or logistical pressure brought two armies face to face in the open field. Even great battles of Louis XIV's reign were seldom decisive, in the sense that they brought the wars to an immediate end. They were often irrelevant unless they helped to determine the outcome of a siege because even total victory in the open field did not necessarily compel the well-defended towns to surrender. Most of the battles of the time were more or less connected to a siege: Fleurus (1680) was linked to the siege of Charleroi; Friedlingen (1702) to the siege of Huningen; Malpaquet (1709) to the siege of Mons; and Denain (1712) to the siege of Landrécies. The generals of the seventeenth century were obliged to respect the dictates of military geography. They were compelled to expend a great deal in time, men, and money in trying to starve out or assault bastioned cities. Fortifications of the later seventeenth century, vast star-shaped complexes which kept the besieging artillery out of range of its prey, continued to be of strategic importance until the 1860s. Wherever they existed, they made battles irrelevant, and therefore unusual. Military geography shaped strategy.

Vauban's fame rests unjustly on his military architecture, for it was he who re-energized the attack, establishing its superiority over for nearly two centuries. It was in the domain of siege warfare that he actually innovated, with more contributions in the offensive realm than the defensive. It was because of his skillful attack on Saint-Menehoud that the young Vauban had been noticed by his superiors. In the second half of the seventeenth century, the bastioned fortification had become a "scientific" construction, which meant that its design was arrived at by a mathematical calculation of how to minimize the wall area that enemy shot could strike and maximize the area of open ground outside it that defending fire could sweep. The attack had therefore to be "scientific" as well. Before Vauban the art of siege existed, of course, but it was often a costly affair with assaulting troops concentrated into too narrow an axis of attack, with too many reckless frontal assaults before enemy defenses had been completely silenced. Siege engineers and Vauban soon worked

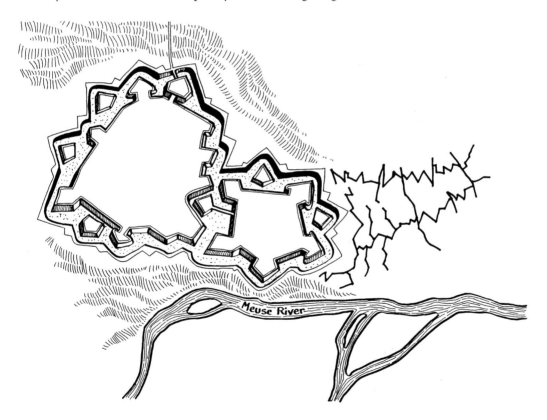

Siege of Stenay 1654. The small city of Stenay, situated north of Verdun in the province of Lorraine, was besieged by Louis XIV's army, commanded by General Fabert, in 1654. It was the first siege operation in which the young (and freshly enlisted in the royal army) Sebastien Vauban took part. On the left of the sketch is the city, in the middle the citadel, and on the right are the zig-zag-shaped approaching trenches and gun batteries established by Louis XIV's army.

out the principles of a classic siege, with attacking troops much less exposed to enemy fire, owing to a well-designed trench system dug on a broad front.

"A city besieged by Vauban is a city conquered!" said a proverb of the time. During the forty years of his military career, Vauban directed about fifty major sieges and published various theoretical books on the subject. During the siege of Maastricht in 1673, he tested a rational method, based on adaptation to the site, of systematic occupation of the ground and skillful use of artillery. Owing to this systematization he reduced casualties. "Let us burn more gunpowder, let us shed less blood!" he liked to say. In March 1672, Vauban delivered to Louvois the manuscript of his treaty about siege warfare titled *Mémoire pour servir d'instruction dans la conduite des sieges*, in which he described an ideal siege. This was later completed in a second book titled *De l'Attaque des Places*, published in 1706. Vauban's method of attacking a place became a codified and formal succession of phases which the French historian Michel Parent did not fear to compare to a classical drama play, characterized by unity of time, action and place.

BLOCKADE

Before laying siege to a place it was obviously wise to know the strength of the fortifications and the defenders' numbers, supplies, intentions and determination. This important information could be obtained from spies, deserters or enemy prisoners. Sometimes, engineering officers were sent on intelligence missions disguised as merchants, travelers or pilgrims. Vauban himself infiltrated in Namur for a secret and close study of the defenses before laying siege in 1691.

As ever, the siege began with a complete encirclement of the place. Cavalrymen blocked all accesses to the town, camps for the troops were erected and siege guns were regrouped in artillery parks. Standard protocol of seventeenth century siege warfare dictated that at this stage the attackers demand the surrender of the defenders, but it was also expected that this would be rejected for reasons of honor. The besieging force then established a *circumvallation line*. This line, facing outwards at about 2,400 meters from the defenses, was composed of fieldworks such as fortlets, redoubts, and earth walls with redans and ditches. It constituted an impenetrable blockade that completely isolated the besieged place from relief, and was intended to drive back any attempt from outside to break the blockade. The besiegers built another similar entrenched line, called *countervallation line*, which faced inwards. This line was meant to protect the camps and to guard against sorties from the garrison. Circumvallation and countervallation were already in use in Roman times, for instance when Julius Caesar besieged Alesia in 52 B.C. Both lines were quite useful because operations were not limited to the place of the siege but spread out in the whole region in the form of counter-attacks, ambushes, convoy-attacks or cavalry raids. However both circumvallation and countervallation lines were not always fully built because their establishment demanded a lot of time and manpower. Moreover the nature of the ground was not always suitable: in mountains for example, they were often impossible to build.

Once the city was totally blockaded, the engineers looked for the weakest spots where attacks would take place. They considered the nature of the ground, available space, waterways and marshland, dominating hills where batteries could be deployed and so on. Theoretically the main attack was directed against a bastioned front and its demi-lune. If the besieging forces were strong enough in soldiers and workers, secondary attacks could be

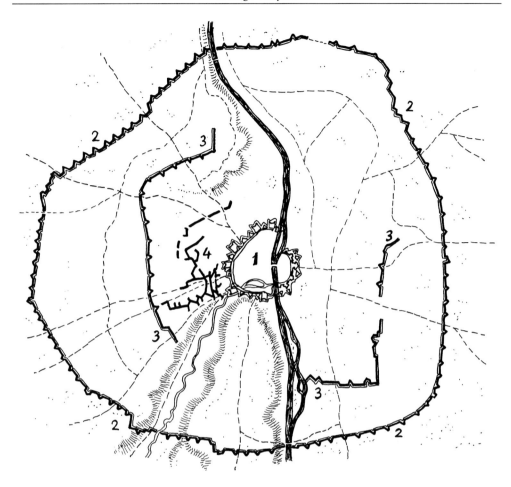

Siege of Maastricht, June 17–29, 1673. The city of Maastricht (1) and its suburb Wijk on the right bank of the river Meuse were totally blockaded by a continuous circumvallation line (2) made of earth walls with redans and a ditch. Sections of countervallation lines (3) were established to protect the camps and supply depots. French approaches (4), consisting of trenches and saps, were then dug to come close to the city. There troops would establish batteries to bombard the defenders and gather assaulting troops under cover.

added to the principal offensive in order to deceive the besieged and to oblige him to scatter his strength.

APPROACHES, PARALLELS AND BATTERIES

Parallels were trenches excavated by the besiegers. Just as the name indicates, they were dug alongside the attacked front, and enabled the besiegers to get closer and closer to their objective in comparative safety until the time appointed for a final, full-scale assault. These tactical elements were already used by Jean de Châtillon (1560–1616), king Henri IV's military engineer at the siege of La Fère in 1595. This method had also been employed in 1669 by Italian mercenary engineers serving the Turks at the siege of Candia (today Heraklion, capital of Crete).

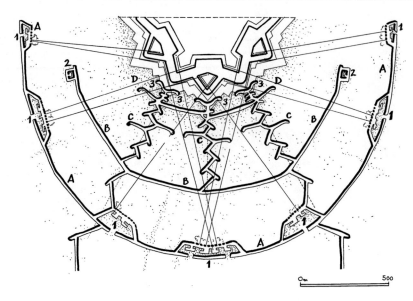

Vauban's theoretical parallels. AA: first parallel with gun batteries (1); BB: second parallel with redoubts (2); CC: half-parallels; DD: third parallel with cavaliers de tranchée (3). This strict geometrical siegecraft, of course, could not always be applied, and most attack works actually built were much simpler and more adapted to the terrain than the idealized examples displayed in textbooks.

Fourth parallel. AA: third parallel; BB: fourth parallel; (1) cavaliers de tranchée; (2) mortar batteries; (3) breach batteries; (4) breach.

Sap digging. Workers used a mantlet (a wheeled shield pushed ahead of the excavation) and a wall of gabions to protect themselves from enemy fire.

*Profile of a sap (**Vauban**'s Traité de l'Attaque des Places). The excavation is reinforced at the enemy's side by an embankment of earth, gabions and fascines.*

Thus the method pre-existed, and it was taken over and systematically codified by Vauban. Parallels had to be broad enough (at least 3 meters) to enable the marching of soldiers but also the coming-and-going of artillery trains, ammunition carts and supply wagons. They had to be deep enough in order to give sufficient protection from the defenders' fire. Their sloping sides were reinforced by gabions, fascines, brushwood or planks. Parallels were linked together by saps. Saps were communication trenches given a zigzag layout in order to avoid enemy enfilade fire. Saps were excavated (when possible) lengthwise to the salients of the bastions because along this imaginary "capital line" were (in theory)

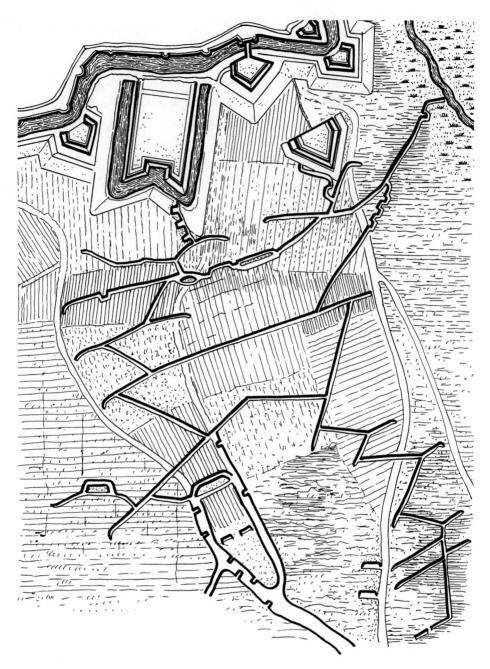

Parallels at the siege of Maastricht, 1673. Because the Dutch had flooded large parts of the countryside around Maastricht, the French attack was concentrated toward the Tongere Gate.

areas where enemy fire was the weakest. Bearing in mind the reduction of casualties among the pioneers, Vauban insisted on protection by night digging, by using mantlets (wheeled shields made of thick planks pushed ahead of the excavation) and by walls of gabions (large cylindrical baskets filled with earth).

Vauban's siege method was characterized by the systematic use of four parallels. The *first parallel* was established at the limit of the defenders' guns' range (about 600 meters); it was used for general communication and could also serve as countervallation line.

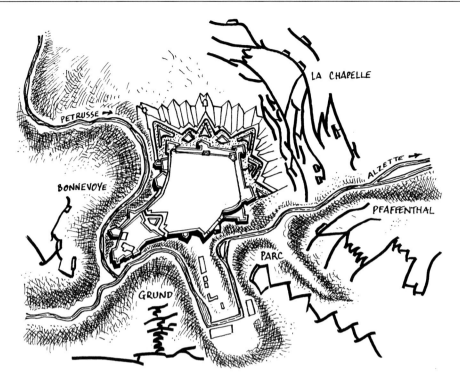

Parallels at the siege of Luxembourg, 1684. The main attack was directed against the southern fronts in the flat plain of La Chapelle. Mortar and gun batteries were positioned on the Pfaffenthal, Parc, Grund and Bonnevoye hills dominating the city.

The *second parallel* was excavated at approximately 350 meters from the defenders' position; there, sheltered batteries were placed lengthwise to bastion faces to give enfilade and ricochet fire which, with a rebound effect, had a great chance of inflicting casualties and damage. Batteries rested on platforms and were protected by earth banks, gabions, fraises, ditches and so on. Batteries could also be deployed on "cavaliers," which were raised terraces giving additional height and better command to the guns.

The *third parallel* was dug at the foot of the glacis; there Vauban advocated building the so-called *cavaliers de tranchée* (trench cavaliers). The purpose of these raised structures, made of three or four tiers of gabions filled with earth, was to dominate and neutralize with grenades the enemies defending the covered way and the arms emplacements. On the third parallel, mortars and batteries were positioned to bombard at close range the lateral outworks and to neutralize the defenders' fire.

Between the second and the third parallels, sections of trenches were excavated (called *half-parallels*) where other gun batteries were deployed and where storming troops were regrouped.

The *fourth parallel*, also called *couronnement du chemin couvert* (crowning of the covered way) was established on the crest of the covered way. In this entrenchment guns were deployed to carry out a breach, as sufficient weight of fire could be mounted to batter a bastion into rubble. Another method was to dig a gallery under the walls and to install a gunpowder mine that was exploded.

However not all sieges progressed with the clockwork precision described above because Vauban adapted his method to the natural particularities of the place he was besieging. The sieges of Maastricht in 1673 and Luxembourg in 1684, for example, were adapted to the sites.

BREACH

A breach is a gap made by the besiegers in a wall or in any other defensive structure. The destruction of the wall could come through bombardment or mining.

Siege battery

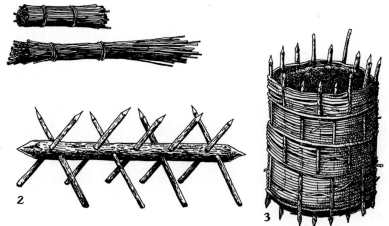

Siege devices. (1) Fascines; (2) frizzy horse; (3) gabion.

In bombardment, the breach was made by gun batteries deployed on the fourth parallel at very close range (less than 50 meters). Vauban advocated cutting out the stonework of the scarp in a letter H pattern. It was calculated that about thousand shots were needed to collapse the scarp wall and fill a part of the ditch with debris.

In mining, the attackers dug a tunnel inside or under the wall foundations. Barrels of gunpowder were then placed in a mine chamber. The explosion of the charges blew away the masonry of the wall. The mine could be simple, double or triple according to what destruction was planned. Vauban considered mining a very important way to breach the defense. Mining was, of course, a dangerous business which had to combine two contradictory aspects: the efficiency of the explosion in performing its function and the safety of the miners. To increase efficiency of this method, Vauban carried out research and study and wrote a manual, *Traité pratique des Mines*. To reduce casualties and accidents, he pleaded for the creation of specialized and well trained companies of miners.

Final Assault

The cannonade reached a climax and the walls crumbled; mines exploded, blowing the ramparts sky-high, opening a pathway into the heart of the besieged fortress. When the breach was made, the following steps led to conquest. First the assaulting party had to get access to the breach. To achieve this, a sloping gallery was excavated from the fourth parallel to the bottom of the moat. The assailants ran across the dry ditch and stormed the breach. The situation was completely different, obviously, if the moat was filled with water.

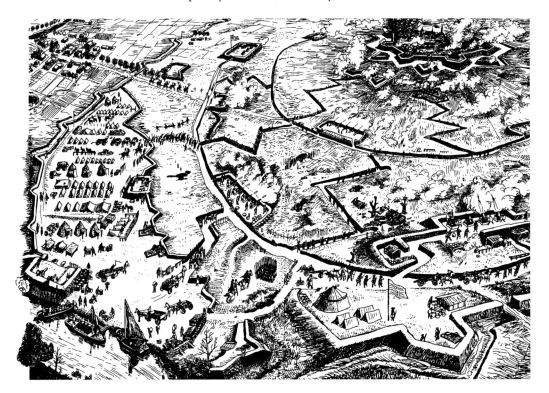

Overview of a siege at the time of Vauban and Louis XIV

The attackers had then to build a kind of dike or bridge using debris of the counterscarp and different materials such as trees, rubble, stones, beams, gabions, fascines, or sacks filled with earth, unless a way could be devised of draining the moat, leaving the besiegers high and dry. To avoid confusion and misunderstanding, Vauban advocated assaults in bright daylight at dawn. If the enemy held on and resisted, he recommended using gabions to form a retrenchment (called *nid-de-pie*).

Infantry assault on a bastioned fortress, however badly it had been knocked about, always remained a desperate business. In the middle of the smoking debris, the assault was a deadly hand-to-hand struggle. It was a crucial, bloody and decisive moment for both parties. A repulsed assault often cost a lot of lives (for example, at Philipsburg in 1676, there were about 1,200 casualties). A successful assault did not necessarily mean the end of the battle. The defenders could continue to resist and build an improvised barricade right behind the breach, while musketeers and gunners from an adjoining bastion directed withering fire on the exposed assault party. When the breach and the barricade were taken, the defenders could retreat into the citadel or the urban castle. In that case, the attackers had to envisage a new siege. A whole new operation might have to deal with the next stronghold or ring of defenses. But stubborn resistance was often punished by the looting of the town and retaliation against the civilians.

CAPITULATION

As we already know, the final objective of seventeenth century warfare was not the extermination of the enemy but his surrender. Most of the time, the final assault was not necessary and a prudent and well-advised fortress governor generally surrendered after a short combat, honor intact, before the breach was effected, and before the horrors of a storming overtook him. According to seventeenth century formalized "rules" of siege warfare, a garrison should be allowed to surrender with honor when it had shown its fighting skill and gallantry until that point. Capitulation could not happen too soon however, otherwise the defenders could be accused of cowardice and their commanders would have to appear before a military court of justice. But surrender had not to occur too late, otherwise the besiegers might decide to retaliate by looting the town. For this delicate and critical decision, the civilian population and urban authorities often brought pressure on the military to choose the right moment. When the governor of the place decided to surrender, a white flag was hoisted and a drummer beat "la chamade," announcing a cease-fire. Hostages and negotiators were then exchanged to discuss the terms. During the truce one could gain time, bargain or haggle over various conditions. Depending on circumstances, when the terms were honorable and acceptable for both parties, an act of surrender was signed.

For the defeated soldiers of the garrison, this document stipulated different matters such as time, conditions and place of departure; destination; fate of the wounded, hostages, prisoners and deserters; as well as conservation or deprivation of flags, baggage, armament and supplies. In the seventeenth century, surrender was normally accompanied by a sort of ritual. If the defenders had fought with gallantry, the defeated garrison was given the honor of war. The men were allowed to leave with waving flag, beating drums and weapons while the victorious party presented arms. Mercenaries had to swear to serve no more until the end of the campaign and were escorted back to the borders. They could also be encouraged to enlist in the victor's army.

Regarding the civilian population, conditions of surrender were extremely various and totally dependent upon the conqueror's further intentions and clemency. The urban authorities had to deliver the city keys, and the town militia was disarmed and its artillery confiscated. According to the new ruler's plan, the population might lose or keep urban rights, exemptions and freedom of economy, administration and religion. They could also be offered liberal terms, and strict discipline could reduce or safeguard the people from the horrors of plunder and rapine. Much depended on whether the capture of the place was temporary or permanent.

After the battle, while the leaders were at the table of negotiation, the dead were buried,

Saint-Denis gate. Saint-Denis gate in Paris (which still exists today at the junction of Saint-Denis Street and Bonne-Nouvelle Boulevard) was erected to commemorate Louis XIV's victories in Holland in 1672. The gate is an arch of triumph designed by the architect François Blondel and decorated by the sculptor Michel Anguier.

and all traces of the siege were removed. Saps and parallels were blocked up again and fortlets, redoubts and batteries were dismantled in order to avoid an eventual re-utilization by the enemy, returning to lay siege to the city. A religious office (*Te Deum*) was celebrated in the cathedral, and a ceremony in the town hall marked officially the transfer of power.

The capitulation was followed by the occupation of the place. Occupation was definitive or temporary according to many political, economic and military factors. Urban fortifications could either be dismantled or repaired or even modernized according to the strategy envisioned by the king. Relationships between the conquered population and the new occupant as well as general strategy often had financial consequences for the city. In some case, the urban authorities were fined, obliged to accept and finance a citadel and were burdened with the maintenance costs of an occupying garrison.

The fall of an important town often excited French enthusiasm and did not stay unnoticed in Europe, particularly when the Sun-King and his court attended the siege. Louis XIV's exploits were invariably compared to those of Alexander the Great, Julius Caesar, and Charlemagne. In order to commemorate the event, but also to underline Louis XIV's glory, various pieces of art were produced such as poems, drawings, engravings, paintings (notably those by the Flemish painter Frans van der Meulen), marble tablets, tapestries, medals or monuments. These works of art, whether they were faithful representations or more subjective interpretations, were just many expressions to help the world remember Louis XIV's prestige.

Advantages and Disadvantages of Vauban's Method

Vauban's method of attacking fortified places, constituted undeniable progress, not only by reducing slaughter but also for improving the certainty of success. If Middle Ages and Renaissance siege warfare was an uncertain undertaking, in the late seventeenth century, a besieged town was, most of the time, going to have to surrender. In normal conditions, Vauban took pride in his ability to predict the exact time each siege would take him, even before the operation had begun. He estimated achieving capitulation within 48 days, only two weeks for a small stronghold. For example, the very well-fortified city of Maastricht was taken after a siege of thirteen days (1673) and Ghent was taken within six days (1678). On the other hand, the relatively weak city of Mons only capitulated after nine months (1691) and Namur after five months (1695). Vauban's siege system represented something of a revolution in the art of poliorcetics since it drastically reduced casualties, and made sieges both predictable and rather short, whereas previously they had too often been the exact opposite.

However, Vauban's method presented very serious drawbacks, and static fortress siege warfare remained a grueling test, particularly for the civilian population, always suffering the most. Vauban's system excluded any possibilities for a sudden surprise attack, allowing the besiegers to concentrate their weapons and men on the attacked front. It required very important resources such as funds, men, food, transportation, artillery and ammunition. For example, the siege of Mons in 1691 required 106,000 rounds; 7,000 bombs; 40,000 grenades; 1,000 pounds of gunpowder; 64,000 tools; and 30,000 sacks filled with earth. Besides, the establishment of fieldworks was time-consuming and laborious. It demanded

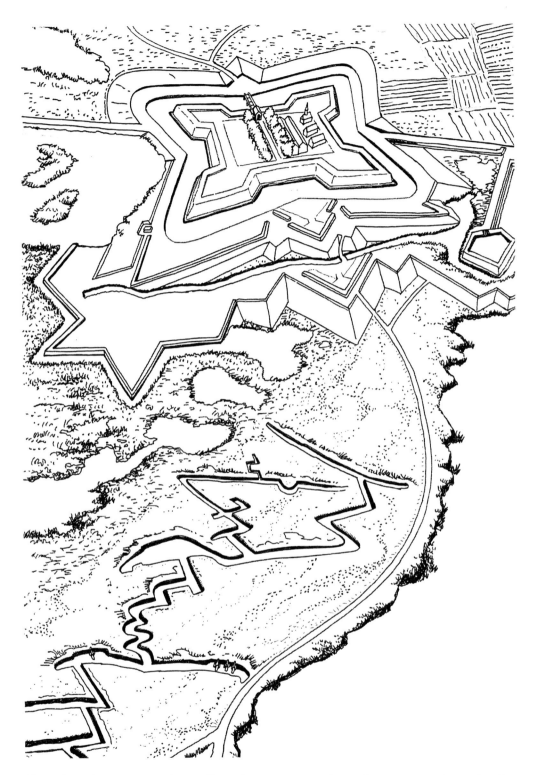

Siege of Fort Roovere 1747. The small Dutch Fort Roovere, situated near Berg-op-Zoom (southern Netherlands), was besieged and taken by the French on July 24 and 25, 1747. The city of Berg-op-Zoom was taken after a siege that lasted from July 12 to September 16, 1747. Forty years after Vauban's death his attack methods were still used.

a lot of manpower and troops ten times the force of the defenders. Obviously all fieldworks were made by hand without any mechanized help and, of course, the nascent French engineering corps never had enough manpower. In this predicament workers were hired, but also rounded up among the local civilian population. At the siege of Maastricht in 1673, more than 20,000 peasants were drafted. At the siege of Mons in March 1691, the French army impressed 20,000 workers into service, who built the 27 km. long circumvallation line and excavated some 30,000 cubic meters of earth. In 1693, at the siege of Charleroi, 12,000 men were arbitrary employed. No need to say, this very dangerous and tiresome forced labor was unpopular. The local peasantry was also obliged to help fabricate gabions, fascines and brushwood. They had to supply horses and oxen, tools, carts and wagons, and often food and billet too. Refusal to collaborate, desertion or unwillingness were punished by fine or imprisonment and, in the worst case, by looting, burning, retaliation and atrocities. For the local population, the approach of an army or a siege was a calamity. War, not only in the seventeenth century, always leaves behind it a track of tears, hatred, desolation, ruin and death, as illustrated by the winter of 1688–1689 that witnessed the cruel and senseless devastation of the German province of the Palatinate perpetrated by the French.

Vauban's fieldworks mobilized huge manpower and took a lot of time. This was the besieged's main trump. A small-but-determined garrison entrenched behind modest fortifications could hold back and delay a whole army. Fortresses, fortified cities, forts and strongholds constituted a network of obstacles opposing enemy progress. The time gained by this war of attrition war was used by diplomats to form new coalitions and by the military to regroup fresh armies. This predominant aspect of siege warfare produced, as a consequence, slow, long, and exhausting campaigns in which logistics (the supply of food, ammunition and other materials and transportation) played a decisive role. Condé-sur-l'Escaut, Ath or Audenarde were repeatedly taken, lost, and reconquered. The small stronghold of Huy near Liege in Belgium was besieged seven times and occupied twelve times between 1672 and 1715. The slow pace of wars was increased by the seasonal nature of the conflicts. Weather conditions played an important role during a siege. If spring and summer were rainy, transport and movements were difficult, gunpowder was wet, and camps and fieldworks became mudpools which lowered efficiency and a degraded morale.

Vauban's principles of siege warfare were rapidly copied by his opponents at the end of the seventeenth century. This was why he was obliged to review his ideas regarding defense and fortification.

Despite its disadvantages, Vauban's method of siegecraft was applied over a century and a half. Examples are plentiful. The siege of Berg-op-Zoom in 1747, and the siege of the Dutch-held citadel of Antwerp by a French army in 1832 were virtually direct applications of his poliorcetical theories. Even aspects of the siege of Dien-Bien-Phu in Indochina (November 1953–May 1954), when the French Colonial Army opposed the Communist Viet Minh, included many of Vauban's siege features such as encirclement, mines, saps, artillery duels, sorties, assaults, counter-attacks... and final surrender of the garrison.

It should also be noted that Vauban was rewarded by Louis XIV for victorious sieges. In 1673, for the siege of Maastricht, Vauban got 80,000 pounds; for Valenciennes in 1677, 75,000 pounds. For his success at Luxembourg in 1684, he received 30,000 pounds, and for the campaign in the Palatinate in 1688, Vauban was granted 2,000 pounds, four guns and a diamond with a worth 1,000 pounds. For the siege of Mons in 1691, he received 100,000 pounds and for the capture of Namur a year later, the sum of 120,000 pounds.

Sieges Directed by Vauban

This list was established by Vauban himself. Only actual sieges are counted, which means those where trenches were dug and cannons fired. According to the traditions of the time, Vauban, although he directed the whole operation, was not considered a military commander. Thus he was always placed under an army senior officer's command. When Louis XIV or a member of the royal family personally attended the operation, the engineer and commander-in-chief stood aside. The king or his relative, even though totally idle and merely passive spectators, were regarded as the actual commanding officers of the operation.

1653 Second siege of Saint-Menehould in Lorraine: Vauban (second engineer under First Engineer Chevalier de Clerville) serving under Marshal du Plessis, duke of Choiseul

1654 Siege of Stenay in Lorraine: Vauban (second engineer under Chevalier de Clerville) serving under Monsieur Abraham de Fabert (marshal in 1658 then governor of Sedan)

Siege of Clermont-en-Argonne in Champagne: Vauban (second engineer under Chevalier de Clerville) serving under Henri de Saint-Nectaire, duke and marshal de la Ferté

1655 Sieges of Landrécies, Condé-sur-l'Escaut, and Saint-Gillain: Vauban (second engineer under Chevalier de Clerville) serving under Henri de Saint-Nectaire, duke and marshal de la Ferté, and Henri de la Tour d'Auvergne, viscount of Turenne

1656 Siege of Valenciennes (from this siege on, Vauban served as first engineer) under Henri de Saint-Nectaire, duke and marshal de la Ferté and Henri de la Tour d'Auvergne, viscount of Turenne

Sieges of Condé-sur-l'Escaut and Saint-Gillain: Vauban placed under leadership of Monsieur du Passage and Monsieur de Schombe

1657 Siege of Montmédy: Vauban serving under Henri de Saint-Nectaire, duke and marshal de la Ferté

Siege of Mardyck: Vauban placed under leadership of Henri de la Tour d'Auvergne, viscount of Turenne

1658 Siege of Gravelines: Vauban serving under Henri de Saint-Nectaire, duke and marshal de la Ferté

Sieges of Ypres and Audenarde: Vauban placed under leadership of Henri de la Tour d'Auvergne, viscount of Turenne

1667 Sieges of Tournai, Douai and Lille: Vauban placed under nominal leadership of Louis XIV

1672 Sieges of Orsoy and Doesburg: Vauban placed under nominal leadership of Louis XIV

1673 Siege of Maastricht: Vauban placed under nominal leadership of Louis XIV

1674 Siege of Besançon (city and citadel): Vauban placed under nominal leadership of Louis XIV

Siege of Audenarde: Vauban serving under Monsieur de Rochepierre

1676 Siege of Condé-sur-l'Escaut: Vauban placed under nominal leadership of Louis XIV

Siege of Bouchain: Vauban placed under nominal leadership of "Monsieur," Philippe of Orléans (Louis XIV's young brother)

Sieges of Aire-sur-la-Lys and Fort François: Vauban serving under Marshal d'Humières

1677 Sieges of Valenciennes and Cambrai (city and citadel): Vauban placed under nominal leadership of Louis XIV

Siege of Saint-Gillain: Vauban serving under Marshal d'Humières

1678 Sieges of Ghent (city and citadel) and Ypres (city and citadel): Vauban placed under nominal leadership of Louis XIV

1683 Siege of Courtrai (city and citadel): Vauban serving under Marshal d'Humières

1684 Siege of Luxembourg: Vauban serving under François De Bonne, Marshal de Créqui

1688 Sieges of Philippsburg, Mannheim (city and citadel) and Frankenthal: Vauban serving under "Monseigneur le Grand Dauphin" (Louis XIV's son)

1691 Siege of Mons: Vauban placed under nominal leadership of Louis XIV

1692 Siege of Namur (city and citadel): Vauban placed under nominal leadership of Louis XIV

1693 Siege of Charleroi: Vauban serving under Monsieur de Luxembourg

1697 Siege of Ath: Vauban serving under Marshal Nicolas de Catinat

1693 Siege of Vieux-Brisach: Vauban serving under Louis of France, Duke of Burgundy (Louis XIV's grandson)

Opposite: Italian bastioned front by F. de Marchi, 1599. Francesco de Marchi (1504–1577) from Bologna was an Italian military engineer and theoretician of the bastioned fortification. On that subject he wrote a treatise titled Architectura Militare *in 1565, which was later published in 1559 at Brescia. The main features advocated by Marchi and other Italian engineers formed the basis of bastioned fortification, including the following: (1) bastion with ears; (2) curtain at the same level as the bastions; (3) ditch; (4) ravelin or demi-lune, a triangular outwork placed between two bastions in front of the curtain; (5) covered way, a broad lane covered by a breastwork; (6) glacis, a wide and bare stretch of ground around the fortress deprived of vegetation and building for defending against fire. The pentagonal and well-armed bastions, projecting from walls and supported by ravelin and covered way, became the key feature in a mutually supporting system of defense, as attacking troops could not reach the foot of bastions and walls without suffering appalling casualties. The pentagonal bastions and the triangular ravelins gave the bastioned fortification a very distinctive, geometric, star-shaped form which, in essence, was dictated by the arcs of fire of the guns within the fortress.*

Chapter 4

Vauban's Bastioned Fortifications

Italian Bastioned Fortifications

The utilization of artillery in the fourteenth century and its progress the following centuries gave rise to an evolution of military architecture. Guns created distance between belligerents. High Middle Ages towers, walls and gatehouses, which were meant to be obstacles and from which defenders could drop missiles and projectiles, only became vulnerable targets. What was now needed was a fortified place from which guns could be fired. As warfare became an ever more costly and destructive business, all aspects of military affairs were

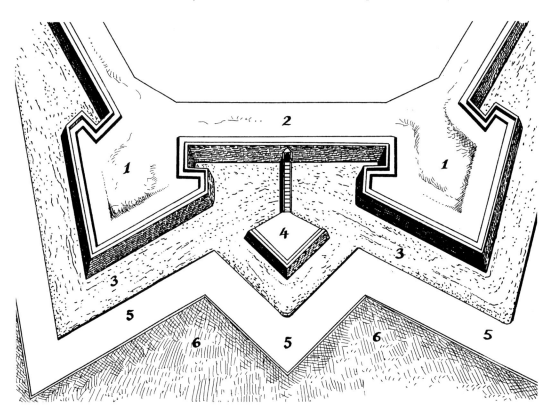

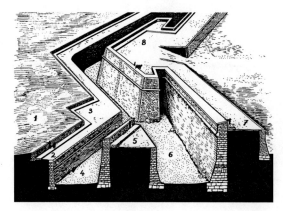
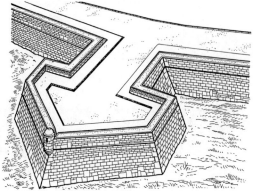

Above, left: Cross-section, bastioned system. *The cross-section shows the most important features of the bastioned fortification: its half-sunk low profile, and the related height of the works given by deep ditches. Works were reveted with stone masonry filled with rammed earth, the whole constituting a structure of immense solidity so as to provide both a solid cannon platform and an outer face on which impacting shot made the least possible impression. (1) Glacis; (2) covered way; (3) place of arms; (4) ditch; (5) ravelin or demi-lune; (6) main ditch; (7) curtain (main wall); (8) bastion.* Right: Italian bastion. *It is not known who invented the bastion. It probably came to several designers at the same time as the most suitable design. The bastion had two faces forming a wedge that pointed out toward the surrounding countryside so as to present a glancing surface to enemy fire. The bastion had two flanks that joined the wedge to the walls, used by the defenders to sweep the ditch and stretches of wall between the bastions.*

subject to analysis. The money to be made invited envy and drew all sorts of practitioners into the market. So scholars, intellectuals, architects and even famous and visionary artists such as Leonardo da Vinci, Michelangelo and Albrecht Dürer subjected fortification to intensive study, launching a whole flood of speculation and arguments about new methods of defense. Proper military architects and engineers began to appear, and with more or less skill, quickly designed more sturdy defenses in the form of low and thick gun-towers to create grazing trajectories

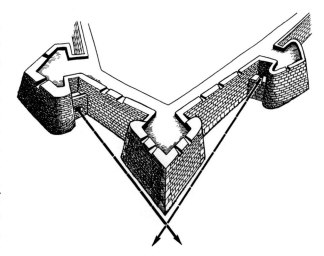

Principle of flanking. The black arrows indicate the line of fire.

and all-round protection. It soon appeared that since cannons did their worst against high walls, new walls to resist them must therefore stand low and be thick, with sloping faces. The result was that fortification became horizontal instead of vertical. Examples of these transitional forms are numerous: the castle of Salses near Perpignan in southern France or Henry VIII's coastal forts such as Deal, Walmer or Sandown in England.

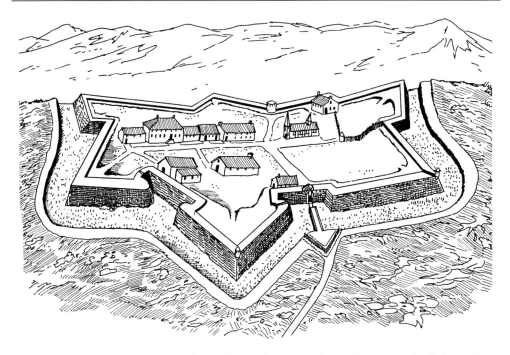

Fort Puymaure. Fort Puymaure, situated near Gap in southern France, was built by engineer Ercole Negro and Jean Sarrazin in 1580.

Fort du Montalban, Nice, 1559–61. Fort Montalban, situated on top of Mount Boron, dominating the city of Nice on the French Riviera, was built between 1559 and 1561 by the Italian engineer Domenico Ponsello. Fort Montalban was intended to control and defend the passage between Nice and Villefranche-sur-Mer. It was a massive square with four bastions placed at the angles.

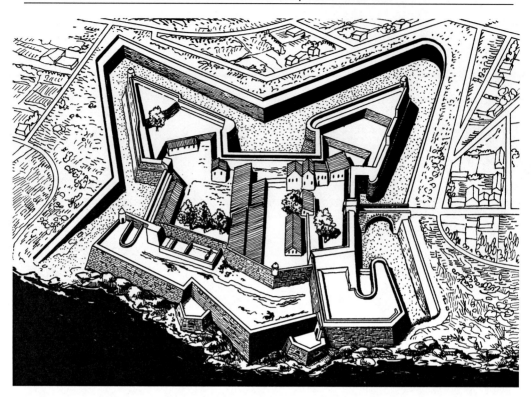

Citadel of Villefranche-sur-Mer. Villefranche was a port possessed by the dukes of Savoy, near Nice. The citadel was built in the beginning of the 1560s by engineer Francesco Paciotto for Duke Emmanuel-Philibert the Great.

Further developments gave birth to a solid, angular, geometrical fortification characterized by a low and half-sunken profile and a bastioned outline. The modern bastioned fortification was created for historical reasons in the Italy of the Renaissance, but it is not known who invented the bastion. It appeared as a response to the highly successful campaign in Italy launched in 1494 by King Charles VIII of France, who had a modern, mobile artillery, which demonstrated that medieval castles with high walls and towers had had their days. Bastioned fortification not only resisted bombardment and held the enemy at a distance, it also served as a defending fire platform. The wonder is that the technique was developed so fast, in the first decade of the sixteenth century, that it developed so rapidly and that it spread so quickly all over Europe, measured against the pace of other adaptations to military innovation. It was an amazing creation and at the same time an enormous undertaking costing a lot of money, as the issue was nothing less than the replacement in a few decades of a continent-wide system of vertical fortification which had been designed and built over many centuries. Bastioned fortification was universally adopted, at least by those who could afford the gigantic costs involved: emperors, kings, popes, and a few wealthy counts, powerful dukes, and rich independent cities. Gunpowder and, the response to it, bastioned fortification, marked the end of an era, the disappearance of private castles, and the monopoly of the state in matters of national defense. There was a scramble among the great powers of Europe to build new defenses around the towns at risk of attack, since whoever held the towns controlled the countryside. There-

Fort Exilles (Turin). Fort Exilles was built between 1600 and 1610 in a pass in the Alps near Turin (Italy).

fore war became a struggle for strongholds, a series of protracted sieges. However the demise of the obsolete medieval castles did not occur overnight. Obviously a medieval fortress could still resist a gang of bandits or a military force not equipped with artillery. In many areas where artillery could not easily be brought in (for example in mountains or marshy places or in coastal situations), old-style medieval fortresses and "transitional" pre-bastioned fortifications retained a significant value.

The basic principle of the bastioned fortification designed by Italian artists, engineers and architects such as Giorgio Martini, Antonio and Guiliano da Sangallo, Michele San Michele, Francesco da Marchi, Girolamo Cataneo, Francesco Paciotto and many others, was further developed by Dutch engineers (Simon Stevin and Adrian Anthoniszoon for example) during the long war of independence against Spain from 1558 to 1648. For the sake of economy, Dutch fortifications were made of earth and wood rather than of stone, but they effectively held back the powerful Spanish offensives of 1605 and 1606.

The bastioned system, a circuit of low, thick walls punctuated by protruding bastions, presented many advantages, the most important being the well-designed flanking, which suppressed all blind spots (zones below and beyond where the ground could not be seen and defended). In a bastioned fortification, every part was always covered by fire coming from neighboring sections; communication was easy along bastions and curtains which were broad and at the same level; and the sunken profile did not offer too obvious a target to enemy fire. The bastioned line with its thick ramparted walls and angular outline

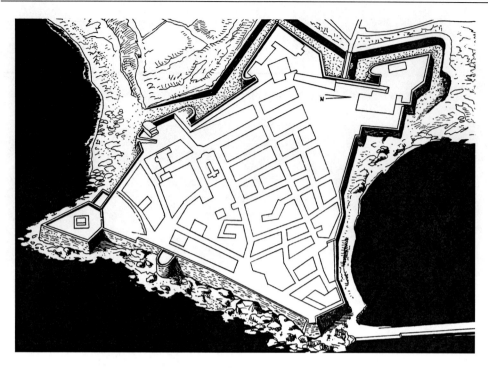

Bastia, Corsica. The citadel of Bastia on the island of Corsica was built between 1480 and 1521. It formed a neighborhood of the city called Terra Nueva. The city of Bastia, founded in 1372, is the capital of the island. Corsica was a possession of the free port-city of Genoa until the French purchased it in 1768.

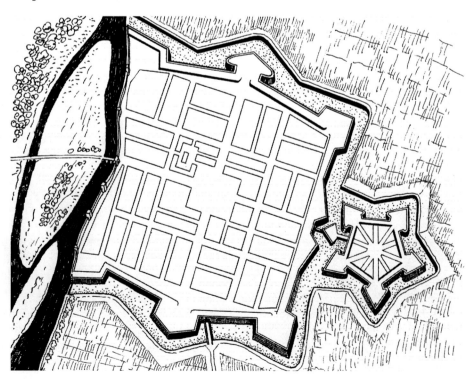

offered a good resistance to enemy fire. Faced with masonry and filled with thick earth layers, it could absorb cannonballs. In other words, the bastioned system restored the balance of arms in favor of defense as rapidly as cannons had reversed it at the end of the fifteenth century. The main disadvantage of bastioned fortification was the extremely high cost involved. This brought an end to private medieval fortification and announced the standardization of military architecture which progressively became the monopoly of the state. While towns in the Middle Ages owned their walls and towers, with the development of expensive guns and bastioned fortifications, cities could no longer pay for these expenses. They asked for help from the king, who had gained in power since Louis XI. In return, the king demanded control, guardianship and then exclusivity over defenses, and only places with a strategic value for the security of the realm were fortified, mostly situated at the borders. The bastioned system remained in use until the early 1870s, at least in France.

Vauban's Predecessors

During the sixteenth century, European fortification was dominated by Italian engineers, who were the first international technical mercenaries. François I and Henri II in France, Carlos V in Germany, in Italy and in the Low Countries, the knight Hospitallers in Malta, and Henry VIII in Britain relied upon Italian architects to build citadels, forts and urban walls. By the end of the sixteenth century, the Italian monopoly gradually decreased and, at the beginning of the following century, new generations of national engineers appeared. By that time every state that aspired to preserve its sovereignty (and that was rich enough) had its frontiers protected at the most vulnerable points — mountain passes, river-crossings, navigable estuaries, communications crossroads, etc. — by bastioned defenses. The modern frontiers of Europe are, indeed, largely the outcome of fortress-building. In France, under Henri IV's reign, Minister Sully founded the embryo of what would later become the *Corps des Ingénieurs du Roi* (King's Engineering Corps). French engineers borrowed the best of Italian and Dutch methods and created a new and original style. One of the first French theorists of the bastioned fortification was a certain Veroil de la Treille. In 1557 he published *Manière de fortifier Villes et Châteaux* (*Manner to Fortify Towns and Castles*) in which he advocated a fortification directly influenced by the Italian method. Three important military engineers were Vauban's predecessors: Jean Errard, Antoine De Ville and Blaise De Pagan.

JEAN ERRARD

Jean Errard (1554–1610) was an experienced soldier who specialized in fortification and siege warfare. After having studied mathematics and geometry, he was trained by Italian engineers working for the duke of Lorraine, Charles III, whom he started to work for in

Opposite: *Groundplan of Vitry-le-François. Vitry was a new town built on the order of King François I in 1544. Located on the River Marne, the city was intended to defend one of the accesses to the province of Champagne. It was a square town (612 meters × 612 meters) with a grid plan and a citadel built by the Italian engineers Girolamo Marini and Aurelio Pasini.*

Jean Errard's fortification, 1594

1580. With his protector siding with the ultra–Catholic League, Errard — who had become a Protestant — had to leave Lorraine in 1584 to take refuge in the Calvinist principality of Sedan, in the service of the duke of Bouillon, where he would gain the title of engineer to the prince of Sedan. Made famous by his long defense of the city of Jametz (1588–1589), Errard's reputation traveled as far as the court of France, and Henri IV's minister, the duke of Sully, called for his service. Errard took part in several battles and sieges, including Amiens in 1597. Two years later, he was promoted to the rank of engineer of the fortifications of Picardie and Île-de-France and was charged with developing and directing the nascent French engineering corps. He took part in most sieges and battles fought by Henri IV to reconquer the throne of France until his death in 1610. Already in 1600, Errard had published his major book called *La fortification réduicte en art et démontrée* (*Fortification Demonstrated and Simplified in Art*). Errard, often

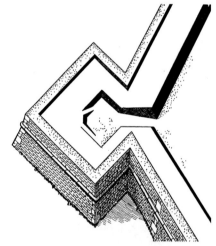

Jean Errard's bastion. Typical of Errard's style was the use of right angle for salients and shoulders of bastions.

called the "father of French fortification," was the first of the great school which was to emerge in France during the seventeenth century, and his treatise became one of the standard texts of the time, running into four editions. His contribution was to combine theoretical erudition with empiric flexibility and to bring a sound appreciation of tactics to the problem of defense. Although he was never dogmatic, his first rule was to use musket fire to defend a place because, according to his experience, infantry fire was more efficient and consumed less powder than artillery, particularly for short-range defense. From this obser-

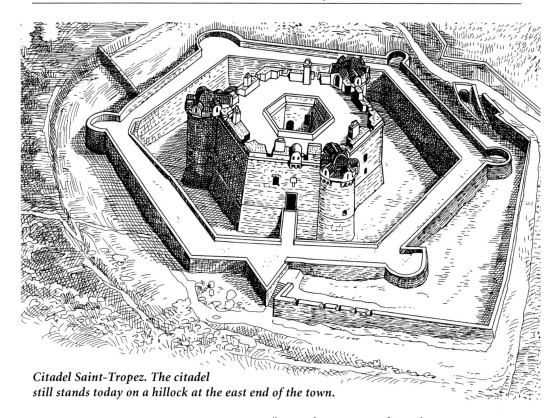

Citadel Saint-Tropez. The citadel still stands today on a hillock at the east end of the town.

vation, Errard advocated that the distance between two bastions be adjusted to musket-range (a maximum of 240 meters). Infantry was deployed on the bastions' faces while artillery was concentrated in the flanks. To prevent escalade with ladders, he advocated deep ditches, resulting in sunken high ramparts. He also recommended the use of *traverse* (an Italian invention that will be further described). Jean Errard insisted on the importance of cavaliers, demi-lunes, cov-

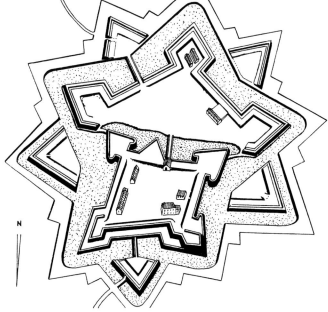

Citadel of Doullens, 1598. Doullens is situated on the River Authie in the departement Somme. The construction of fortifications was decided by King François I. The quadrangular citadel (bottom) was built by the Italian engineer Antonio de Castello in 1525. During Henri IV's reign the citadel was reshaped by Jean Errard, who added a crownwork (top) in 1598.

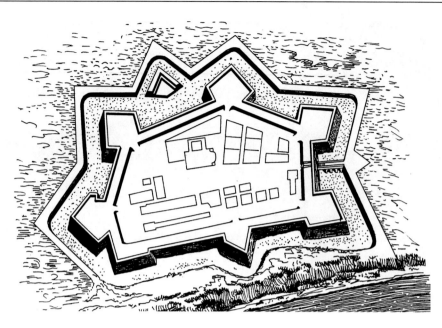

Citadel of Verdun by Jean Errard. Verdun, Toul and Metz were annexed to France under Henri II's reign in 1552. The Verdun citadel was built in 1640 after a design by Jean Errard. The shape of the bastion flanks illustrated very well Errard's typical style.

ered ways and glacis. However, his system was far from perfect because he advocated salients and shoulders with right angles. This outline, far inferior to the Italian orillon and even the Dutch 90-degree flank angle, reduced the space in the gorge of the bastion, and his geometrical construction could easily be splintered by enemy fire. Moreover it gave poor flanking fire. Jean Errard was a theorist but also an experienced soldier and a builder. Henri IV entrusted him with the establishment of fortifications on the realm's borders. Errard modernized several places in northern France, namely Doullens, Montreuil, Laon and

Citadel of Sisteron. Situated in a steep canyon of the river Durance, Sisteron was a strategic gate between the Dauphiné and the Provence. The impressive citadel, which still exists today, was designed by Jean Errard for King Henri IV.

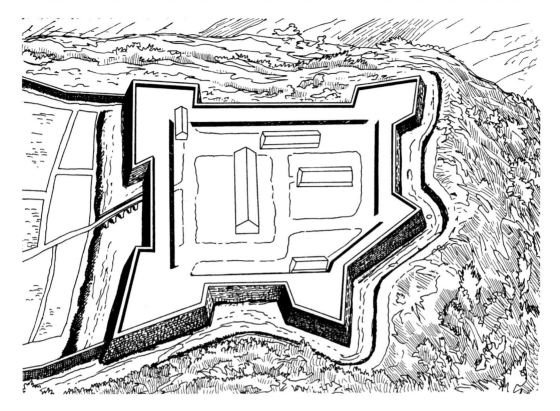

Citadel of Laon by Jean Errard. Laon, the old Carolingian town and capital of France at the time of Charlemagne, is situated at the point were the provinces of Île-de-France, Picardy and Champagne meet. The citadel was designed by Jean Errard for King Henri IV.

Sedan. He designed the citadels of Verdun, Amiens, Sisteron and a part of the urban fortifications of Bayonne.

Henri IV had other good, qualified engineers such as Raymond de Bonnefons and Jean de Beins. De Bonnefons, assisted by his son Jean, built many installations on the Mediterranean seacoast, including Antibes, Toulon, the citadel of Saint-Tropez, Fort Port-de-Bouc near Martigues and defense works at Marseille.

ANTOINE DE VILLE

Jean Errard's principles were taken over by Chevalier Antoine De Ville (1596–1656) under Louis XIII. De Ville, born in Toulouse, was a great traveler and a man of war who participated in many sieges. In 1628 he wrote a theoretical treaty titled *Les Fortifications du Chevalier De Ville*. Antoine De Ville's treaty was a useful text which became the standard work of the time. His system, closely inspired by Italian and Spanish works, introduced a strict geometry and calculated proportions into the design of fortification. He insisted on giving dimensions governed by the effective range of the contemporary weapons. His bastioned front was characterized by bastions with *orillons* (ears), a demi-lune, ditch and covered way on the counterscarp. Nothing really new, but De Ville's main contribution was adaptation to the local site and various advice about defense based on geometry but also

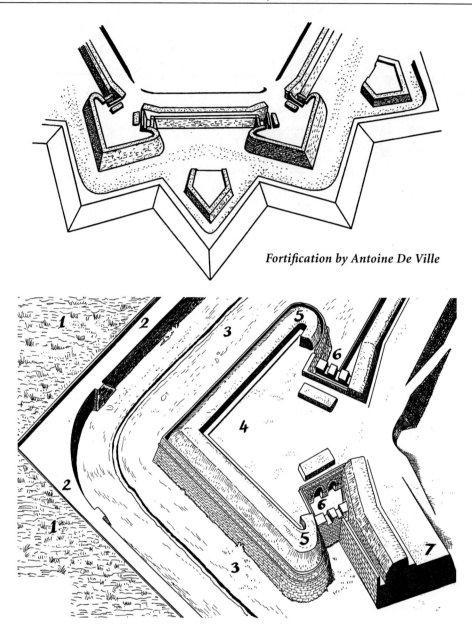

Fortification by Antoine De Ville

Bastion by Antoine De Ville. (1) Glacis; (2) covered way; (3) ditch; (4) bastion; (5) orillon (ear); (6) two-story flank; (7) curtain, seen here in cross-section.

Opposite: *Citadel of Saint-Jean-Pied-de-Port. Probably built by Antoine de Ville between 1643 and 1647, the citadel included the Saint-Michel bastion (1); Saint-Jean bastion (2); Royal gate with Royal demi-lune (3); Royal bastion (4); Saint-Jacques bastion (5); and Porte de Secours gate and demi-lune (6). Obviously, like all other citadels, forts and fortresses, the citadel of Saint-Jean-Pied-de-Port included barracks, supply-stores, a powder house and service buildings.*

on experience and flexibility. He probably created the citadel of Saint-Jean-Pied-de-Port (Pyrénées Atlantiques). In 1639, he published a manual called *De la charge des gouverneurs des places par Messire Antoine De Ville*. This book, intended for commanding officers and defenders of besieged places, remained valuable for nearly two centuries.

Blaise de Pagan

Like Errard and De Ville, Blaise François de Pagan, count of Merveilles (1604–1665), was an experienced soldier who specialized in siege warfare and fortification. After many years of active service, Pagan became blind in 1643 and therefore was forced to retire, having achieved the rank of *maréchal-de-camp*. He devoted the rest of his life to the study of mathematics and astronomy. In 1645 he published a theoretical treaty titled *Les Fortifications* in which he summed up his experiences and reflections on the subject. This masterly work soon eclipsed all previous works. Pagan's theoretical designs were characterized by a clever and competent use of geometry. He advocated a much more refined system than his predecessors, including vast bastions often fitted with cavaliers, and with two-story flanks to increase firepower. One of his major contributions was the design of a very accurate flank disposition enabling a complete flanking of the ditch and the faces of adjacent bastions. Pagan's scarp was slightly sloped to give a good stability to wall and bastion. He advocated a deep ditch, which gave the rampart a height of about 8 meters in order to oppose enemy scaling with ladders. Pagan's other important features were outworks: counterguard and demi-lune, the latter being furnished with a *réduit* (a sort of entrenchment). Outworks could also be linked together to form a complete and continuous line of fortification (the so-called *envelope*) using a double-ditch system. Pagan's work was entirely theoretical, although part of the fortifications of the fortress of Blaye near Bordeaux (Gironde) is sometimes attributed to him. It also seemed that Pagan was asked by the Knights of Saint John

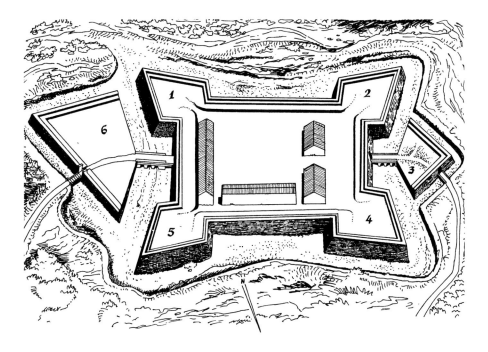

***Pagan's fortification. Pagan's theoretical system of fortification was particularly marked by
the introduction of strong bastions with well-armed flanks (1); counterguards (2) placed in
front of the salient points of bastions; and demi-lunes fitted with an entrenchment (3).***

of the Hospital to make a design in 1645 for the fortification of the suburb of Valetta (later
known as Floriana) on the island of Malta. Pagan apparently made a report but his work
was not retained for unknown reasons. Nevertheless, his conceptions were specially important because of the influence they had on French military engineers and more particularly
Vauban. Pagan's bastioned method contained almost all of Vauban's "first system" features.
Pagan was also a great traveler who explored a part of the Amazon River. From this journey he published in 1655 a report titled "Relation historique et géographique de la Grande
rivière des Amazones dans l'Amérique."

Vauban's Three "Systems"

The period between the end of the sixteenth century and the beginning of the seventeenth century was marked by the Wars of Religion (from 1559 to 1598, which came to an
end thanks to Henri IV's Edict of Nantes); by the submission of the Protestants as a military and political power within the realm due to the energetic efforts of Cardinal Richelieu
under Louis XIII (1610–1643); and finally by the troubles and civil war of the Fronde, during Louis XIV's minority. As can be imagined, those internal difficulties and turmoil did
not create a favorable context for the establishment of coherent national fortifications.
These reigns were characterized by the maturation and proliferation of theories but finally
by few significant realizations. One must wait until 1661, the actual beginning of Louis
XIV's direct rule, to see conditions ripen to produce the complete and full development of
French bastioned fortification.

"A city fortified by Vauban is an impregnable town!" affirmed a common saying of the
time. However Vauban himself never showed such self-confidence nor submitted to such

over-optimism, because he knew by experience that a besieged city's fate was almost always capitulation. Vauban's main talent was to cleverly get the best out of his subordinates, out of circumstances and out of a very favorable context. In the second half of the seventeenth century, bastioned fortification began to reach its full development. Vauban was certainly not the creator of French bastioned fortification, as an erroneous but persistent legend says, but merely a rightful heir, a skilled and a brilliant link to techniques created by sixteenth century Italian, Dutch and French precursors. As he himself readily admitted, his designs sprang less from pure creation than from adaptation of existing figures into a logical and homogenous whole. Vauban was highly inspired by the heritage of the military engineers and architects that had preceded him as well as by his own experience of all the techniques of siege warfare. Besides, Vauban was not alone. Posterity has retained his name, but he was assisted by numerous talented engineers whose names have fallen into oblivion. Late seventeenth century classical French fortification was a collective undertaking ordered by King Louis XIV and Minister Louvois, and designed and built by many anonymous or far less famous collaborators. French bastioned fortification reached the apogee of its fame during Louis XIV's reign. No other age saw the construction of such elaborate bastioned fortification on so vast a scale. Vauban was talented, of course, but he was also a lucky man because his life and work corresponded to a period of balance when funds and technical possibilities coincided with the demands of royal politicy. As a result Vauban had a comfortable budget and freedom of action enabling him to apply his principles for the defense of France. The borders of Louis XIV's realm became a training ground for generations of military engineers, leading to significant changes with a multitude of consequences for the urban landscape.

Traditionally (and quite wrongly), Vauban's work is divided into three fortification "systems." Vauban never designed or attempted to propagate any "system" at all. He was a practical artisan who had no interest in converting fortification into a dry, academic subject. Vauban was a pragmatist, a man of action who based his designs on experience and the demands of the terrain. He never did see his work as progressing from a first style to a second and then a third. His own approach was always to design a fortification that paid the fullest attention to the local conditions and was the most appropriate to the particular problem in hand. He deeply distrusted fortresses designed in a study by some intellectual who had never toiled in muddy trenches under enemy fire in actual combat.

Vauban was less an innovator than a popularizer of existing themes, yet the quantity and the quality of his work formed an innovation in themselves, as for the first time in France's history, a single individual imprinted his style and vision on a national defensive scheme. The theoretical but highly questionable classification system was not done by Vauban himself but deduced and codified by eighteenth century analysts who admired his work and followers who apparently could not understand his work unless they could reduce it to a series of simplified theoretical concepts.

FIRST SYSTEM

The so-called *first system*, as we have just seen, was the synthesis of various predecessors' works, especially those of De Ville and Blaise de Pagan. This fortification was characterized by a masonry bastioned front (about 330 meters long) composed of bastions with or without orillons, outworks in the ditch, a covered way with arms emplacements, advance

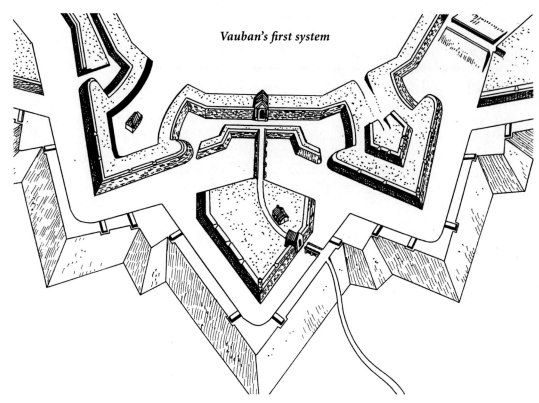

Vauban's first system

works and a glacis. This "system" was applied in most of Vauban's realizations, however, with many local adaptations and modulations. Brilliant examples are preserved in the citadels of Lille and Bayonne, as well as in the urban defenses of Saint-Martin-de-Ré, Blaye, Montdauphin, Mont-Louis and many others.

SECOND SYSTEM

The disadvantage of the "first system" was to organize defenses around one single main wall. Basically, should the defenders of one bastion be put out of action, this meant that both adjacent bastions were no longer defended, which produced disorganization and then the collapse of the defense. The so-called *second system*, allegedly conceived about 1687, tended to solve this problem — so said the eighteenth- and nineteenth-century theorists. Vauban designed a front of considerable depth by dividing the main wall into two autonomous parts separated by a ditch. The first external line — called *enceinte de combat* (fighting line) — included a covered way, detached bastions (or counterguards), tenailles and demi-lunes; it worked as an external envelope, as elements were separated by narrow ditches crossed by small bridges which gave an almost continuous effect. The second internal line — called *enceinte de sureté* (safety line) — was higher than the first one in order to command it. This second wall was intended for close range defense with two-story, polygonal bastioned towers, stoutly built to contain artillery within bombproof casemates and allowing firing through portholes. The second and most important walled enclosure was still intact even when the first line was breeched and conquered. As a result, the besiegers had to undertake a second siege to lay hold of it. This "second system," Vauban's principal inno-

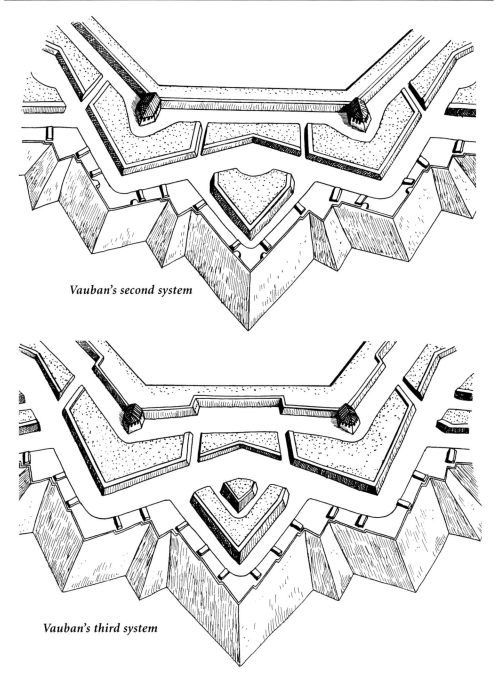

Vauban's second system

Vauban's third system

vation, was very expensive and not widely applied (e.g. Oléron, Besançon, Landau and Belfort).

THIRD SYSTEM

The *third system* was merely an improvement on the second. The curtain of the internal walled enclosure was casemated and its line was fitted with small flanks which increased the defense of the ditch. The demi-lunes were enhanced by a reduit and their own ditch. The superior parts of the internal main walls were made of thick earth layers, which reduced the volumes of masonry and offered an efficient resistance to enemy fire. Neuf-Brisach, created in 1698, is the magnificent but one and only application of the very expensive "third system." This arrangement was never copied or re-used elsewhere, so it must surely be counted as an experiment or oddity rather than a "system."

ADAPTATION TO THE SITE

The simplistic threefold systematization of Vauban's fortifications neither properly reflects the richness of his conceptions nor the diversity of his realizations. It is true that Vauban's fortification was largely governed by geometry, but it is also true that he was opposed to strict doctrines, systems and dogmatism. In his numerous works one can find a technical scheme applied with skill, intelligence and flexibility. He observed only one rule: adaptation to the site, which was one of the fundamental laws of fortification. Vauban applied one principle: to follow good sense and experience in order to achieve maximum efficiency. The pursuit of the best solution to every particular situation was illustrated, for example, by the unorthodox profile built at Briançon or by the irregularity of the outline of Montdauphin, both being dictated by a mountainous site. Vauban did not confine himself to bastioned construction and — for the sake of efficiency — did not fear to re-introduce ancient concepts such as high and roundish, medieval-like towers as part of coastal forts or mountain fortresses.

Vauban, who all his life was a very prolific author, paradoxically wrote rather little on fortification and defense. In the knowledge that every place presented its own problems, which could only be solved by adaptation and local adjustments, he insisted on fundamental rules such as *command* by means of cavalier in order to dominate an area of other works by virtue of height. A work commands another when it is situated higher. This principle enables superposition and simultaneity of firing from an inner-high position into or above an outer-low one. Vauban gave only general advice: opposing enfilade fire by using traverses; increasing the defense in depth by means of outworks, which multiplied the number of obstacles ahead of the main wall; the use of counter-mine networks; and night counter-attacks to harass the besiegers. Vauban's theoretical conceptions concerning defense proper and fortifications are known by a few writings, but mostly by his secretary

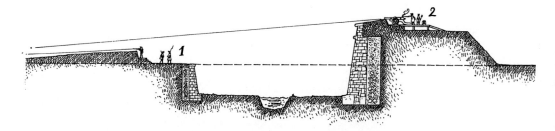

Principle of command. The covered way (1) is commanded by the main wall (2) because the latter is slightly higher than the former. The slope of the glacis was—as it were—an extension of the superior slope of the rampart so that the whole of the glacis was open to firing from the parapet on the main rampart.

Tower at Saint-Vaast-La-Hougue. This coastal tower is an example of the reintroduction of medieval work by Vauban.

Thomassin's memoires, and, of course by his numerous constructions themselves which have come down to us.

The late seventeenth century was a time of codification and formalism, and the story of military architecture became a babel of technical terms applied to a bizarre geometry. The following sections take a close and detailed look at French classical bastioned fortification, and describe its compositional elements.

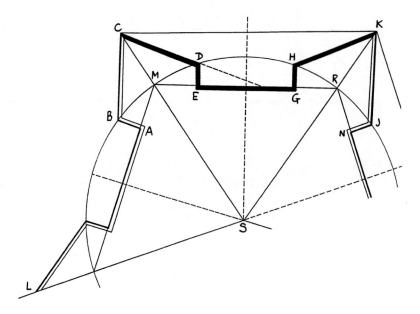

Basic lines and angles of bastioned fortification. The bastioned front CDEGHK is composed of a curtain, EG, and two half-bastions, CDE and GHK; BC, CD, HK and KJ are the faces of the bastions; AB, DE, GH and JN are the flanks of the bastions; AE and GN are the gorges of bastions ABCDE and GHKJN; SC and SK are the capitals, imaginary lines bisecting the salient angles BCD and HKJ; ABC, CDE, GHK and KJN are the shoulder angles; DEG and EGH are the flank angles; CK is the external polygonal line linking both salients; MR is the internal polygonal line. The length of the lines and the value given to the angles, of course, could endlessly vary.

Bastioned Front

The basis of the bastioned system was the front, which included a portion of wall (called the rampart or curtain) and two adjacent half-bastions. This basic unit was the result of a technical evolution originating from Italy about 1500. The bastioned front was an ensemble of five fundamental lines related by rules and geometrical ratios. The unit could be repeated at will to form a fort or enclose a city. Endlessly, the five lines of the unit could vary in length and be connected with various angles. These infinite variations were determined by engineers according to local conditions to adapt fortifications to the site, but also caused by a sort of fashion or style created by currents, schools of thought or movements. This phenomenon, particularly in late sixteenth-century Italy, gave birth to countless theoretical bastioned fronts each with its own style. Of course there were endless futile disputes between engineers of opposing cliques, each engineer or school of engineers asserting that his method was the best. In Vauban's fortification, the distance between the tips of two adjacent bastions (the so-called external polygon line, or length of the bastioned front) was generally equal to 180 *toises* (about 360 yards).

Bastion

The term bastion seems to come from the French word *bastille*, which was a defensive stronghold placed in front of the entrance to a medieval castle or city. A small bastille was

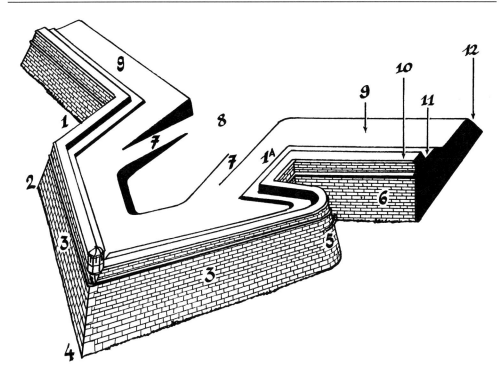

The main parts of a bastion. (1) Flank; (1a) flank with ear; (2) shoulder; (3) face; (4) salient; (5) orillon or ear; (6) curtain; (7) ascent, sloping access; (8) gorge; (9) wallwalk; (10) breast-work; (11) banket; (12) interior slope.

a *bastillon* (an artillery tower), and this word was shortened to *bastion*. Another term was *bulwark*, coming from the Dutch *bolwerk*, which was originally a gun-emplacement made of earth. This word also spawned the Italian *balovardo* and the French and English *boule-vard* (which is now a broad avenue created when the bulwarks were dismantled). Bastions were given a name, often linked to the royal family, such as Bastion du Roi (king's bastion), Bastion de la Reine (queen's bastion), Bastion du Dauphin (heir to the throne bastion). Bastions could also be named for the neighborhood or the gate that they protected, for example, Bastion Saint-Paul, Saint-Martin, Sainte-Croix, Saint-Jacques, Sainte-Marie, etc. Or they could be named after particular buildings located in the vicinity, such as Bastion de la Poudrière (powder house), Bastion de l'Hôpital, (hospital), etc. These are only examples and many other names were used.

A bastion was a protruding, terraced platform, most generally as high as the main wall. It was distinguishable by two essential characteristics: first, a low, ramparted profile, and second, a pentagonal, arrow-headed groundplan.

The bastion's profile was ramparted, which meant that it was made up of a rampart, two relatively thin masonry walls (called revetments) holding a thick mass of earth, and a backfill which absorbed artillery fire like a sponge. The bastion was rather low to the ground in order not to be an easy target, while the depth of the moat prevented climbing. In addition to being solidly constructed and so difficult to damage or destroy, bastions offered defenders excellent combat emplacements for crossfire, and enabled them to return in equal measure a besieger's artillery fire.

The bastion pentagonal outline was formed by two *faces* turned outwards to the enemy; both faces joined at the jutting-out *salient*. They were connected to the curtain by two sections of wall called *flanks*. The meeting point of face and flank was called *shoulder*. The *gorge* was the open space at the rear turned to the inside of the city or fort. The surface enclosed by those five lines was called *terreplein*.

From the faces one could fire at long range with artillery or prevent enemy progress by musket fire. This was mostly the case in Vauban's fortifications. He copied this over from Jean Errard because frontal musket fire was more accurate and cheaper than cannon fire. In Vauban's fortifications, the face of a bastion measured an average of 60 to 90 meters (but only 44 at Montroyal and 160 at Strasburg). This length was dictated by the range of the musket but also by various local conditions.

FLANKS

Each flank was placed so that it could fire into the ditch along the curtain and face of the adjacent bastion. This disposition, called flanking, was very useful. Indeed, a shot fired across an enemy line was far more effective than a direct frontal barrage. Owing to flanking, precise accuracy and range was less important: a small armed group could defend a large area, depending naturally upon the range of the weapons used. Vauban's flank length — on the whole — varied from 16 to 50 meters. Vauban took over Pagan's flank design. The angle formed by flank and curtain measured about 120 degrees, which enabled the defenders to fire right in front of them and to give an excellent flanking.

Inspired by sixteenth-century Italian techniques, Vauban used two sorts

Flanking. The black arrows indicate the line of fire. Each bastion depended on its neighboring bastion for protection in interlocking fields of fire.

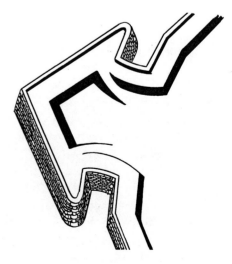

Bastion with ears

of flanks. First, a single flank, which was
connected to the curtain by a straight,
plain portion of wall, generally referred
to as a right flank. Second, a flank with
orillon, which increased the defenders'
safety. The *orillon* or *ear* was a protruding screen built on the shoulder, preventing the defenders in the flank from
oblique enemy bombardment, but allowing them to enfilade the ditch. This protective element was round or square,
shapes which gave bastions their charac-
teristic arrowhead or ace-of-spade form.
Vauban appeared to have no particular
preference between the two sorts.

The flank was often slightly curved
and sometimes fitted with two floors. The
upper story was open and at the same

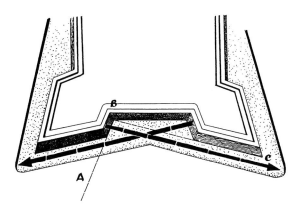

*Flank angle (ABC= 90 degrees). The points A, B
and C form together the curtain angle or flank
angle of 90 degrees, enabling a perfect flanking
of the ditch. The black arrows show the firing
lines.*

level as the terrace. The lower flank was situated below and could be casemated. A *casemate* was a closed, vaulted gun chamber with a firing port built in the thickness of a masonry
wall, which perfectly protected gunners, cannons and ammunitions. But its use was not
without disadvantages. The angle of fire was limited and observation was considerably

*Cross-section, casemate. (1) Casemate; (2) embrasure; (3) ventilation shafts; (4) earth cover;
(5) corridor.*

Casemate at Neuf-Brisach

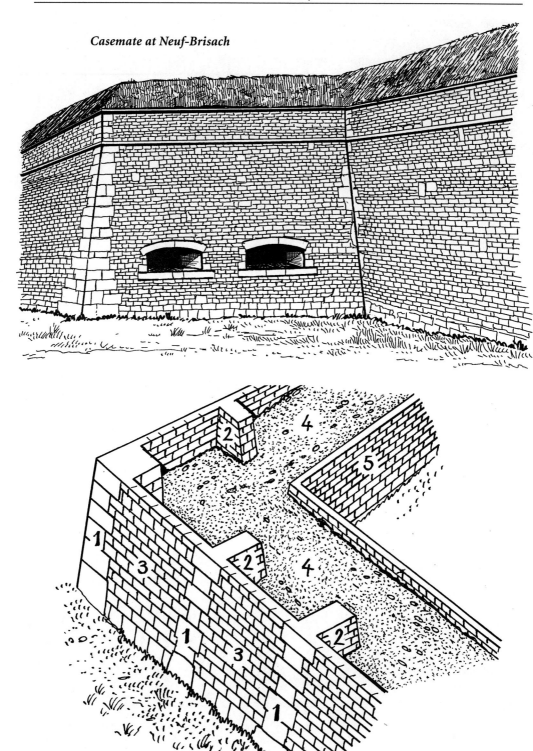

Clamps and buttresses. The sketch shows a rampart in cut-away. (1) Vertical clamp; (2) interior buttress; (3) outer revetement; (4) rampart filled with earth; (5) inner revetement.

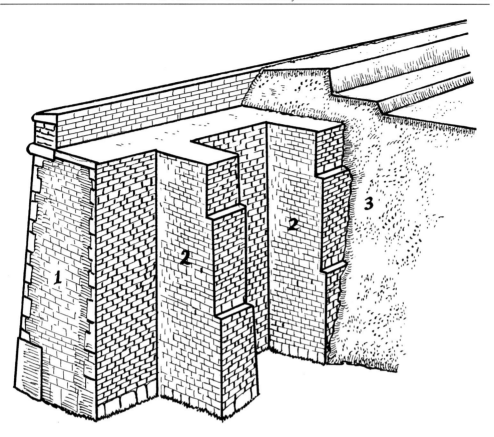

Counterforts (buttresses). Counterforts were sections of masonry built perpendicularly against a wall for extra support. (1) Wall seen here in cross-section; (2) buttress; (3) mass of piled earth shown in cross-section.

reduced. The ventilation of a casemate was a difficult problem to solve. In spite of vents, vertical chimneys and other air channels intended to evacuate smoke, after a few shots the chamber was usually full of choking fumes, making it very difficult and unhealthy for the gunners to operate. It was also a dark and cold cave. Because of these disadvantages, Vauban preferred gun batteries in the open air and scarcely used firing chambers. However casemates were used in Briançon and Neuf-Brisach.

The masonry at the angles of a bastion (salient and shoulders) was the most vulnerable part, therefore it was clamped. *Clampings* or ties were vertical superstructures of heavy and strong stones which formed pillars holding the masonry together and increasing the stability of the walls. Revetments were also reinforced by counterforts, which were buttresses built inside the walls.

SHAPES OF BASTIONS

The bastion's outline was mostly symmetrical and corresponded to precise geometrical rules. However, depending on adaptation to the nature of the ground and local conditions, in order to avoid *dead angles* (blind spots), the plan of the bastions could follow an irregular outline. In certain cases, a *half-bastion* was built: this meant that one of its faces

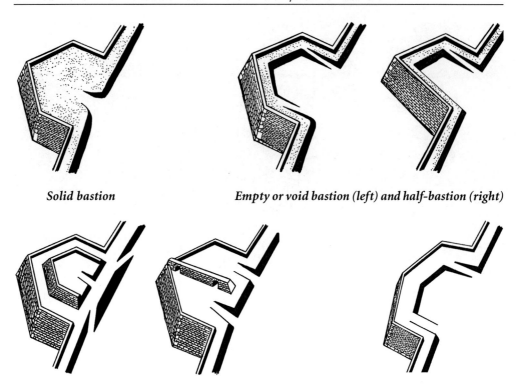

Solid bastion   *Empty or void bastion (left) and half-bastion (right)*

Bastion with cavalier (left) and bastion with   *Flat bastion*
traverse (right)

was directly linked to the curtain without a flank. A bastion was said to be *void* (or empty) when it was terraced only along its revetments; this hollow and protected terreplein was a suitable spot for a powder house for example. A bastion was called *solid* (or full) when its terreplein was completely filled with earth. On the upper surface of a solid bastion, a windmill could be placed, or a cavalier. A *cavalier* was a raised structure higher than the rampart whose plan was similar to that of the bastion. The purpose of this inner work was for observation, to give additional firepower by providing an additional layer of musketry or guns, and to increase the height of the bastion so as to command the surroundings. The cavalier also acted as a kind of shield, preventing enfilade fire and protecting buildings in the town or fort. On the other hand, because of its height, the cavalier could be an easy target.

A bastion was sometimes *traversed*, which meant that its terreplein was divided into two or more parts by a *traverse*, a thick and solid masonry wall built generally on its capital line. The purpose was to protect the defenders from enemy fire. The traverse was pierced with one or more vaulted passages, which enabled the garrison to circulate from one compartment to another. This feature was often used by Vauban in mountain fortifications. The bastion could also be *flat*: in this case its two faces formed together an unprotruberant angle with little or no salient at all.

In rare cases, a bastion could be arranged as a harbor, as in the citadel of Saint-Martin on the Isle of Ré.

In certain large cities, one of the bastions of the principal enclosure, situated opposite the citadel, could be used as a *reduit*, as a fort or as a secondary citadel. Its gorge was then fitted with an enclosing wall, a rear moat and a drawbridge. Vauban used this feature at Gravelines, Landau, Besançon (Fort Griffon) and Lille (Fort Saint-Sauveur).

BASTIONED TOWER

In Vauban's second and third "systems," bastions were detached from the main enclosure by a ditch. In this case the separated bastion could be considered and termed a *counterguard*. Behind this element, Vauban conceived a *bastioned tower*. This was meant to provide flanking fire and protect the main wall. Because of its relatively small dimensions, the bastioned tower was not an easy target for enemy mortars and was not vulnerable to enfilade and ricochet fire. It was provided with two casemated floors: the casemates in the lower tier flanked the ditch and the upper ones covered and commanded the detached bastion placed before it. The top of the tower was either arranged as an artillery platform or fitted with a roof to protect men and guns from bad weather and enemy fire. The casemated, totally masonry bastioned tower

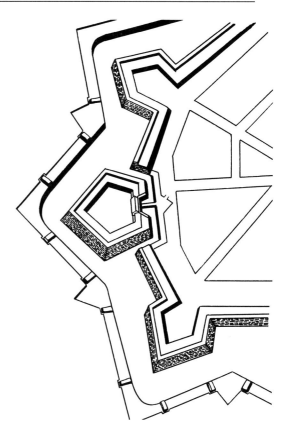

Entrenched bastion. The gorge was closed by a wall and defended by a ditch. The bastion was then transformed into a small fort or reduit.

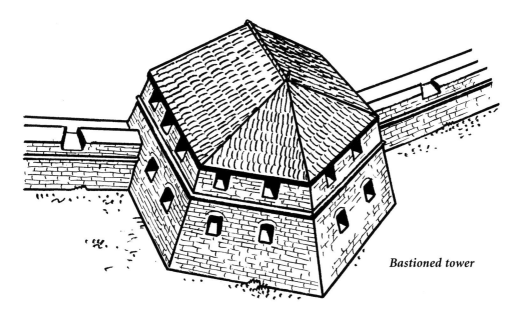

Bastioned tower

was, however, much more expensive to build than the earth-filled or solid bastion, and — although fitted with ventilating flues and vents intended to clear the choking smoke from the guns in the casemates — the crucial problem of ventilation remained unsolved. Bastioned towers were used at Besançon, Landau, Belfort and Neuf-Brisach, but they never caught on with other fortress builders.

Curtain

The *courtine* (curtain) was the section of rampart between two bastions. Its length depended on the range of the weapons used by the defenders and of the nature of the ground. In Vauban's fortifications an average of 350 meters was common (but only 160 at Montroyal and 628 at Maubeuge). Its height was the same as the bastion, usually 8 to 10 meters, to oppose scaling ladders. Its width varied according to the thickness of the breast-work and the importance of the wallwalk. Its shape was mostly straight, but in Neuf-Brisach, Vauban furnished it with two small recessed casemated walls to increase the flanking capacity. This feature, called *ordre renforcé* (reinforced order), was created by the Italian engineer Zanchi in 1554. The curtain was protected by outworks such as fausse-braie, tenaille

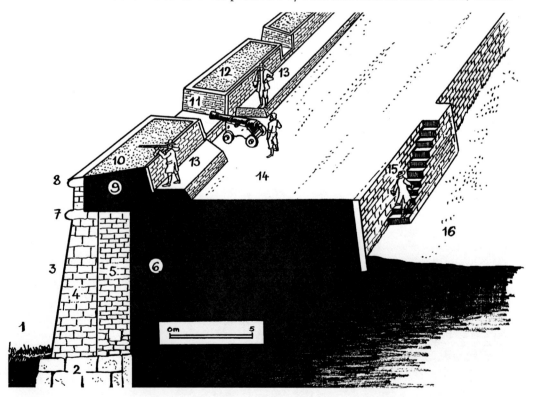

Cross-section, rampart. The area at the level of the surrounding country was called datum. The height of any element over this was its command. (1) Ditch; (2) foundations; (3) scarp; (4) external revetement; (5) buttress; (6) rampart made of earth; (7) cordon; (8) tablet; (9) breastwork or parapet; (10) plongée or superior slope of parapet; (11) embrasure; (12) merlon; (13) banquet or fire-step; (14) wallwalk; (15) internal revetement; (16) terreplein or datum.

or demi-lune which, will be described further. In the groundplan, curtains and bastions formed the outline of the main enclosure, also called the *magistral line*. In cross-section, the external part of the curtain was called the *scarp* and the inner section was called the *interior slope*.

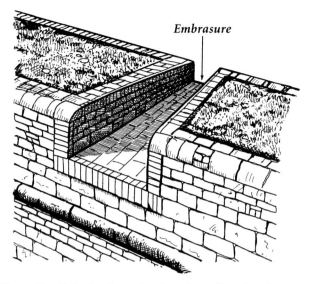

WALLWALK AND BREASTWORK

The *wallwalk* was a continuous alley arranged on top of curtains and bastions. Its purpose was to allow for an observation post, uninterrupted communication and a combat emplacement protected by a breastwork. The wallwalk had to be rather broad to allow the circulation of troops, guns and supply carts. Besides, it had to make possible the firing of cannons, which meant including sufficient room for muzzle loading and space behind the gun for recoil.

Access to the wallwalk was by ramps or ascents (inclined planes), whose slope and breadth were calculated in order to accommodate guns and supply wagons. Ascents were obviously placed in the gorge of bastions to facilitate movement and flexibility. At the foot

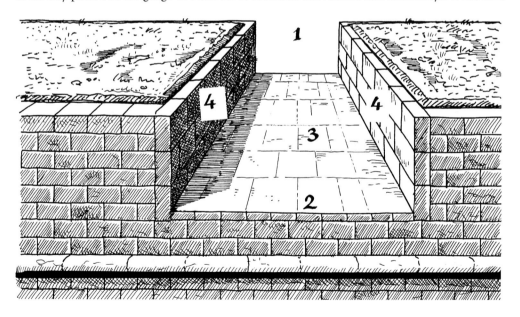

Parts of the embrasure. An embrasure or gun-port was an opening in the parapet to allow artillery to fire. It was divided into the following: (1) throat, the interior opening wide enough to admit the muzzle of the gun; (2) mouth, the exterior opening governed by the amount of lateral coverage required; (3) sole, the bottom surface, the outward slope; (4) cheek, each side wall of the opening.

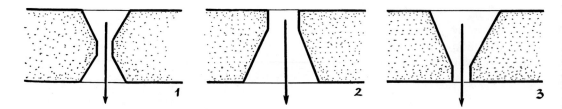

Shapes of embrasures (seen from above). (1) Strangled or X-shaped; (2) flared or inverted V-shaped; (3) splayed or V-shaped.

of the inner slope of the rampart, there was an alley or *rampart street* which was arranged to allow quick, easy and continuous communication to all fronts of the fortress. Foot-soldiers reached the wallwalk by means of staircases arranged in the inner slope of the wall.

The breastwork, also called *parapet*, was a thick, man-high, massive wall protecting the wallwalk. A *banquette*, a continuous step, allowed soldiers to fire over it. This firing position over the parapet without using the cutting of an embrasure was called fire "en barbette." The superior slope of the parapet, the so-called *plongée*, was limited on the outside by the external crest and on the inside by the firing crest.

To allow artillery fire through the parapet, *embrasures* were cut off. Those openings were modern adaptations of medieval crenellation (the solid mass between two void embrasures was called the *merlon*). They gave servants, guns and ammunition good protection, but although their shape was flared outward, the traverse of the gun was reduced. Embrasures were placed to enable enfilading fire.

The wallwalk was paved with tiles; parapet and embrasures were reveted with stones. However, engineers knew from experience that, when heavily bombarded, masonry produced dangerous stone splinters. To avoid this, wallwalks were often made of stamped earth. For the very same reason, breastworks and merlons were often made of comparatively thin layers of bricks filled with earth; it was observed that brick splinters were less dangerous than stone splinters. Guns deployed on the wallwalk were often placed on a wooden platform made of thick planks resting on beams to be at the correct height and to avoid sinking in loose ground, for example after a heavy rainfall.

ECHAUGUETTE

The *echauguette* or *guérite* was a small turret or sentry-box built of masonry on top of a wall. The purpose was to have an observation post to watch over the ditch. For this reason echauguettes were placed on corbels at the salients and shoulders of bastions and outworks. The jutting out turret sheltered a single standing guard from wind and rain. The sentrybox was fitted with small and narrow loopholes for observation and firing, should the occasion arise. Access was by a narrow corridor arranged in the thickness of the breastwork. In floorplan the echauguette was circular or polygonal and its roof was covered by a decorated, domed cupola. Echauguettes had also a decorative function due to their elegant shapes, their gracious silhouettes and their coupling with cordon and tablette. Some were elaborately decorated with heraldic devices and other ornamentation. More prosaically their floors (overlooking the ditch) could be fitted with an opening and used as a latrine.

Echauguette (sentry-box). (1) Echauguette; (2) tablette; (3) cordon; (4) scarp

Round sentry-box on bastion Desmourier at Port-Louis (Bretagne)

Echauguette (sentry-box), Brouage. The scarp was made of thick stones while the parapet and the embrasures were constructed of brick revetments filled with earth to avoid splinters. Note the strong cordon and the echauguette.

Echauguette at Rochefort

Sentry boxes were quite fragile though. Many have been destroyed and, in many cases, only bases are visible today.

SCARP

The *scarp* was the interior wall or, if the ditch was wet, the inner bank of the moat. Its plan followed the main enclosure made by curtains and bastions. Vertically, it formed the external wall from the bottom of the ditch to the cordon. The scarp was always reveted by masonry holding back masses of earth, and was slightly sloped to ensure its stability. On top of the scarp, the wall was furnished with two semi-circular projections of masonry: the *cordon* and the *tablette*. The practical purpose of these elements is unclear. Were they intended to repel rain and also those who tried to scale the wall? The author is inclined to think that both cordon and tablette were actually merely ornaments, aesthetical concessions in an architecture based on solidity, functionality and efficiency. Cordons and tablettes were also placed on top of counterscarps and even on top of outworks. At the foot of the scarp, a *berm* (or roundway) could be established. This space (a few meters broad) prevented dislodged earth from the rampart from filling the ditch. The ramparts on top of the scarp (both bastions and curtains) could be planted with trees, which provided a shady promenade for the population of the town in peacetime. Timber was always in great demand by any garrison, with different uses ranging from firewood to building materials. In times of crisis, trees provided a reserve of timber that could be converted into a *palisade* (an obstacle in the shape of a fence made of wooden posts), or an *abatis* (an improvised defense made of tree branches laid on top of each other facing the enemy, working sort of like barbed wires). These obstacles could also be permanent, but — being perishable — they could not be left unattended for years, and therefore had to be constantly reviewed, maintained and renewed.

Ditch

The ditch was a passive, excavated defense surrounding a fort. In Vauban's fortifications, it hemmed bastions and curtains. Its width varied from 10 to 30 meters and its depth was about 8 to 10 meters. The ditch was limited by the scarp on the inside and by the counterscarp on the outside. The *counterscarp* was often masonry to retard natural erosion and collapse effected on purpose by besiegers. The defense of the ditch was done from the bastions' flanks and from outworks. Ditches could be dry or wet depending on the availability of water supply.

A *dry ditch* was mostly deep and relatively narrow. It formed a continuous obstacle around the whole fortress. It had to be wide enough to hold a sizable raiding party and make bridging and filling difficult, but not so wide as to allow the besieger to breach the base of the scarp with artillery fire. The dry ditch could be used in peacetime as a training ground. In wartime it could be used as a refuge for the fleeing inhabitants of the countryside and for cattle, or as a means of communication and as an assembling place for a party getting ready to make a sortie. Access to the dry ditch was done by *posterns* or sally ports, which were vaulted tunnels or gateways built of masonry under the ramparts. A dry ditch was often furnished with a *cunette*, a narrow, V-shaped canal dug in its middle with the purpose of draining rainwater, and to act as a further barrier. Where water was available, the dry ditch could be flooded through sluices from a nearby river to produce a sudden torrent of water able to wash away any temporary bridge made by the besiegers in their attempt to cross the moat.

A *wet ditch* was permanently filled with water. It formed a serious and very efficient obstacle protecting against a surprise attack and discouraging mining. If clean of rubbish and excrement, the moat could provide the garrison with fresh fish. On the other hand, the wet ditch could erode the bottom of the masonry and often was a hazard to the health of the garrison if the water was stagnant. Disease, it is well known, was always a greater killer in those times than weapons. Besides, in winter the water could freeze, rendering the wet ditch useless as it provided the enemy with a platform of approach. In a wet moat, the cunette was also dug: the purpose was to keep a deep running current of water which did not easily freeze. In very frosty weather the garrison had to break up the ice. The water supply was regulated by hydrological elements such as batardeaus, sluices and watergates.

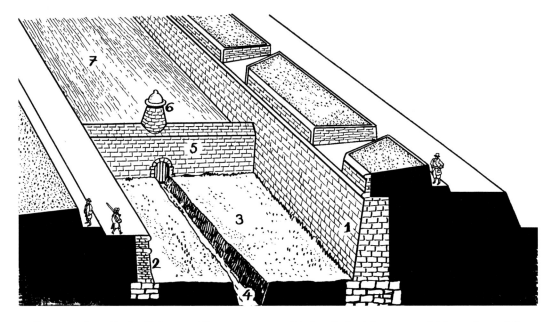

Cross-section, ditch. (1) Scarp; (2) counterscarp; (3) dry ditch; (4) cunette; (5) batardeau; (6) dame or monk; (7) wet ditch.

A *batardeau* was a kind of dam intended to separate dry and wet ditches or to isolate running sea or river waters from standing moat waters. It was built in masonry crosswise in the ditch and thus formed a dangerous weakness in the defensive system. To prevent its use as means of crossing the moat, its superior part was usually topped as a *dos d'âne* (knife-edge) and fitted with a *dame* (a "lady" or monk), a solid obstacle of circular masonry. A batardeau could be hollow and fitted with galleries in which sluices and watergates were placed.

Gatehouse

Obviously the gate was the most vulnerable part of a fortress, thus the number of accesses to forts, citadels, and fortified cities were limited as much as possible. In late seventeenth-century fortification, the gate was always placed in the middle of a curtain in order to be defended from both adjacent bastions. The access was a tunnel passing under the rampart. For security reasons its width allowed passage for only one wagon or cart at a time; therefore busy market days in town were often characterized by traffic jams. The tunnel passed through a building, called a *porte* (gatehouse), in which various premises were available, particularly for guards and urban toll officers. At both ends, the tunnel was closed by a heavy, double-leaved door reinforced by metal parts and huge nails and locked by a strong transverse beam. A *wicket*, a small door, was arranged in the main door in order to let pedestrians walk in without having to open the main gate. Above the doorway hung a *herse* (also called *orgue*): this adaptation of the medieval *portcullis* was a heavy barrier made of

Briançon: Pignerol Gate

Above, left: *Campani gate (Saint-Martin-de-Ré)*. Right: *Blaye: Porte Royale. Reflecting Louis XIV's glory, the Porte Royale at Blay was a beautiful arch of triumph. It also concealed various traps for possible attackers. It was preceded by a demi-lune, and furnished with a swing-back drawbridge and a strong wooden door. Behind it, a curious circular yard was placed in order to communicate with the fausse-braie; the yard was dominated by a sentry-box and fitted with loopholes allowing musket fire. The gatehouse was lengthened by a tunnel passing under the rampart; the access to the tunnel could be closed by a portcullis and a second strong wooden door. The height of the vault was calculated in order to allow the passage of a horseman, and its width was arranged to admit a coach and a row of soldiers presenting arms on every side.*

strong wooden balks which could be raised by machinery placed in a chamber in the first floor of the gatehouse. Should the occasion arise, the *orgue* could be slid very rapidly down by means of its own weight and side-grooves.

The gatehouse was also the expression of Louis XIV's greatness, power and splendor. Marking the entrance of a town, the portes, protected by more advanced construction and obstacles, were often adorned with decorative finery. The magnificence and the quality of the decorations sculpted on the gatehouses are witnesses of the golden age of the town in the seventeenth century. The front side of the gatehouse frequently looked like an ostentatious arch of triumph in baroque or French classical style, representative of an architecture in which the solemn measures of classical antiquity and the worldly splendor of the Renaissance blended with Spanish gravity and French grace and frivolity. The façade was always nicely proportioned, lavishly framed with columns and pilasters, and crowned with a decorated pediment displaying allegorical statues, military trophies, classical ornaments based on Greco-Roman patterns, heraldry and coats with royal arms. French classical architecture combined grace and dignity to produce an effect of monumental grandeur. In spite

Gate at Le Quesnoy

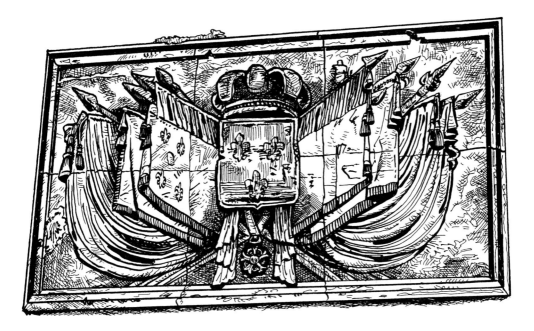

Coat-of-arms with flags at Rochefort

Above, left: *Trophy with Sun-King ornament at Longwy (Lorraine).* Right: *Ornament at Neuf-Brisach.*

of Louvois's protestations, Vauban did not hesitate to engage famous sculptors and talented artists to design and decorate gatehouses. As for Louis XIV, he regarded ostentious pomp and prestige as quite as important as security. Gates, like bastions, were always given a name, often honoring the royal family, such as Porte Royale (royal gate), Porte de la Reine (queen's gate), Porte Dauphine (heir to the throne gate). The gate could also be named for a religious figure such as Saint-Martin, Saint-Louis, Saint-Jacques, Saint André, etc. Or it could be named after a neighborhood, a direction, or the road leading to another town, such as Porte de Paris, Porte de Grenoble, Porte de Colmar, etc.

DRAWBRIDGE

Because of its vulnerability, the gatehouse was particularly well defended. Its access was protected by one or more outworks (almost always a demi-lune), and the ditch was crossed by means of a bridge. In Vauban's time, a bridge was composed of a non-movable section, called the *pont dormant*, made of wood resting on stone piles (this part was mostly rebuilt in masonry arches in the following century). At about 4.50 meters from the gate, this permanent part was interrupted by a *pont-levis* (drawbridge), which could be quickly raised in moments of crisis. Two main types were in use. The first kind was inherited from the Middle Ages and composed of a roadway held by chains attached on strong beams and

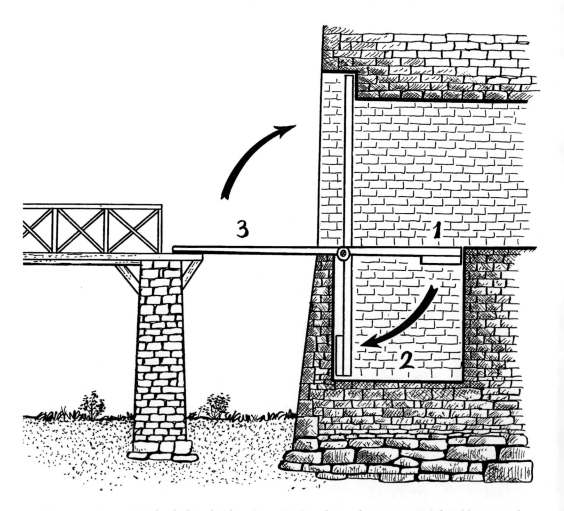

Cross-section, swing-back drawbridge. By swinging down the counterweights (1) set on the drawbridge beams, they come down in two pits (2) arranged on both side of the passage and the mobile bridge (3) moves into vertical, closed position.

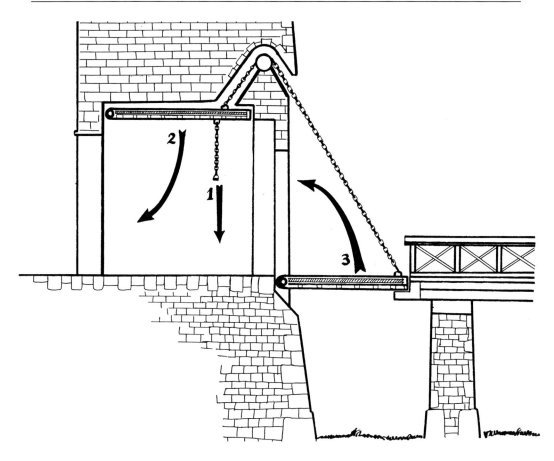

Cross-section, drawbridge with counterweight. By pulling down the chain (1), the mobile heavy door (2), working as a counterweight, lifts up the mobile bridge roadway (3).

counterweight. The closed position was obtained by lifting; the vertically moved bridge constituted a second door and beams were housed in two grooves cut out in the façade above the gate; a variation of this lifting method used a rear door as counterweight. Vauban disliked this system, criticizing the vulnerability of beams, chains and grooves. Instead he advocated and used from 1680 onward another method consisting of counterweights fixed at the rear of the bridge. It closed by swinging back counterweights which were lodged in two pits arranged sidewise behind the doorway. Unfortunately today, most original draw-bridges have been removed and the approaches filled with a permanent roadway. A modern tourist can with some imagination see how strong the original arrangements must have been.

WATERGATE

When a river crossed a fortified place, defenses were adapted. One must not forget the economic and commercial importance of waterways. Riverbanks were reinforced by dikes, running waters were impounded by batardeaus or retained by dams. A watergate was arranged in the middle of the curtain. It could take the form of a masonry gatehouse with

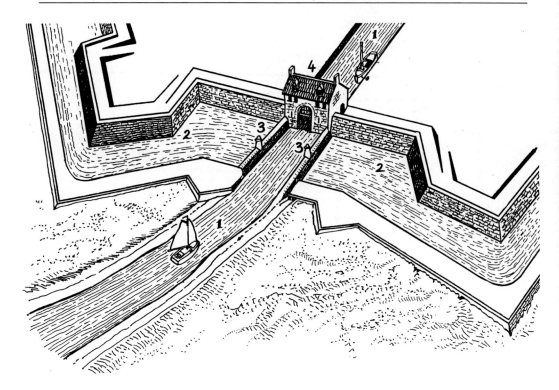

Schematical view of a watergate. (1) River; (2) wet ditch; (3) batardeau with monk; (4) watergate house.

one or more arches to allow boats to circulate. Should the occasion arise, navigation could be blocked by sliding down a portcullis as described above.

Outworks

Outworks were various fortified elements placed into the ditch, inside the perimeter of the covered way. Outworks formed a tangled skein and their ditches a kind of labyrinth. Their sheer number, scale and complexity may often be as awesome to modern tourists as they were supposed to be to seventeenth-century besiegers. They were built in depth, often extending over very wide areas. They protected each other with cross-fire and made an external line of resistance; theoretically each outwork needed a siege, or at least a fight, to be taken before the besiegers could reach the main enclosure. If the enemy managed to conquer one, he would always find that there was another one covering it from the rear, so the time of final victory would be frustratingly postponed. Their height, outline and positioning were cautiously designed so that no blind spots could exist; their alignment was intended to create in the ditch large and efficient firing lanes turned into killing grounds to smash attackers so foolhardy as to have descended there. Outworks were furnished with parapets and ascents and surrounded by secondary moats which were less wide than the main ditch. The gorge of these works was always open, which meant not protected by a parapet; so if an outwork was conquered it offered no protection to the besiegers. Of course the height

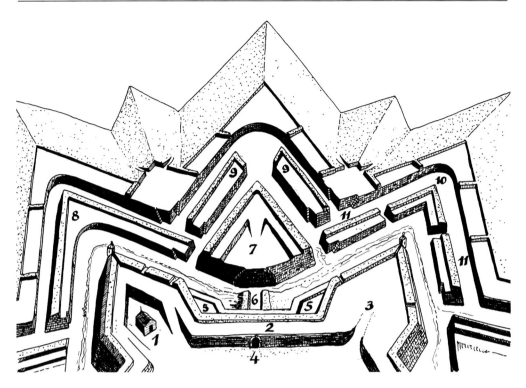

General view of outworks. (1) Void bastion; (2) curtain; (3) solid bastion; (4) postern giving access under the curtain to the tenaille and caponier; (5) tenaille; (6) caponier; (7) ravelin or demi-lune; (8) counterguard or couvre-face; (9) tenaillon; (10) bonnet; (11) lunettes.

of every outwork was calculated in order to command the next. Communication between outworks and the main body was effected through the ditches when these were dry and by means of wooden foot bridges and rowboats when ditches were wet. In French bastioned classical fortification, outworks were often masonry and decorated with cordon and tablette. Outworks included the fausse-braie, the tenaille, the caponier, the demi-lune, the counterguard and its variations as well as the tenaillons and the envelope.

FAUSSE-BRAIE

The *fausse-braie* was a low, continuous parapet placed in front of the ditch, on the berm at the foot of the main rampart. It formed a line of communication and a combat emplacement, enabling grazing fire at intruders in the ditch. Communication between outworks and the main enceinte was done by a postern placed under the rampart. Widely and successfully used in the old Dutch fortification system, where ditches were very broad and always wet, the fausse-braie presented serious disadvantages in French (comparatively) narrow and dry ditches. Indeed if the enemy had taken possession of the counterscarp, then he dominated the defenders deployed in the fausse-braie and could fire at them because the fausse-braie was lower than the counterscarp. Moreover the defenders of the fausse-braie were dangerously exposed to splinters and possible collapse of the main wall behind and above them when this was submitted to heavy breaching fire. For this reason Vauban

Fausse-braie as used in the old Dutch fortification

preferred to use tenailles and counterguards and only made use of the fausse-braie when conditions were suitable, in Blaye for example, or in mountainous sites such as in Briançon or Besançon.

TENAILLE

The *tenaille* was created — it is often said — by Vauban, who considered it the replacement of the fausse-braie. It was a low wall placed in the ditch at the foot of the main curtain between both flanks of bastions. This outwork was formed by two walls built in the alignment of the faces of the bastions together making a re-entering angle. Other forms were used though, for instance the shape of a bastioned front or a protruding redan placed

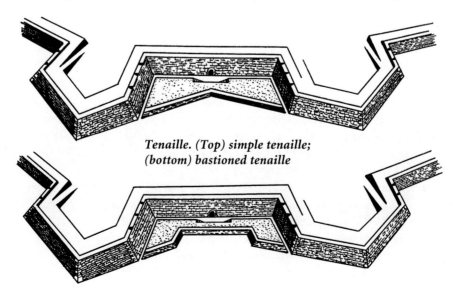

Tenaille. (Top) simple tenaille; (bottom) bastioned tenaille

in its middle. The purpose was to protect the base of the curtain and flanks of adjacent bastions from bombardment and to oblige the besiegers to attack the faces, which were held under heavy fire from the flanks (if everything was right). The tenaille was also slightly higher than the ravelin, and infantrymen could fire into it, should that outwork be taken. The tenaille was often fitted with a breastwork, which helped active ditch flanking; behind it a party of defenders preparing a sally could be regrouped. For this purpose an exit (named the *postern* or sally port) was pierced under the main enceinte, allowing the garrison to move around the defenses while remaining under cover from enemy sight and fire.

In Vauban's first and second "systems," the tenaille was a broad and vast detached work. In rare cases, a tenaille could be coupled with a demi-lune as seen in the fortifications of the arsenal of Lorient (Morbihan).

DEMI-LUNE

The *demi-lune* (literally half-moon) was an Italian invention also called *ravelin*. It was the most important outwork. It was placed in the ditch, in front of the curtain, between two bastions. The demi-lune was systematically placed in front of a gate and also built in the gorge or ahead of crown and hornworks, as we shall further see. The demi-lune thus shielded a curtain or the entrance to a fort, a citadel or a city. It also covered the flank of the bastion and formed an additional obstacle before the main fortification. It was very often triangular, composed of two faces protruding towards the enemy; but it could also be given two flanks and thus have a pentagonal shape. Its gorge, as we have just seen, was always open. Its dimensions were carefully defined. According to the fundamental principle of command, its profile had to be lower than the main wall but higher than the covered way. The outline of its gorge had to be built so as not to hinder crossfire from the flanks. In its gorge, one or two staircases were arranged in order to access to its terreplein from the bottom of the ditch. The demi-lune could be traversed with a thick wall built on its capital line; for example, Vauban used this feature in Briançon (the demi-lune west of the porte Dauphine) and in Besançon (the demi-lunes of front Saint-Etienne and front Royal). The

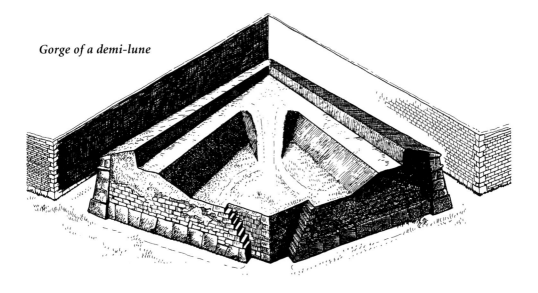

Gorge of a demi-lune

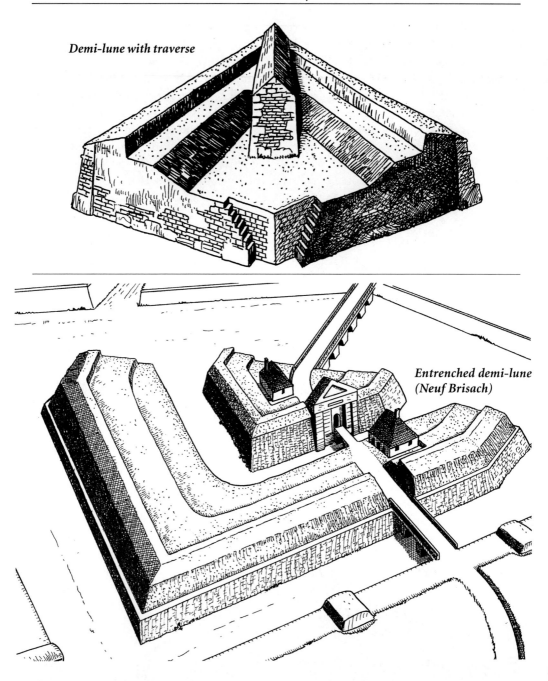

Demi-lune with traverse

Entrenched demi-lune (Neuf Brisach)

demi-lune could also be fitted with a reduit; it was then divided into two parts by an inner ditch, as one can see in Neuf-Brisach.

CAPONIER

The *caponier* was a protected corridor enabling the communication between the main enceinte and a demi-lune. It was placed across the ditch and extended by a postern (a small

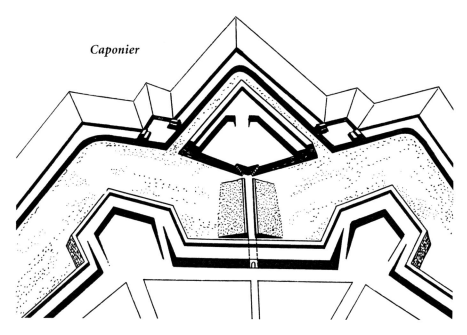

Caponier

tunnel closed by heavy doors) passing under the rampart. From the front, the corridor was protected by the volume of the demi-lune and, sidewise by two breastworks which were commonly fitted with infantry firing steps enabling musket fire to expand the active flanking of the ditch. In some cases, the caponier could be covered by vaulted masonry and earth, thus forming a subterranean gallery.

COUNTERGUARD

The *counterguard* was an outwork placed in front of a bastion or a demi-lune. The purpose was to protect the salient point and both faces. The counterguard was an active

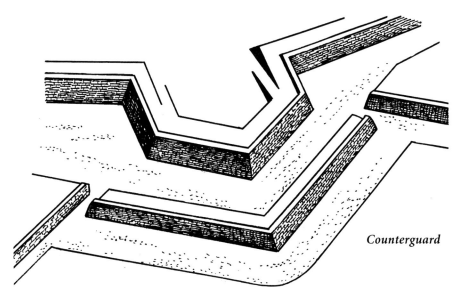

Counterguard

combat emplacement fitted with a breastwork and an infantry banquette as well as a wide wallwalk suitable for artillery, ascents and staircases. If this was not the case, when the width of the wallwalk was only suitable for infantry fire, then the outwork was called a *couvre-face*.

OTHER OUTWORKS

In order to multiply the number of obstacles opposing the advance of besiegers, counterguards could be divided into secondary works. Two autonomous parts were called *tenaillons*, which only gave protection to the faces; depending on local adaptation, one of these could be omitted. The structure was then called a *half-counterguard*. The counterguard could also be split in three parts: a *bonnet* ahead of the salient and two *lunets* protecting the faces. As already said, in Vauban's first and second "systems," counterguards could also be considered as detached bastions.

Above, left: *Tenaillons*. Right: *Counterguard divided into three parts. (1) Bonnet; (2) lunet.*

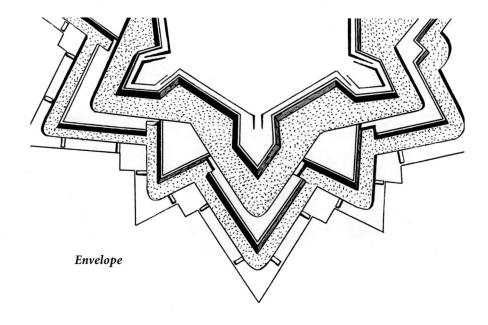

Envelope

Counterguards, demi-lunes or any secondary outworks could be linked together by small bridges to form an *envelope*. This succession of connected elements allowed a rapid communication all around the fortress and constituted another continuous external line of defense. Good examples can be seen at the citadel of Le Palais on the island Belle-Île-en-Mer, at the citadel of Lille and at Neuf-brisach.

COUNTERSCARP AND COUNTER-MINE NETWORK

The *counterscarp* was the outer wall of a dry ditch or the exterior bank of a wet moat. However the term sometimes included the outer wall, covered way and glacis. In classical French bastioned fortification, counterscarp walls were almost always masonry, reinforced by buttresses and decorated with cordon and tablette. The element could be fitted with a *coursière* (counterscarp gallery), which was a covered communication corridor built within the thickness of the masonry; the gallery could be furnished with loopholes allowing reverse fire, which meant firing behind the back of attackers already in the ditch.

From this gallery a maze of *counter-mine tunnels* could be dug under the glacis, obviously provided the soil was suitable. A counter-mine network was composed of underground listening-posts (prepared chambers, called *ecoutes*, from which observers could detect enemy mining activity) and masonry galleries dug under the glacis. These subterranean branches, arranged in an asymmetrical, irregular pattern, were designed and built together with the fortress. They would have their entrances on the fortress side of the covered way or of the ravelin. From the main galleries, secondary branches could be dug when enemy activities had been detected and located. Then gunpowder was placed and ignited with the purpose of blasting enemy galleries, killing attacking miners and exploding defense

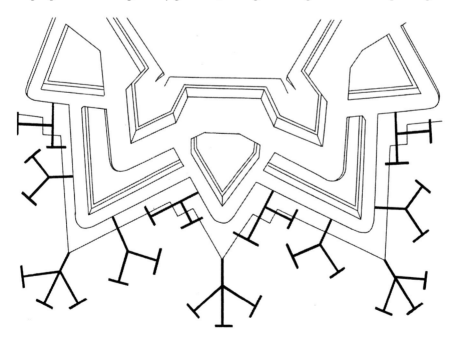

Counter-mine network. The black lines indicate permanent masonry tunnels under the glacis from which secondary counter-mine galleries could be dug.

works taken by the besiegers. It could also happen that both mine and counter-mine struck each other, either inadvertently or on purpose. Then attackers and defenders fought a ter-rifying and creepy hand-to-hand battle in subterranean darkness. The grimness, danger and immense labor entailed in such underground warfare can easily be imagined. This dark, subterranean, dangerous and gruesome kind of warfare was still used for attacking and defending entrenched positions during the First World War (1914–1918).

Covered Way and Place of Arms

The *covered way* was a continuous broad lane placed on top of the counterscarp all around the fortress. It formed a first line of combat as the alley was "covered" by an unin-terrupted breastwork. The crest of the parapet was aligned on the slope of the glacis to give grazing fire. Defenders posted on the covered way gained a fire range equal to the width of the ditch. The idea of protecting this outer lane beyond the ditch was said to have been invented by the Italian military engineer Nicolo Tartaglia. The soldiers got access to the covered way by mean of narrow staircases in the counterscarp-wall. These were called *pas-de-souris* and often their lowest step was 1.50 or 2 meters from the bottom of the ditch. Therefore one had to use a ladder (which, of course, retreating defenders took away with them), otherwise the stair was rather difficult if not impossible to use.

In the angles formed by the covered way, *places of arms* were arranged: at a salient angle, the *salient place of arms* and to a re-entering angle, *re-entering place of arms*. Re-entering

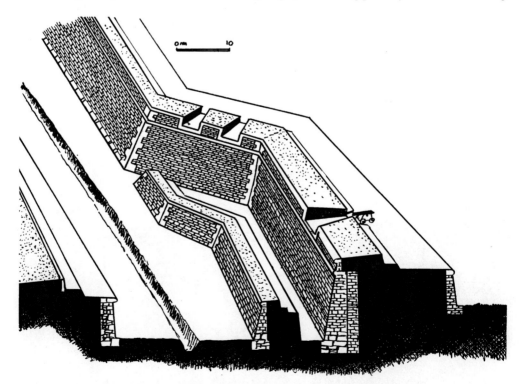

Cross-section covered way, ditch, tenaille and rampart

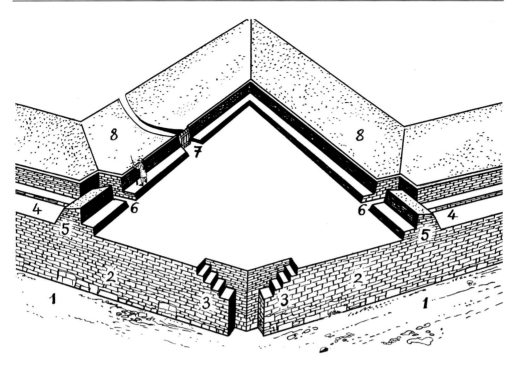

Place of arms. The re-entering place of arms is seen here from the gorge. (1) Ditch; (2) counterscarp; (3) pas-de-souris stair; (4) covered way; (5) traverse; (6) chicane passage; (7) sortie; (8) glacis.

places of arms were the most important. Placed on each side of a demi-lune, they were formed by two protruding faces and could be possibly strengthened to some kind of fortlets called *lunettes*. By the way, a place of arms was also a central square in a fort or a citadel as we shall further see.

The covered way and places of arms were essential elements of the bastioned fortification. They were actually the defenders' ears and eyes. Patrols were sent, sentries were posted and observers were deployed. The covered way and places of arms played a communications and defense role at the periphery of

Pas-de-souris stair

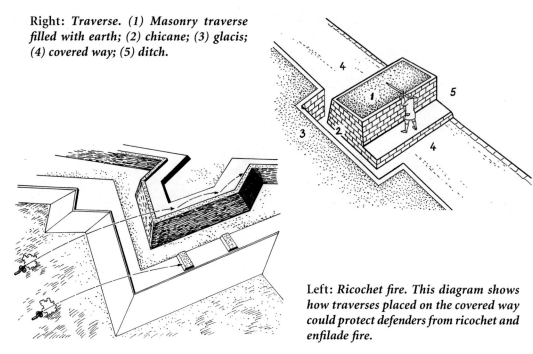

Right: *Traverse. (1) Masonry traverse filled with earth; (2) chicane; (3) glacis; (4) covered way; (5) ditch.*

Left: *Ricochet fire. This diagram shows how traverses placed on the covered way could protect defenders from ricochet and enfilade fire.*

the fortress. They could be reinforced by fences, palisades, fraises (wooden poles planted horizontally), or thorn hedges acting as primitive barbed wires in order to deter escalades. Furthermore, the covered way and places of arms allowed the besieged a more active role. It was indeed practically impossible or at least very difficult to regroup troops exiting the main enceinte. It was thus from the covered way and from the places of arms (and from the dry ditch) that sally parties were concentrated to launch organized counter-attacks which could destroy or capture the besieger's artillery and break up his advance approaches. Psychologically, offensive sorties and counter-attacks were important for the defenders' morale, and tactically speaking, a successful sally could turn the tide of the siege. For this purpose, re-entering places of arms included *sorties*, which were passages opened in the breastworks which, when not in use, were closed by a barrier or a strong gate and guarded by a sentry. As ever, according to the fundamental principle of command, the covered way and places of arms were always lower than the outworks but higher than the glacis.

To avoid enfilade and ricochet-fire, particularly effective on the long branches of the covered way, Vauban recommended *traverses*. These elements, probably created by unknown Italians and adopted by Jean Errard, presented the advantage of chopping the covered way into separate sections. They were earth or masonry works of equal height to the crest of the parapet and placed crosswise at regular intervals on the covered way. Traverses were also fitted with an infantry banquette, allowing thus a stepwise resistance. To make communication possible, traverses were furnished with *chicanes* (angle-shaped, narrow corridors) which generally enabled the passage of only one soldier at a time. As we have seen above, traverses were also placed on the capital lines of bastions and outworks.

GLACIS

The *glacis* was a wide zone entirely surrounding a fortified place. It was limited by the crest of the covered way and the natural level of the countryside. Its width was determined by the range of arms employed, with muskets, about 150 meters. The glacis had to be as

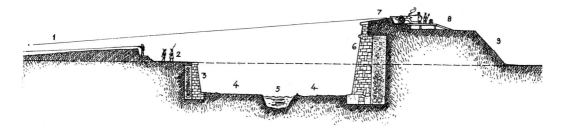

Profile glacis. (1) Glacis; (2) covered way; (3) counterscarp; (4) ditch; (5) cunette; (6) scarp;
(7) parapet; (8) rampart; (9) inner slope.

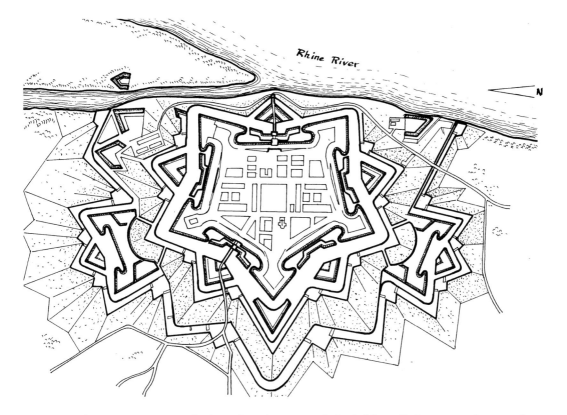

Double glacis at Huningen. The fort of Huningen was defended by a ditch, a covered way and
a glacis with two hornworks, and a second outer covered way and a second outer glacis (dot-
ted areas).

even as possible and completely bare, thus neither planted with vegetation nor with any
buildings in order to provide maximal field of fire. Its gentle declivity was smoothed on
the general profile of all the other defense works and intended to conceal from view and
therefore from the enemy's fire all walls of the fortress. The glacis could be reinforced by
an exterior ditch and sometimes by an outer covered way and a second glacis (examples
are numerous, such as at the citadel of Lille and at Huningen). However the glacis was a
very seductive area, right outside the town. In peacetime, the glacis of fortified places were
often used by the citizens as fields, allotments, kitchen gardens or meadows. In spite of

municipal interdictions, even a new suburb could spread into the glacis, but the unprotected settlement was certain to be looted or destroyed when a siege occurred.

Advance Works

One implication of Vauban's belief in tactical defense in depth was the establishment of advance defenses outside the main center of resistance. Such elements had of course existed in earlier times, but with him the practice became widespread and quasi-systematic. Vauban made a clear distinction between *dehors* (outworks) placed in the main ditch inside the perimeter of the covered way and *ouvrages avancés* (advance works) which were placed ahead of the main ditch. Advance works were projecting combat positions which occupied a portion of the glacis ahead of a curtain or ahead of a bastion. They were designed to force the besiegers to begin a siege from a greater distance and to cover parts of the ground not easily seen from the main wall. They formed external fortified positions which were still in direct defensive connection with the main enceinte, outworks and counterscarp. For this reason their gorges (rear) were always open. They significantly increased the defensive perimeter and therefore obliged the besiegers to multiply the development of approaches and thus the number of workers and troops. They safely set the combat zone far ahead of the main enceinte. A siege was actually a succession of battles and combats beginning in the advance works, continuing in the covered way and the places of arms, then in the outworks and finally in the main enceinte. As a last resort, the besieged — should they really want to fight to the last man — could retreat into the citadel. Advance works could be temporary, hastily constructed just before or during a siege. Some of them were permanent and built at the same time as the fortress and constantly maintained. Others were semi-permanent, which meant that they were overhauled, re-occupied and re-armed only in periods of war when the threat of a siege was likely. In the late seventeenth century, the age of formalism, advance works were codified. The most commonly used were the hornwork and the crownwork, the flèche, the redan, the lunette and various forms of tenailles.

HORN- AND CROWNWORK

A *hornwork* (*ouvrage à corne*) was formed by a bastioned front (one curtain and two half-bastions) which was linked backwards to the main ditch by two parallel *ailes* (wings or walls). Along the wings — which could be up to 200 meters long — many guns could be positioned to flank the adjoining works and the glacis. A permanent hornwork was fitted with the same features as the main enceinte: wallwalk, parapet, ascents, cordon and so on. It was always surrounded by its own ditch and its own covered way. A demi-lune could be added to cover the front curtain and its large terreplein could be divided into several entrenchments including a second bastioned front, a tenaille or a demi-lune in order to oppose a defense in depth. Hornworks were widely used in seventeenth-century fortification and are easily distinguishable by their typical outline. Worthy of mention is the *cornichon* ("gherkin"), which was a hornwork with short wings. Vauban used this adaptation due to lack of space in the mountainous fortifications of Luxembourg.

A *crownwork* (*ouvrage à couronne*) was the union of two hornworks, thus including

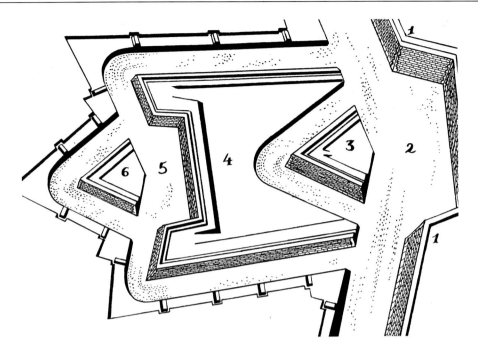

Hornwork. (1) Main wall; (2) main ditch; (3) demi-lune placed in the open gorge of the horn-work; (4) hornwork; (5) hornwork ditch; (6) demi-lune ahead of the hornwork.

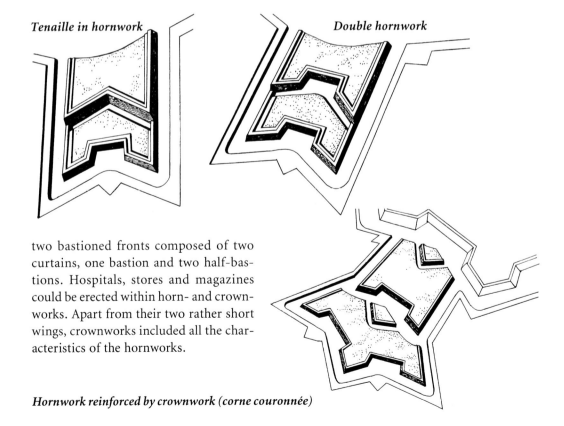

Tenaille in hornwork

Double hornwork

two bastioned fronts composed of two curtains, one bastion and two half-bastions. Hospitals, stores and magazines could be erected within horn- and crown-works. Apart from their two rather short wings, crownworks included all the characteristics of the hornworks.

Hornwork reinforced by crownwork (corne couronnée)

Entrenched hornwork at Huningen   *Entrenched hornwork (Breda, 1674)*

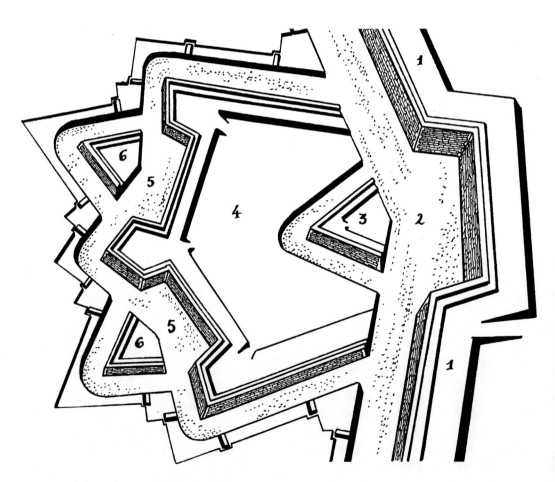

Groundplan of a crownwork. (1) Main wall; (2) main ditch; (3) demi-lune placed in the open gorge of the crownwork; (4) crownwork; (5) crownwork ditch; (6) demi-lune placed ahead of the crownwork.

ARROW, REDAN AND LUNETTE

A *flèche*, also called *freccia* or *arrow*, was a small, arrow-shaped advanced work, an entrenchment formed by two protruding faces. Vauban made great use of this element, which he placed either ahead of the salient of a bastion as support for a salient place of arms or ahead of a re-entering place of arms. In both cases, the rear of the flèche was connected to the covered way by a narrow sunken passageway.

A *redan* was a small work, formed by two protruding faces. The redan was incorporated into a defensive wall such as a countervallation, a circumvallation or an entrenchment linking two redoubts. It

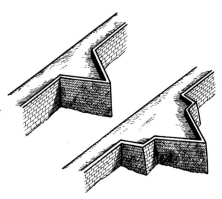

Simple redan (left) and reinforced redan (right)

could also be used to replace a bastion in a fortress. Its gorge was always open and its outline was said to be *renforcé* when its faces were reinforced by two small brisures.

A *lunette* was an advanced work which had the form of a bastion. It was placed ahead on the glacis to oppose besiegers' approaches. The lunette often possessed its own ditch and covered way. It could be closed in the gorge by a parapet and was accessible by means of a drawbridge, which is why one may also consider it a detached work.

TENAILLE

Advance works also existed based on the form of a *tenaille*. The front of these works was composed of two walls forming together a re-entering angle. One distinguished the

Schematic view of advance works. (1) Hornwork; (2) crownwork; (3) tenaille; (4) bishop's miter; (5) swallow's tail; (6) redan; (7) flèche; (8) lunette.

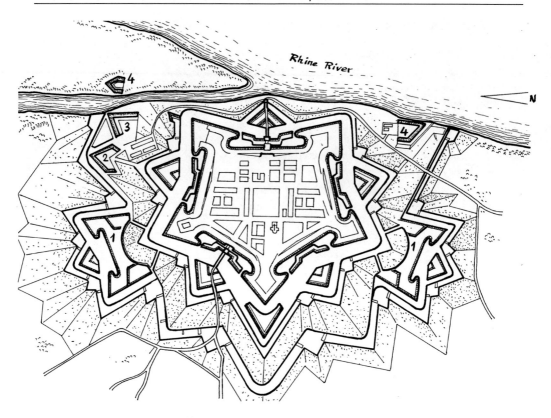

***Advance works at Huningen. When Vauban created the fortress of Huningen between 1679
and 1682 he built two hornworks (1). To protect the banks of the river Rhine, he added one
flèche (2), one redan (3) and two detached lunettes (4).***

single tenaille and the *double tenaille*, both with two long parallel wings; the *bonnet de prêtre*
(bishop's miter or priest's cap), with diverging wings; and the *queue d'aronde* (swallow's
tail), with converging wings. These advance works were, however, not often used and, when
constructed, were merely temporary counterapproaches. Exception could be seen in the first
citadel of Saint-Martin-de-Ré (built in 1624 and dismantled in 1629), which included two
bishop's miters and two swallow's tails, all four permanent.

CONTROVERSY ABOUT ADVANCE WORKS

About the efficiency of advance works, the greatest theorists of fortifications had controversial opinions. Marolois (the great commentator on the old Dutch fortification system) favored their use and Vauban extended them as far as possible, with the aim of
compelling the attacker to begin his siege operations at a distance. Outworks and advance
works, supported by other defenses behind and beside them, multiplied the obstacles in his
way so that the difficulties in gaining ground never ceased. Repeated complexes of
fortification of this type often extended 300 yards ahead from the central enceinte and constituted powerful obstacles to a siege. Vauban built many hornworks, for example in Huningen, Fort-Louis-du-Rhin, Le Quesnoy, and Lille, just to name a few. He built a large
crownwork in front of the Belfort Gate in Neuf-Brisach. Horn- and crownworks enabled

occupation of a section of ground which otherwise might prove useful to the enemy; they could cover the entrance to a town, or they could be used to fortify a new suburb. They could form a *bridgehead*, when a town was established on two banks of a river.

On the other hand, Simon Stevin (the Dutch mathematician and military engineer), Daniel Specklin (an Alsatian fortification expert) and Menno van Coehoorn (creator of the new Dutch bastioned system) were radically opposed to their employ, objecting that they were useless, much too expensive to build and to maintain and that they dangerously scattered the defender's forces. Hornworks were criticized because of the limited number of guns their half-bastions could contain and because of the long vulnerable wings, where guns and crews were dangerously exposed to enfilade fire. Critics observed that the purpose of horn and crownworks was more to terrify or deter the enemy than actually strengthen the defense. Advance works were also unpopular because defenders posted there could feel left alone or sent to sacrifice. They might be tempted not to fight tooth and nail and retreat soon, after a few rounds had been shot at them. Besides, once conquered, advance works provided the besiegers with captured guns, space and material to carry on the siege.

As for the other advance works, flèche, redan, lunette and tenailles, most theoreticians and military engineers agreed that they had little defensive power as they had insufficient room to mount many guns, that enemy batteries of superior strength could easily defeat them, and that they could be outflanked and attacked from behind. They could at best confuse the enemy and play only a delaying role in the first phase of a siege.

Detached Works

While outworks and advance works were always related to the main enceinte, and therefore were always provided with opened gorges, *detached works* were isolated fortified positions. When a fortified town (*place forte*) included a civilian population, detached works were exclusively military. Because they could be attacked from all sides, they needed to be given a complete enclosure and full autonomy. They were built in important strategic places such as crossroads, waterways, dominating hills, passages, mountains, valleys and so on. They were also widely used as coastal defenses, both for observation and combat. Detached works could be built permanently as parts of an organized defensive system, or temporarily constructed during the time of a campaign or during a siege. Dimensions, shape and strength depended on the importance of objectives to be defended. One distinguished various detached works from small to large: post, lunette, battery, redoubt and fort.

A *post* was a small position manned by a few soldiers who had a control, observation or surveillance mission — a sort of checkpoint, in modern parlance. The post could be a simple entrenchment such as a lunette, a flèche or a redan.

A *battery* was an artillery emplacement specially arranged to receive guns of the same type firing in the same direction and towards a common objective. If permanent, the battery could be completed by a barrack for the gunners, a store, a powder house and a fortified enclosure, in which case it could grow to the capacity of a redoubt or a fort.

A *redoubt* was a fortlet. When temporary, the redoubt was an earthwork used, for example, in a siege. When permanent, it was masonry, and completely self-supporting, with a ditch, a drawbridge and a covered way. In seventeenth-century fortification, the redoubt (also named *sconce* in English, *schans* in Dutch, and *redoute* in French) was built

Shapes of redoubt. (1) Closed hornwork; (2) tenailled redoubt; (3) bastioned square redoubt; (4) triangular redoubt with half-bastions; (5) square redoubt with half-bastions; (6) simple square redoubt.

Lines of fire. Theoretical studies in geometry and mathematics, but also the nature of the terrain and local conditions established what form a fortress or a walled city should take. Properly built, bastioned fortification ensured that every angle of wall, ditch and approach was covered by defensive fire, mowing down the attackers as they struggled through a maze of outworks and advance works.

according to a codified combination of regular bastioned forms: triangular, square or rectangular, with three or four bastions or half-bastions. They could have a stellar outline when made of tenailles but also, depending on natural site conditions, a completely irregular groundplan.

A *fort* distinguished itself from a redoubt only by its larger dimensions, its superior capacities and firepower and by the fact that it often had its own garrison. In many cases, a fort was an old medieval castle which was modernized and adapted to modern warfare (Brest, Collioure castle, Château-Queyras, for example). If the fort was completely new and if conditions were favorable, its shape was commonly rectangular or pentagonal, with four or five bastions and fitted with a ditch, outworks, covered way and glacis. Forts and redoubts were also given the form of crown- or hornworks— in this case then with a closed gorge.

COASTAL FORT

Vauban, the protector of Louis XIV's territorial borders, was also passionate about the defense of the French coasts. As much on the landside as on the seaside, nothing escaped the notice of the fortification commissioner general. The defense of naval bases and sensitive spots on shores demanded a different approach than the northeastern border, where the dense maze of strongholds and fortified towns could support each other. In Louis XIV's

Fort Lupin, 1683. The coastal Fort Lupin was built in 1683 to protect the approaches near the military port of Rochefort (see also Chapter 5).

Corps de garde at Saint-Germain-sur-Ay (Normandy)

time, landing techniques and large-scale amphibious operations were at a very elementary stage. The scale of attack to be expected from the sea was usually much smaller than that on a land front. To watch over about 3,000 km. of French coastline and to defend the most strategically important and most vulnerable points such as islands, harbors, straits, anchorages, or beaches which could be attacked by Anglo-Dutch raiders, Vauban designed a special kind of detached coastal work. A *fort de côte* (sea fort) was usually composed of a low, masonry semicircular gun battery with a thick breastwork pierced with embrasures for grazing fire. In Vauban's time one cannon on land (provided it was sheltered behind a fortified emplacement) was estimated to be five to ten times more valuable than one gun embarked on an unsteady ship. Very often a high tower was built in the gorge of the battery. The various floors were arranged as powder magazine, food and water storage, and lodging for the garrison and it was equipped with loopholes for close-range defense. The top of the building was covered with a roof or arranged as a terrace used as an observation post, an armed emplacement and possibly as a lighthouse. On the land front, the fort was often surrounded by a wet ditch, a covered way and a glacis. Combining long-range grazing fire and short-range plunging fire, Vauban's coastal forts were efficient units, such as the hexagonal, four-story Tour Dorée in Camaret-sur-Mer (Finistère) or forts Chapus and Lupin (Charente-Maritime). Vauban also re-used and overhauled old medieval coastal watchtowers such as the Dungeon of Fouras (Charente-Maritime) or Castle La Latte (Côtes-d'Armor). Vauban's new-built or re-shaped coastal forts were good examples of an unorthodox use of Middle Ages fortifications, intelligently adapted to special conditions. Medieval works retained much of their value in coastal defense as well as in mountainous sites because attackers met tremendous difficulties in trying to bring supplies and heavy siege artillery into position.

In 1680, Louis XIV enacted an ordinance creating a special coast guard militia. Organized along paramilitary lines, it was composed of *Capitaineries* (units made up of able men

Coastal gun tower at Port-en-Bessin (Normandy). The tower was probably designed by engineer Descombes in 1694.

from about 12 or 15 parishes situated on the coastline) headed by a captain, generally a local aristocrat or a retired officer. Corporals and sergeants, who had to be literate, were recruited among the population. In peacetime, activities were limited to training and maintenance of batteries and redoubts once a fortnight. In wartime or when raiders were detected, the *Capitaineries* were mobilized for patrols along the shores—either on foot or on horseback (for the richest)—and manning watch posts and coastal gun emplacements. Alarm was given by means of waving a flag, by sounding a trumpet or firing a shot, or by fire signals at night. Watch posts consisted of *Corps de Gardes* (watch-houses) built on promontories or cliffs or on top of a dune, where a panoramic view was possible. There was no standard building but a watch-post was generally a simple, rectangular stone house composed of two rooms: one for the men with a fireplace and bunks; the other arranged as an ammunition and weapon store. Some watch posts had a lookout in the form of a small tower or watch-turret, for example at Cancale (Bretagne). Of course watch-posts (and sea forts as well) were only established in seaboard sections suitable for an amphibious operation—beachy shores without steep cliffs, strong streams and currents, or dangerous reefs. But given the large spread of French coasts, it was impossible to fortify efficiently: in case of a landing, the coast guard militias—at least those composed of determined men—could only fight a delaying combat. Indeed, as civilian militiamen were not paid, were poorly trained, and had to provide for their own weapons, most of them were merely Sunday combatants with a low military value. Their main trump was their knowledge of the terrain of operation, and the fact that they defended their own villages. But, on the whole, the system did not work smoothly, particularly during the periods of the year when military operations could interfere with agriculture activities.

*Citadel. (1) Governor's residence; (2) arsenal; (3) chapel; (4) central place of arms; (5) officers'
house; (6) soldiers' barrack; (7) powder house; (8) main gate-house; (9) secondary postern.*

CITADEL

A *citadel* was a very particular kind of detached work. Like a detached fort, a citadel was purely military but it was a fortress built within a fortified city. The citadel was placed on a dominating position inside the town or overlapping the urban fortifications, which allowed its access to be independent from the city gates. The citadel was accessible by a main gate turned toward the city (porte de Ville) and a secondary access leading directly to the countryside (porte de Secours or porte des Champs). In certain cases, the citadel was an old medieval castle (*château*) which was modernized (Brest or Briançon, for example) or a former foreign work adapted to modern warfare (Perpignan, for example). If the defensive structure was entirely new, a geometrical bastioned form was often chosen. In the absence of constraints (unfavorable site conditions or a lack of funds) Vauban preferred a regular pentagon based on the classical example of the citadel of Antwerp (Belgium) built for the Spaniards by the Italian engineer Pacciotto in 1567. Indeed the pentagon fulfilled military demands, reduced dead angles and offered a practical and efficient internal organization. The inner space of the citadel was divided according to a classical radial plan in which streets regularly diverged from a central square (called place of arms) to curtains and bastions. This use of space, invented and codified by Renaissance Italian architects and urbanists, presented a sober, well-ordered and majestic aspect which suited military requirements. However, due to lack of funds, rectangular citadels with four bastions were also built (in Bayonne and Saint-Martin-de-Ré, for example) and, due to natural conditions, irregular citadels were erected (in Besançon and Bitche, for example). Between the city and the citadel, a wide and bare glacis was established; this space, called the *esplanade*, served as an

Citadel, Bayonne. The square citadel of Castelnau in Bayonne was designed by Vauban in 1680.

open field of fire and could be used as a military training ground. A citadel, esplanade and new fortified enceinte cost a lot of money and, sometimes, required the destruction of houses or even larger urban sections.

The citadel fulfilled three distinctive roles. The first function was improved logistics. The citadel contained everything needed in order to resist a long siege, such as barracks; food, water and foraging-stores; an arsenal; a powder house; workshops and so on. It was also a supply point for armies in campaign, and provided winter quarters and a military administrative center.

Secondly, the citadel was a powerful military bulwark. Just like the keep in the medieval castle, it acted as a final fallback position, a reduit from which to continue the defense even when the town was conquered; therefore it was always constructed on a high position in order to both command and protect the city. It was strongly fortified with powerful bastions, complete with surrounding ditches with outworks, a covered way, external glacis and internal esplanade. This display of strength was also meant to deter enemies from laying siege.

The third and most important role was political. A citadel was intended to subjugate, control and overawe recently conquered populations with questionable loyalty or a rebellious propensity. A part of the weaponry was directed towards the esplanade and the city to repress insurrections. Its garrison might sally forth to persecute or bombard dissidents at any time, and could also discourage the inhabitants by force from surrendering at a premature stage in a siege. Very often the construction of the expensive citadel as well as the occupying garrison's pay was financed by citizens' money. For all these reasons, the citadel represented a threat. It was an unpopular and hated place, an object of terror and dictatorship as well as a financial burden. As soon as relationships between the occupiers and the conquered population got better, urban authorities would ask for it to be dismantled or at least that the military take over expenditures.

In France the phenomenon of citadel-building was directly linked with the consolidation of the royal power and the territorial expansion which principally began under Louis XI's reign (Beaune, Dijon and Auxonne citadels, for example, were built after the annexation of Burgundy in 1577). During Louis XIV's reign, Vauban and his collaborators reshaped a lot of older fortifications and built ten entirely new citadels (Lille, Arras, Strasburg, Valenciennes, Mont-Louis, Fort-Louis, Marseille, Bayonne, Besançon and Saint-Martin-de-Ré). In the eighteenth century, citadels lost some of their political role because of population's loyalty, but the long-standing association of royal fortification with naked oppression of urban populations erupted in the events that led to the Revolution of 1789. In the nineteenth century, citadels lost some of their military role because of the creation of outer rings of detached forts. Citadels remained military administrative centers and many were transformed into prisons. For example, the citadel of Saint-Martin-de-Ré became a place of departure to overseas convict prisons, such as the labor camp of Cayenne in French Guyana, about which Léo Ferré wrote a song with the famous quotation "*Merde à Vauban!*"

Flooding

Vauban paid particular attention to water obstacles, and was always ready to "get his feet wet." Inundation (flooding, the creation of artificial lakes) was the voluntary and controlled submersion of more or less broad zones in order to cut off access in moments of crisis. Flooding presented many advantages. On a large scale it was very cost effective because fortifications and defensive troops were only needed on high ground. On a small scale it made impossible the establishment and digging of entrenched approaches to lay siege to a place. It also made impossible the use of underground mines. To be effective, the water had to be deep enough to prevent the access of foot-soldiers, horsemen, artillery trains and supply wagons; on the other hand it had to be shallow enough to prevent navigation. As can easily be imagined, the use of military tactical inundation required great technical knowledge and sophisticated hydrologic installations in order to control such a dangerous element as water. For example, one had to calculate the surface to flood, supply enough water, take into account ground-absorption and evaporation, estimate erosion, and build and maintain water-gates, dams, sluices, batardeaus and supply canals. Low-lying grounds had to be flooded quickly in moments of crisis, but left totally dry for more productive use in ordinary times. To these huge civilian engineering works were added military considerations such as surveillance of opposing sabotage or counter-works and dispositions to facilitate combat conditions.

Inundation also presented serious disadvantages. Obviously it could be effected only on low or marshy lands. It facilitated delay or could even stop enemy progress but made a counter-offensive very difficult too. It took a long time to build and to effect, especially on a large scale. Besides, as we have seen, when it froze, a water defense lost a great part or the totality of its value. Flooding was also extremely unpopular. For the local peasantry, it could mean the destruction of homes, the loss of the harvest, the death of cattle and durable degradation or even infertility of the inundated fields and meadows, especially when corrosive sea water was used.

Throughout history of warfare, flooding played an important role, especially in the Low Countries. This strategy was the basis of Dutch defense from the sixteenth century until the 1950s. Dutch Protestant independents and Spanish troops used it in sieges (in Den Briel in 1572, Alkmaar in 1573, Leiden in 1574 and Den Bosch in 1629). Large scale inundations around Amsterdam stopped Louis XIV's army and saved the Dutch Republic in 1672. In 1702, Marshal de Boufflers considered laying siege to the small fortified city of Hulst in the south of Holland. Vauban, whom he asked for advice, declared the city untakeable because of its impassable water defenses.

Vauban, as early as 1668, was much interested by this form of defense and employed it wherever possible in the low and marshy countrysides of northeast France: at Gravelines near Dunkirk, Condé-sur-l'Escaut, Maubeuge and Verdun, for example. Flooding was used until the twentieth century in the Maginot line, in Dutch defense in 1940 and in the German Atlantic Wall (1942–1944).

Entrenched Camp

From 1692 on, Vauban — responding to the fact that the fate of a besieged town was always surrender — advocated the establishment of entrenched camps. The aim was to abandon minor fortresses and strengthen major ones by the addition of temporary exterior lines. These would be composed of field works or semi-permanent fortifications including redoubts, and earth walls flanked by bastions and redans and preceded by ditches. In doing so he intended to accommodate whole armies in addition to the fortress garrisons, and increase the defensive zone by using field fortification. Having numerous troops available enabled the besieged to make successful sallies and counter-offensives. Besides, increasing the defensive perimeter obliged the besiegers to multiply its approaches. In both cases this could help protract the defense until an intervention army came to the besiegers' rescue. The concept bought extra time for the defender to bring his troops from a distance and concentrate them at the threatened point. Vauban proposed the establishment of such camps in the Alps in Montdauphin and Seyne-les-Alpes, as well as in Langres, Belfort, Menin, Furnes, Philippeville, Mons, and Namur. Such camps were actually established at Dunkirk, Givet and Brest. In 1701, Louis XIV ordered engineers Joinville and Girval to build a continuous line of field works; the huge entrenched camp, about 200 km. in length, linked Saas-van-Ghent to Huy to defend Belgium. Another famous example was the Wissemburg line at the northeast corner of France, which followed the valley of the Lauter River.

The entrenched camp concept gradually became a common feature in the eighteenth and nineteenth centuries, Belfort, Langres, Verdun and Toul being good examples.

Military Buildings

Fortifications were completed by various buildings, premises and installations which made possible the operation of weapons and the spartan daily life of a military community. In a fort or a citadel, military buildings were constructed around a central square, called *place of arms*, where ceremonies, assemblies and parades were held and where maneuvers, drill and training took place. Despite his readiness to adapt in a pragmatic fashion to the local terrain and particular conditions, Vauban relied on a number of standardized buildings, regardless of whether they were built on a plain or in a mountainous region. These buildings were always sturdy, and intended to be practical and long-lasting. Many were usually beautifully decorated and designed in French classical baroque style based on a strict system of rules emphasizing the harmony of proportions and geometric regularity. Together with the gate-houses, military buildings expressed Louis XIV's absolutism over the country, his glory that was intended to last forever, the grandeur of France, and also man's rule over nature.

Living Quarters

For much of history, due to the lack of enough barracks, soldiers were billeted in civilians' homes in garrison-towns, the unfortunate inhabitants being obliged to provide food and sleeping accommodation for one or more men. The expense was (often but not always) reimbursed by the crown to the householder at a fixed rate. Campaigning soldiers were often accommodated piecemeal in the loft of an inn, in livery stables, or in damp and frequently unsanitary bivouacs and tent camps. This method was unhandy for the troops (as it always took some time to assemble them when needed), and, understandably, was very unpopular for civilians. Billeting often generated abuse, quarrels and complaints, even fights when things went wrong. In order to suppress or at least reduce this trouble, Vauban and Louvois advocated the construction of *casernes* (barracks) especially in existing forts and citadels. The construction of buildings especially designed to provide accommodation for military personnel was a revolution in warfare. It paralleled and exemplified the rise of standing armies. Barracks, like fortresses, were embodiments of Louis XIV's royal authority, which their imposing architecture was meant to reflect. They also enabled a strict control of the men by the NCOs, and guaranteed that soldiers were supervised, correct, present, ready and armed any time when needed. Vauban designed a standard barrack composed of a central staircase leading to four identical sleeping rooms. This basic unit could be repeated at length, could have multiple floors to increase capacity and could be vertically shifted to adapt to a sloping site. However, if Vauban's barracks generally displayed an imposing exterior façade, the internal layout was rather primitive. Barracks were overcrowded, uncomfortable, ill-ventilated, badly heated and without easy longitudinal communication because of the room partitions. Recreation was non-existent and privacy was scarce. Corporals and sergeants normally had a screened-off bunk. As for the troops, every dormitory was equipped with several beds which were shared. The dormitory was fitted with a fireplace intended both for heating and cooking. In Vauban's time, living, sleeping, cooking and eating took place in the barrack-room because refectories and kitchens were not always available. Hygiene at the time of Louis XIV was unbelievably crude and even the royal palace of Versailles did not smell of roses. Latrines and primitive washing facilities were placed outside the barracks. Latrines were also placed on the walls, in small areas shaped like medieval machicolation, a series of voids and corbels hanging above the wall with defecation falling into the ditch. An example can still be seen at Fouras Castle (Bretagne).

Barracks were built behind and parallel along sections of curtains for a rapid deployment of the soldiers to their combat emplacements. Sometimes barracks were integrated within a curtain or acted as a protective traverse (in Belfort and Montlouis, for example);

Latrine

Cross-section, latrine

in this case the barrack qualified as "defensive" and was constructed with thick walls pierced with loopholes for infantry fire on its external façade.

A cavalry barrack was composed of stalls on the ground floor and accommodations for men on the first floor. The unit was completed with various service premises including barns, forage stores, workshops for a blacksmith and harness-maker as well as for a veterinary surgeon.

Barracks could not, however, take care of all the troops, and the billeting remained a common practice. Nevertheless the progressive housing of soldiers in barracks that started during Louis XIV's reign would mark the urban landscape of many *villes de garnison* (garrison towns).

Near the barracks were the officers' pavilions, which had one or two floors with a central staircase giving access to a corridor leading to a number of rooms. Officers were noble-

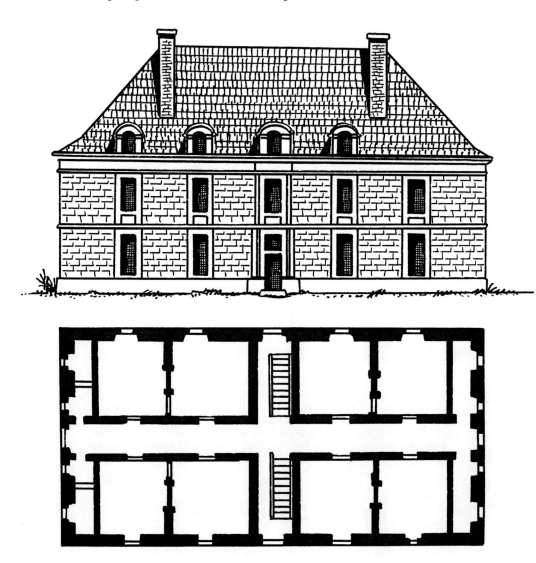

Officers' house designed by Vauban at Montdauphin about 1700

men who enjoyed privileges such as free time, better food, and larger living spaces. Their servants were lodged in the attic, several of them packed into tiny rooms.

The commanding officer of the place was called the *gouverneur* (governor). His residence, called an *hôtel,* was often rather luxurious. It was sometimes a kind of palace with a garden *à la Française* and it usually included administrative annexes and offices. The governor was not always present because, just like a colonel, he had purchased the title and the office (which brought significant income), or he had received the function as a reward from the king. Vauban, for example, was governor of Lille and Douai. Often the actual commanding officer was a subordinate, called the *lieutenant du roy* (king's lieutenant), who lived with his family in a house or in an apartment in or near the governor's residence.

Garrison and barrack life was rather dull and boring, and — at least for the troops — was in some respects not wholly unlike prison life, particularly in remote forts far from anything. The situation was somewhat different in a fortified town where a static garrison could have the opportunity to mingle with the local population. In peacetime, soldiers could supplement their wages by hiring themselves out to local artisans and as part-time agricultural laborers for the harvest and wine-making. Love affairs could develop, and women could be invited to dwell in the barracks. Although marriage was not encouraged, wives and mistresses could be adopted as part of the unit. Though not directly on the payroll, they could make a living by carrying out menial and domestic tasks. Children born from these legitimate or illegal unions could be signed up officially as paid *enfants de troupe.* They would serve as kitchen boys and junior drummers, and — when they got old enough — would become full-time soldiers.

ARSENAL

The need for centralized control over weapons saw arsenals concentrated within strongholds or other places of importance. The arsenal was an essential building. It was the logistical base of a fortified town, a fort or a citadel. Shape, dimensions and capacity depended on the importance of the place. The arsenal was often composed of a central yard with buildings around it. These included vast magazines on the ground floor where guns, carriages, wheels and carts were stored. Small arms (muskets, swords, etc.) and equipment were generally stored in the upper floors. The highly dangerous gunpowder was never stored in the arsenal but kept apart in special powder houses. The arsenal was completed by various premises and workshops (e.g. masons, smiths and carpenters) who built, repaired and maintained military equipment, artillery and fortifications. The arsenal was meant to provide everything the local garrison needed but also be able to supply and support armies in campaign. Their sitting was thus of enormous strategic importance, and they often were located in frontier fortresses.

In a military harbor (e.g. Toulon, Brest, Rochefort, Dunkirk), the arsenal was a huge zone including shipyards and rope, carpenter and sail workshops where warships were constructed, repaired, armed and supplied.

POWDER HOUSE

Powder houses were often built in a standard, single-story design. For obvious security reasons, powder houses were located as far as possible from living quarters and for

Powder house

tactical reasons as close as possible to combat emplacements. Powder-magazines were therefore often placed in the protected terreplein of void bastions. They were, of course, always guarded by sentries, and their access was strictly restricted to those having legitimate business. Capacity varied according to the importance of the place and several powder houses were scattered all over the fortress to supply different sections of the defense. The building was surrounded by a stone or earth wall or a palisade. The magazine had to be protected against plunging mortar fire. The measures taken included strong and highly resistant vaulted chambers covered with a bomb-proof roof supported by buttresses, brick and stone arches, and earth or grass cover intended to absorb explosion. Walls were very thick and strengthened by buttresses. Windows were few, small, narrow and cunningly fitted with chicanes (masonry blocks) around which air could circulate but through which sparks and missiles from the outside could not pass. Inside the powder house, kegs and barrels rested on wooden shelves and timber to ensure dryness. Nails, hinge-pins and locks were made of bronze (a metal that does not spark) to prevent accidental explosions. For this very same reason, soldiers working in the powder house were asked to wear clogs. The powder house often included an *armurerie* (workshop) where shells, petards, cartridges and grenades were filled.

GUARDHOUSE

The *corps de garde* (guardhouse) was a post intended to shelter the soldiers checking the entrance of a fortified city, fort or citadel. The gates formed weak points in a defensive perimeter, since they were by definition points of access. In the case of a fortified town, the

Guardhouse

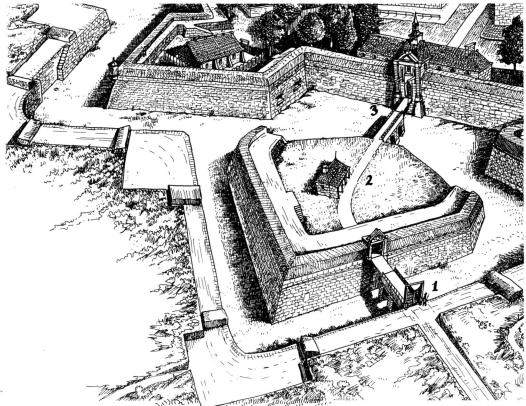

Guardhouse placed in a demi-lune. There were generally several check-points before one could have access to a fortified place. The first one was on the counterscarp (1); the second at the guardhouse in the demi-lune (2); and a third one was at the drawbridge and main gate-house in the curtain (3).

personnel controlling accesses included guards and soldiers but also customs officers who levied taxes and tolls on all persons and goods coming in or going out of the town. The gate taxes were one of the major forms of income for cities in the Ancient Regime. Access to a fortress was usually restricted to those having legitimate business within, particularly in time of war. The guardhouse could be a chamber integrated in the gate-house or an independent detached building constructed on a demi-lune. The guardhouse, often of a universal, standard design, was not a combat emplacement but a useful building for day-to-day police purposes. It included a chamber with bunks for the sentries, a room/office heated by a fireplace for the officer and an exterior gallery or porch roof resting on wooden beams (e.g. Briançon, Montdauphin) or stone arches (e.g. Thionville, Saint-Martin-de-Ré).

HOSPITAL

Under Louis XIV's reign an effort was made in the domain of medical care. When possible, Vauban constructed a military hospital. The building was mostly built far from living quarters to prevent contagion. It included an operating room, several wards for the sick and wounded and an apothecary. The hospital was often self-contained, with its own medical and nursing staff, kitchen, baker and wash house. Its capacity was calculated on a ratio of one sick man out of twenty-five soldiers. Theoretically each patient had an individual bed and appropriate food and received medical care and nursing. However, in spite of progress by the military surgeon Ambroise Paré (1509–1590), medical knowledge and care remained rudimentary. A wound, even light and superficial, often resulted in infection, which necessitated amputation, illness and sometimes death. Survival and healing depended much more on a strong individual physical constitution than on medical intervention. The main soldier-killer was sickness due to lack of hygiene, profound medical ignorance or promiscuity. Until the decisive medical progress at the end of the nineteenth century, epidemics and diseases were more lethal than wars. Under the weight of a major battle or during a siege, medical arrangements often collapsed, with wounded hastily packed into improvised hospitals, generally monasteries or convents, where they were nursed by monks and nuns.

HÔTEL DES INVALIDES

Until Louis XIV's reign, there was no specific institution for housing invalid soldiers and disabled veterans. Crippled and old combatants were abandoned to their unfortunate fate. The luckiest among them might be assisted by charitable Christian institutions but most of these poor souls survived miserably as beggars or thieves. A small effort was made under Henri IV to care for them with the foundation in 1596 of the *Maison de la Charité Chrétienne* (Home of Christian Charity) to comfort, house, dress and feed veterans. On Vauban's request, Louvois convinced Louis XIV to follow his grandfather's example by building a home for veterans. For this purpose, the gigantic and magnificent "Hôtel Royal des officiers et soldats invalides et estropiez au service de Sa Majesté," commonly called the *Hôtel des Invalides,* was designed by the architect Liberal Bruant, and built in Paris from 1671 to 1706. The Invalides formed a miniature town governed according to both a military and religious system. The first residents, who came in 1674, were divided into three groups: *invalides parfaits* (total invalids) and *invalides imparfaits* (non-total invalids) who could not serve at all anymore; these two categories were the blind, the legless cripples and the maimed who were housed in the Hôtel des Invalides. The building had a capacity of 3,000 long-termed disabled, but by the end of the seventeenth century it was rather overcrowded, with about 4,000 residents. Pensioners in the Hôtel des Invalides were divided into companies supervised by veteran NCOs and officers. They wore a blue coat lined in red with pewter buttons, and ran shoe-mending, tapestry and illumination workshops.

The third category were *invalides de service* (duty-invalids), the least disabled, who were regrouped into special companies. The more able veterans— any soldier still capable of loading his musket — were employed in minor auxiliary service including keeping watch, and maintenance of a peace-time fortress-garrison. Of course, this function was more charitable than military.

Saint-Louis Church, Invalides at Paris. Also called Dome Church or Soldiers' Church, the Invalides church opens onto a large cour d'honneur and represents a fine example of classical architecture.

Today the Hôtel des Invalides houses the Museum of the French Army. In the Dome Church (designed by Jules Hardouin-Mansart, a part of which is called Soldiers' Church) lies the body of Napoléon I in an imposing red porphyry sarcophagus beneath the golden dome. It has been there since 1840, when the British allowed the transfer of the emperor's body from the island of St. Helena to Paris. A wing of the building, however, continues to provide the very service for which the institution was initially created: the care of French disabled soldiers and veterans.

WATER SUPPLY

Water supply was a matter of major concern to any garrison. Obviously a besieged place without sufficient water was doomed to rapid surrender. Each fort or citadel was equipped with a well, sometimes very deep. At Fort Joux in the Jura, the well is 132 meters deep. In the citadel of Besançon, the well is 120 meters, and in the citadel of Bitche, 80 meters. Given its essential importance, the well was commonly protected by a bomb-proof roof

Well and chapel, Besançon

resting on strong pillars (e.g. at Besançon and Fort Barreaux), or even included inside a fortified vaulted building (e.g. at Longwy). The well was guarded by a sentry and fitted with a hoisting wheel. When a well was not available, water tanks were arranged to collect rain. Vauban paid particular attention to wells and water tanks and wrote a theoretical treaty about how to construct and maintain them.

MISCELLANEOUS BUILDINGS

Each important fortified town, fort or citadel had a *poste de police* (prison) for undisciplined soldiers, captured deserters, and criminals. It could also happen that a whole fortress (generally a citadel or a remote fort) would be arranged as a detention center for enemy prisoners-of-war who would be detained in spartan conditions until the end of the conflict. Being enclosed spaces with high walls and deep ditches, and guarded by a armed

Church at Briançon. The Collégiale Notre-Dame was designed by Vauban and built between 1703 and 1718. The conspicuous church was curiously placed in the middle of a bastion, totally exposed, perhaps with the naïve hope that a Christian enemy would have scruples about firing at God's house?

garrison, a fortress could easily accommodate a large number of prisoners at little additional cost to the king. A *pillory* and a scaffold for the death penalty (hanging) were displayed on the busy square to serve as a deterrent. The logistical capacity of a fortified place was further completed by various accommodations without direct military connections but essential for the daily life of a community. Each fortress had food stores matching the importance of the garrison, one or more mills (moved by wind or horse power), bakers and wash-houses. For horses, stalls, forage stores and a blacksmith's workshop were arranged. A fortified place had to be as much as possible self-sufficient, living in a kind of autarchy. It thus possessed meadows for cattle, kitchen-gardens, orchards, cattle sheds, poultry houses, and rabbit hutches as well as a butchery.

The garrison could worship in a parish church (in a town) or a chapel (in a fort or a citadel). Louis XIV considered himself as the defender of the Roman Catholic faith, and France was named *la fille ainée de l'Église Catholique* (the eldest daughter of the Catholic Church). The garrison church was the focus for spiritual life, and soldiers were supposed to attend religious services, observe Christian morality, and behave decently. Vauban never forgot to reserve a space for a place of worship and himself designed churches in the citadel of Strasburg (1681), Montdauphin (1699) and Briançon (1700). The garrison church or chapel were often solidly built in a sober style, and the top of the bell tower provided an excellent lookout post.

Design of Fortifications

On Louis XIV's order, transmitted by Louvois, Vauban went to such-and-such a region or such-in-such a city to inspect, survey, report, build, improve or dismantle fortifications. The tireless gentleman of Morvan made in the king's service numerous journeys across France, as we have seen in Chapter One. As a young man, he traveled on horseback but when he got older he arranged for himself a *chaise de poste* (a sort of wheel-less coach carried by two horses) in which he could travel and work in a precarious comfort. Historians estimate that Vauban traveled an average of 1,500 to 2,000 km. every year in all weather along the bad roads of the realm. Vauban was usually accompanied by a team of secretaries and escorted by a platoon of horsemen because, even for him, roads were not always safe from bandits, highwaymen and hijackers. Vauban's visit to a fortress commonly took place as follows. Accompanied by the provincial director-engineer of fortifications, Vauban was welcomed by the local urban and military authorities. After an official reception and rest, he met with the king's ordinary engineer posted there and for a few days discussed problems with him, inspected, studied, took notes and drew sketches about the local fortifications. After this active work on the spot, Vauban, assisted by his secretaries, wrote a report. The first part of this document was a survey describing geographical particularities, strategic importance and resources of the population. The second part was the *Projet des ouvrages à faire* (project of works to be made), which included estimates, proposals, advice, specification of the costs and completion time. Fortifications were very expensive, and this often gave rise to anger from Louvois and protestations demanding reduction of the cost, while Vauban asked for more funds. The project was illustrated by watercolor groundplans, cross-sections and drawings explained by legends and keys. Proposed fortifications were colored in yellow, existing ones in red or rose, military buildings in grey and artillery depots in purple. Slopes and relief were indicated by hatches and shadows; gardens, meadows and orchards were shown in green and fields in brown. Scales were given in Ancient Regime measurement, as the metric system was only introduced during the French Revolution of 1789. One toise or *fathom* was equal to about 1.92 meters. It was divided into six feet. Each foot was approximately equal to 32 cm. Plans, maps and drawings, though intended for a pure military-technical use, were often very beautiful and formed a rich illustration of historic urbanism and architecture. Many of them are preserved today in the *Archives du Génie* (Engineering Corps Archives) and in the *Bibliothèque Historique de l'Armée de Terre* (Ground Troops' Historical Library) located in Vincennes Castle near Paris. Texts and illustrations, after review and correction, were reproduced in three fair copies. The original stayed on location, a duplicate went to the provincial department and the third copy was sent to the War Department's head in Versailles: Louvois (and from 1691 on, Le Peletier). The document was presented to the king, who devoted several hours a week to this task. Louis XIV read the files, examined the projects, studied the propositions, estimated the costs and finally — all alone — made a decision. The king had received a special education in the art of fortifications and was undeniably able to make an intelligent analysis and a competent choice.

Vauban was the creator of entirely new fortified cities: two in Lorraine (Longwy and Sarrelouis), four in Alsace (the new town of Saint-Louis in Vieux-Brisach, Huningen, Fort-Louis-du-Rhin and his *chef-d'œuvre*, Neuf-Brisach), one in the Alps (Montdauphin), one in the Pyrenees (Montlouis) and one in Germany (Montroyal). The chosen site was either an empty space in open field or a small village, or even a hamlet without possible other uses. Making a clean sweep of existing elements, Vauban designed both the bastioned fortifications and the civilian city. In these places created ex nihilo, the competent fortress builder revealed himself a talented urbanist. Vauban's creations are characterized by adaptation to mountainous or marshy sites (Fort-Louis-du-Rhin, the new town of Saint-Louis in Old-Brisach, Montlouis, Montdauphin and Montroyal) and by perfect regular fortifications as well as regular urban plans when on neutral sites (Longwy, Sarrelouis, Huningen and Neuf-Brisach). While the Italian Renaissance radial groundplan was suitable for a fort or a citadel, in practice, it was very uncertain for a large city. In this case, Vauban chose a grid plan in which streets cut each other with right angles, dividing habitation spaces into regular square or rectangular quarters. This rational urbanization was inherited from the classical Roman town. It was used in the Middle Ages *bastides*, as well as in newly created cities.

Construction of Fortifications

When Louis XIV had taken a favorable decision and when the project had been restudied and possibly modified, preliminary works could begin. In the meantime, Vauban was gone and the construction of the fortress was entrusted to the local military engineer. The provincial administrator called upon the services of civilian building contractors, with whom prices were discussed and negotiated: systematically the contract was awarded to the cheapest. This odd procedure — only considering cost — did not always guarantee satisfactory quality. It could also cause the contractor's bankruptcy when his estimate was too low. On the other hand, this kind of business dealing, involving huge sums of money, was

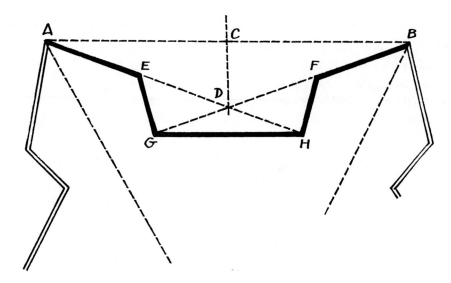

Construction of a bastioned front according to Vauban. On one of the external sides AB of a regular polygon, one draws a perpendicular line CD equal to 1/6th of AB when the polygon has six faces or more (for a pentagon 1/7th and for a square 1/8th). From D, one draws the defense-lines AD and BD. On each of them, one determines to a distance from the points A and B (corresponding to 2/7th of the polygon side) the points E and F which are the shoulder points of the bastions. Measuring on each defense-line, the length EF from points E and F, one determines G and H, which are the internal limits of the bastion flanks (EF = EH = GF). Finally one traces the curtain line GH.

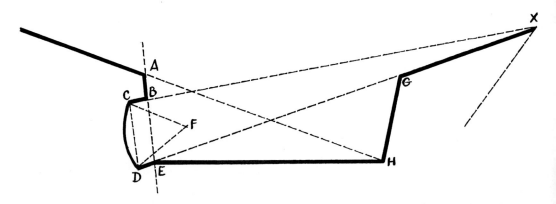

Construction of ear in flank. The right flank AE is divided into three equal parts. From the salient point X of the adjacent bastion, a line XB is drawn and prolonged 10 meters to give point C. Then one draws the line XE, equally prolonged to 10 meters to get point D. The line CD forms the base of an equilateral triangle with F as the top. From F one traces the arc of circle CD, which gives the flank-curve. The inner part of the flank CB is called "retrait" and the section of rampart DE is called "courtine retirée."

often accompanied by corruption, favoritism or misappropriation of funds. Vauban, who was devoted to painstaking work and proper use of the royal treasury, disapproved of this prejudicial detrimental, penny-pinching economy, abuses and embezzlement.

Once matters were concluded, the building contractor recruited laborers and specialized manpower (quarrymen, stone hewers, brick makers, masons, carpenters and other

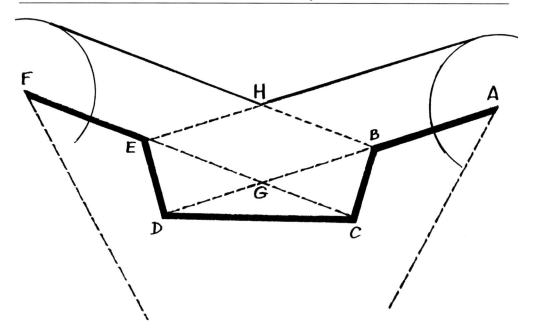

Construction of ditch. In front of a bastioned front ABCDEF, one draws, from the salients A and F, two circles with radius equal to the width of the desired ditch (generally between 10 and 20 meters). Then from the shoulder points B and E, one draws tangential lines to the arcs which give the counterscarp outline and the gorge of the demi-lune. Doing so, one is assured of a good ditch flanking. Prolonging line GH to the outside, one gets the capital line of the demi-lune.

craftsmen). The number of workers as well as the duration of the construction depended on the importance of the task. Certain construction sites were enormous, lasted for years and needed thousands of laborers. Even soldiers were hired and paid as common workers. The construction tangled the whole city and even sometimes the entire region. It necessitated huge infrastructure: stone quarries, transportation (wagons and inland boats for which roads and canals had to be created), brick factories, chalk ovens, numerous tools, scaffold timber, shelters, sheds and barns. Furthermore the mobilized workers needed food, camps and huts. The citadel of Lille, built between 1668 and 1671, required the work of 60 professional master masons, 400 specialized laborers and 1,400 peasants; some 12,000 blocks of sandstone were delivered and 60 million bricks were baked on the spot. To bring the stones from the Lezennes quarry, a canal was created. The total cost was estimated to be 1.5 million pounds.

Before construction, it was sometimes necessary to partially or completely demolish old fortifications, fill up ancient ditches, even destroy certain parts of the city (especially if a citadel was to be erected). As we already have pointed out, while medieval defenses were vertical, bastioned fortifications were characterized by horizontality and depth: they spread out and occupied areas which were sometimes larger than the spots reserved for inhabitation. For example, the fortifications of Lille, including the citadel and esplanade, represented about one-third of the area of the inhabited city. The fortifications of Huningen represented seven times the size of the city. Therefore land had to be purchased under compulsion and compensation paid. Expropriation, disputes and land speculation gave rise to complicated proceedings and endless lawsuits. When all these (sometimes) long and boring formalities were completed, the work could actually begin. Workers and the building site were subject to military regulations stipulating, for example, working hours (generally from dawn to dusk), labor organization and precautions to be taken when demolition explosives were used. Under an engineer's supervision and according to plan, land surveyors prepared the plan, usually starting from the salient point of two bastions. Through chains to mark off distances and stakes pushed into the ground, gradually the whole outline was pegged out. Crowds of workers then dug the ditches and removed huge volumes of soil with means which today look ridiculous: shovels, picks, baskets, hampers, wheelbarrows and tip-carts. Explosives were used to clear rocks away. When a section of ditch was dug, teams of masons built the foundations of the walls. In good ground conditions, large flat stones were tilted inwards to take the thrust of the wall above. When the ground was less stable, masons started with a framed-up timber raft. On marshy ground they installed timber piles driven deep. When the foundations were laid, the masons began to build the clampings at the angles of bastions and outworks, then they built buttresses and revetments of scarps and counterscarps. Scaffolds were progressively raised and materials, stones and bricks were carried up by men or hoisting devices. Constantly, engineers, architects and master builders supervised the whole construction by following and directing operations, by controlling alignments, by checking the quality of material and by clocking workers' hours for payroll. The *déblai* (excavated earth from the ditch) was used to fill up the revetments. This soil, called *remblai*, was piled behind the rampart and well tamped. Meshes of tree branches were embedded in the earth as reinforcement. Calculations and estimations were made by engineers in order that the amount of *déblai* dug from the ditch would match the amount of *remblai* piled up behind the rampart because bringing additional earth from elsewhere was quite expensive. To this, enormous works were added: the smoothing of the glacis and the construction of underground counter-mine galleries, *echauguettes*, gatehouses, barracks, powder houses, guardhouses and so on. Conception and construction of fortifications were even more complicated in mountainous sites where transport was difficult and weather unpredictable. Spectacular difficulties were met in sea-sites and harbors or when a flooding system was planned.

Vauban was regularly informed about the evolution of the construction sites by letters and reports. He also went on inspection tours to see for himself if the works proceeded on schedule and to check whether his designs were well executed. He controlled everything and paid attention to the smallest details. He motivated the builders by giving technical advice and wrote a lot of practical manuals such as "Memory of Things to Do in a Town Menaced by Bombardments," "General Profile of Revetments with Explicative Table," "Instruction on Making Underground Cement Coverings," "Making Masonry Foundations in Water," and "Treatise on Good and Bad Palisades." Vauban did not fear criticizing poor execution, pointing out incompetence or putting down carelessness. On the other hand, he knew and understood what difficulties occurred on sites. When he was satisfied, he was grateful and warmly recommended to Louvois and Louis XIV his honest, intelligent and skillful collaborators.

The reader will have already understood: fortifications swallowed up vast sums. While Vauban was opposed to the unnecessary multiplication of fortresses, Louis XIV did not follow his wise advice. In spite of Colbert's efforts to balance the royal treasury, Louis XIV's luxurious standard of living, war budget and defense expenditures brought France to bankruptcy. According to the Belgian historian Jean-Pierre Rorive, fortification costs from 1671 to 1715 are estimated to have totaled the colossal amount of 105. 543, 368 livres (French pounds).

The Relief Maps Collection

Obviously, military authorities were much concerned by geographical representation, and as a result military cartography underwent a great development in the early sixteenth century. Relief and ground conditions, roads and distances, waterways, bridges, towns and forts were represented in numerous illustrated publications such as Antoine du Pinet's atlas, published in Paris in 1564, or Georg Braun and Franz Hogenberg's *Civitates Orbis Terrarum*, published in 1576. The most important European cartographers were Jacob van Deventer, Nicolas Tassin, Claude Chastillon, Mattheus Merian, Joan Blaeu, Sébastien de Pontault de Beaulieu, Nicolaus Person and Nicolas Fer. For Louis XIV, a sumptuous atlas, *Recueil des Plans des Places Fortes* was made in 1683 by the artists Joubert and Lebrun.

Data provided by accurate maps enabled rulers to have a detailed knowledge of their territories, and allowed them to make important decisions about planning a war or a campaign. Maps were top-secret state documents, and the very specialized cartographers were courted by rival sovereigns, as they carried with them visual knowledge of the land. A cartographer who changed employers could do significant harm to his former master by revealing strategic secrets.

In the domain of cartography, relief maps occupy a particular position. Relief maps are architectural documents in the form of scale models giving three-dimensional volume, position and the extent of fortifications. The collection was created in 1668 on Louvois's instigation. Most of the fortified places conquered, constructed or re-shaped by Vauban and his collaborators were reduced to models with a scale of one foot per hundred toises which approximately corresponds to a scale of 1/600th. A spectator has the illusion of flying over the work at an altitude of about 400 or 500 meters. The collection was displayed in a gallery in the Louvre Palace in Paris. For Louis XIV, it was a document to estimate the strength of the borders, to use for war games or to follow an actual siege. Besides, if a stronghold was taken, the king and his headquarters had its defenses on record to help retake it. The scale models also served to educate engineers by a remarkable visualization of their art. They compensated for the lack of topographical maps with three-dimensional groundplans and drawings. The collection was Louis XIV's private property, kept secret with restricted access. However the proud monarch was pleased to show it off as warning or deterrent to ambassadors or important foreign visitors. Not only fortifications were depicted but also, with exceptional precision, houses, public buildings and the surrounding countryside within gun range. Every model, like a large jigsaw puzzle, was composed of several wooden plates assembled by means of iron bars. Certain scale models are huge. Some of them weigh more than 2,000 kilograms. The relief map of Saint-Omer covers a surface of 50 square meters; that of Namur is composed of fourteen plates; that of Strasburg is 10.86 meters in length and 6.66 meters in width. The production of the relief maps was very expensive and Vauban was displeased with Louvois's toys, objecting that funds would be better employed to build real defenses. However he later recognized their educational value.

Louvois's work was continued and intensified under Louis XV and Napoleon's reigns. From 1870 on though, due to the progress of the science of topography and the use of photography, scale models lost their military value and their fabrication was discontinued. During three centuries, the fragile and vulnerable collection has suffered a lot because of lack of maintenance, several moves, looting in 1815 and war damage in 1940 and 1944. Since 1927, the collection, because of its priceless historical value, is listed as an "historic monument" and protected by the French Ministry of Culture. Relief maps make possible tracing changes in the way cities were defended. They are a valuable source of information about the history of urban development and changing landscapes. Today about hundred relief plans are preserved and a selection is brilliantly exhibited in the attic (fourth floor) of the Musée de l'Armée in the Hôtel des Invalides in Paris. The reader is warmly encouraged to visit it, if possible. The scale models are really beautiful, and are intelligently and nicely exhibited and will appeal to fortification and architecture enthusiasts as well as general history amateurs. Do not forget to take a sweater with you even in the summer because of the rather cool air conditioning. Another part of the relief plan collection (including several Belgian and northern French cities like Lille, Calais, Ath, Maubeuge, Tournai, Charleroi, Bouchain, Bergues, Namur, and many others) is exhibited at Lille (Northern France) in the Musée des Beaux-Arts, Place de la République.

CHAPTER 5

France Fortified by Vauban

The indefatigable Vauban is estimated to have fortified, either completely or partially, between 92 and 150 places, some historians like Wenzler and Haettel respectively going as far as 300 and 330. Estimates vary wildly and the exact figure is in doubt, though the lower estimate seems the more likely. Obviously a great deal depends on exactly how one counts. There are enormous differences between the number of totally new fortresses built ex nihilo; the number of improvements, additions and modification brought to existing places; and the number of plans designed for future works that were later carried out by other engineers. A number of pre-existing major fortresses like Amiens, Saint Quentin or Haguenau were only inspected and approved by Vauban. Another variable factor is whether one considers as a "fortress" a simple battery, a small fort, a redoubt, or merely a project (e.g. Metz completed in 1752, or Toul and Verdun completed in 1850). The exact number is therefore open to discussion, but this does not really matter. The point is that Vauban achieved such a high reputation that any bastioned work in France or in Belgium, and sometimes even further afield, is likely to be attributed to him. Like King Arthur and Robin Hood in Britain, Vauban has become a somewhat mythic figure in France, and the modern historian must proceed with great caution. It should be noted that many fortified works from this period — as well as others from before Vauban — have come down to us due to their continued use for military purposes. To keep up with the progress made in artillery and siege warfare, these fortifications were later modified, and underwent a series of successive adaptations. When the defensive works were de-listed in the late eighteenth or in the nineteenth century, they were very often maintained — not through any historical wish to keep them for posterity, but simply because local authorities had no funds to dismantle them.

It must also be borne in mind that all fortresses built at the frontiers of France were the result of a collective work, Vauban being at the forefront it is true, but with the assistance of many collaborators such as Christophe Rousselot in the province of Roussillon, Thomas de Choisy in Champagne and in Lorraine, François Ferry on the Atlantic shores, Jacques Tarade in Alsace or Antoine Niquet in Provence, to name only a few of Vauban's most important collaborators. Obviously Vauban was not the only royal fortification designer and builder. At times collaborators could be rivals having lively and acrimonious disagreements with him. Vauban first had had to fight a long and sneaky struggle to get rid of his superior and rival, Chevalier de Clerville, but it was never all over, even after Clerville's death in 1677. Regularly, he had to assert his authority over his engineers to maintain his position. In spite of Vauban's influence, it cannot be said that he always got his way. In spite of this caveat, and although the two world wars of the twentieth century have also taken a heavy toll on Vauban's works such as Bouchain, Béthune, and several other places, it remains true that French borders are dotted with Vauban's strongholds, an amazingly large number of them, which provided a unified system of defense in accordance with Louis XIV's strategic priorities.

Although often shifting and changing, the king's aim, on the whole, was to give France natural frontiers: the Alps in the Southeast, the Pyrenees in the South and the Rhine River in the North. The frontiers of France, particularly at the time of Louis XIV, were not the achievement of a strategic plan, however, but the result of an astonishing succession of unpredicted events marked by sudden annexations, territorial secessions, armed seizures, negotiated exchanges and violent conquests of regions and cities, punctuated by the treaties of Pyrenees (1659), Aix-la-Chapelle (1668), Nimegue (1678), Ryswick (1697) and Utrecht (1713). The key to France's foreign policy must be sought primarily in the king's psychological makeup: The love of glory and war which was Louis XIV's ruling passion.

Within Louis XIV's semi-improvised foreign policy, Vauban's intentions were clear and characterized by three main concerns. First Vauban wanted to improve and modernize important but outdated fortified places set up by preceding generations. Second, he supported creating new and modern places according to strategic need, and citadels to control recently conquered places with populations whose loyalty to the crown was yet to be tested and proven. Third, Vauban always looked for the most coherent and most efficient defenses. Therefore he repeatedly pleaded for dismantling or exchanging places with poor strategic importance, which cost a lot to maintain and vainly scattered efforts, resources and troops. Vauban was no construction maniac but a realistic strategist who — with insight — advocated defending France with a centralized system of strongholds to control communication and possible paths of invasion (e.g. highways, major rivers, strategic ports, and mountain passes). In December 1672 he wrote to Louvois: "I am not for the greater number of places, we already have too many, and please God that we had half of that but all in good condition!" In 1694, he suggested destroying, or exchanging for a serious peace guarantee, a certain number of places in Italy and Savoy (Casal, Suse, Pignerol and Mont-mélian), in Germany (Huningen, Freiburg, Brisach, Fort Kehl, Philippsburg, Kaiserslautern, Kirn, Mont-Royal, Trèves and Longwy), in Belgium (Dinant, Namur and Charleroi) and in Spanish Catalonia (Roses and Belver). He proposed to give Nancy back to Lorraine provided the duke concluded an alliance with Louis XIV. On that matter Vauban was absolutely right. Many forts, strongholds and castles inherited from the late Middle Ages and Renaissance were strategically useless, and only maintained on the official list of state-sponsored defensive fortifications out of bureaucratic inertia. However fortification was the exclusive domain of the Sun-King who — alone — decided what would be done and undone. The fortifications of Mont-Olympe, Maubert-Fontaine, Mont-Hulin, Saint-Venant, La Fère, Menin and Stenay were actually dismantled. Other deliberate demolition actions took place later; for example, Aire-sur-la-Lys (dismantled between 1893 and 1897), Ardres (fortified by Vauban in 1677 and dismantled in the nineteenth century), Valenciennes (fortified by Vauban in the 1670s and dismantled in 1889), and Cambrai (dismantled in the nineteenth century). However, France, in 1705, still maintained at high cost 119 fortified cities, 58 forts, 34 citadels, 57 fortlets and castles, and 29 redoubts. Of these 297 fortresses, Vauban wished to exchange, demolish or abandon no fewer than 110 of them.

Vauban's work, directed by Louis XIV and closely controlled by the succeeding Director General of Fortifications Seignelay, Louvois and Le Peletier de Souzy, is noticeable in Lorraine, Alsace, Franche-Comté, in the Alps and Pyrenees and particularly along the vulnerable northeastern border which is the eternal invasion route to Paris.

Vauban fortified French harbors and gave special attention to the islands in the Mediterranean Sea and in the Atlantic Ocean which, if taken and occupied by enemies, formed dangerous and threatening bridgeheads. Because of later frontier modifications, many of his construction sites are now situated abroad: for example, Furnes, Courtrai, Charleroi, Namur, Huy and Dinant are in Belgium; Sarrelouis, Landau and Philipsburg are in Germany; and Suze, Fenestrelles and Pignerol are in Italy. In particular circumstances, directed by Louis XIV's short-term policy, Vauban was forced to fortify foreign cities such as Maastricht, Luxembourg, Verceil or Turin. Finally it must be added that not all Vauban's projects were retained by Louis XIV, such as Le Havre, Belle-Île or Antibes.

Vauban also planned to fortify Paris. The concept was to bring the capital of France up to the same level of defense as the strongest frontier fortresses with a continuous bastioned enceinte reinforced by detached works in the villages on the surrounding hills: Belleville, Montmartre, Chaillot and the suburbs Saint-Jacques and Saint-Victor. Vauban also drew up plans for the construction of two powerful citadels to subdue the rebellious population. This project was not carried out. On the contrary, Parisian fortifications built under the preceding reigns were demolished on Louis XIV's order for political reasons: the king apparently had never forgotten nor forgiven the *Fronde* revolt. In fact Paris would be properly defended only in the 1840s.

The following section takes us on a journey along the French borders, clockwise from Pas-de-Calais to Normandy. It seeks to draw out the common themes and contrasting aspects of each region's history and fortifications. Pre-Vauban fortifications are briefly considered, with a short introduction summarizing the historical development of the provinces, and the towns and their fortifications. Very little attention, though, will be paid to eighteenth-, nineteenth- and twentieth-century defense works, because they fall outside the time limit of this study.

Northeast Frontier

From ancient Roman times to the 1930s, the Maginot Line, across the large northern European plain, had a territorial and historical unity which was used and tested at war throughout history as a fortification "research laboratory." The flat territory from the North Sea to the River Meuse still offers today a dense and varied catalogue of strongholds. It is really an open air museum displaying the development of fortification. During the sixteenth and seventeenth centuries, the northeastern provinces of West-Flanders, Picardy, Hainaut, Artois and the south of the Ardennes were Flemish territory and part of the Netherlands, which by inheritance came under the rule of Spain. These regions formed constant battlefields opposing France to Spain. This area, close to the sensitive location of Paris, was the most important for the French to bar, as it is a large plain where enemies could converge their forces and operate unimpeded by natural obstacles. A region of shifting borders, great battles and countless sieges, the numerous historic fortifications form an outstanding legacy. In 1659, the Treaty of the Pyrenees gave Artois (and its capital Arras) to France and decided the marriage of Louis XIV with Maria-Theresa of Austria, Infanta of Spain. This union eventually provoked the War of Devolution in 1663, when Louis XIV demanded the queen's right over Brabant. In 1667, the French took Charleroi, Tournai, Douai and Lille. The Treaty of Aix-la-Chapelle in 1668 gave a part of Flanders to France and the Treaty of Nimegue in 1678 allowed Louis XIV to annex many cities. The Treaty of Utrecht in 1713 permanently regulated the French northern border.

During Louis XIV's reign, these regions without natural barriers were heavily fortified with numerous fortresses termed *Pré Carré* (literally "square meadow," but Vauban of course meant "defended state"). Vauban's "Pré Carré" was designed in the years 1672–1674 and occupied him most of his career. The expression, coined by Vauban himself, originally referred to the northeastern border but soon came to indicate the whole of France's defenses. In January 1673, Vauban wrote to Louvois: "Seriously my lord, His Majesty should think of making his pré carré. This confusion of enemy places overlapping ours displeases me; we are obliged to maintain three instead of one." The Pré Carré represented an innovative way of considering the defense of France. Before Vauban, fortifications were mostly seen as local or regional systems, and for the first time a scheme at a national level was undertaken. In peacetime, the places showed off the limits of France; in wartime they formed a prepared battlefield. They could play a defensive role to avoid invasion but were also advanced positions from which an aggressive operation could be launched. In fact they were designed to extend French power step-by-step into the Spanish-Austrian Habsburg lands. The chain of fortresses was thus not only defensive, but acted as logistics bases for the launching of offensives. They were strategically situated and close enough from each other in order that, if need be, the garrison of the one could come to the other's rescue. The context was quite favorable for Vauban to set up his Pré Carré in the Northeast. The fortification was in existence before he undertook any action. A dense network of towns already existed, situated at the very heart of the geopolitical and economic struggle at that time. The towns needed to be tailored to new requirements with regard to society and warfare, but behind Vauban there was wealth and, most importantly, a determined political will. Louis XIV considered his conquests as everlasting and therefore backed his engineers with all his power.

The Pré Carré can be compared — to a certain extent if one considers only its defensive function — to the Maginot Line built in the 1930s. It was constituted in depth, with two main networks of fortified cities. The first line included Dunkirk, Bergues, Furnes, Fort Knocke (La Kénoque), Ypres, Ménin, Lille, Tournai, Fort Mortagne, Condé-sur-l'Escaut, Valencienne, Le Quesnoy, Maubeuge, Philippeville and Dinant (later Givet-Charlemont). This first line could be reinforced by canal-floodings from Ypres to the River Leies and from the Leies to the River Scheldt. In peacetime, rivers and canals were very important commercial waterways for economic development and trade exchanges. The first line included several towns in the Spanish Low-Countries (actually Belgium) acting as outposts: Nieuwpoort, Audenarde, Ath, Mons, Charleroi, Namur and Huy, all of which were untenable over the long term, and which Vauban proposed to give back to Spain in exchange for political compensation. As for the port of Boulogne, by order of Louis XIV, Vauban dismantled its defensive works in favor of rebuilding the fortifications of Calais.

At the rear, a second line was composed of Gravelines, Saint-Omer, Aire-sur-la-Lys, Béthune (later Saint-Venant), Arras, Douai, Bouchain, Cambrai, Landrécies, Avesnes, Marienburg, Rocroi and Mézières. The defenses continued eastwards to Sedan and Stenay.

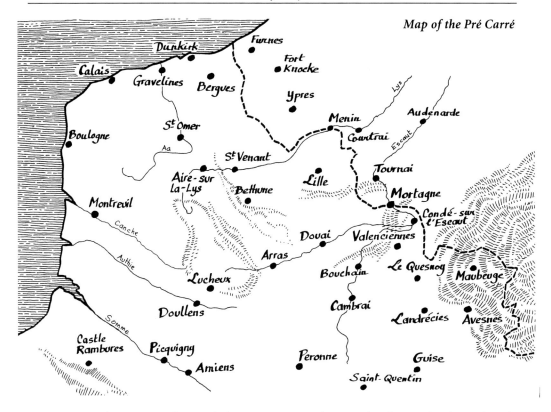

Map of the Pré Carré

Further east, the Meuse valley, and the mountainous forests of Ardennes (with an altitude from 400 to 700 meters) constituted a natural and impenetrable shield, denying the advance of an army with artillery.

The double-lined Pré Carré was backed up by a third line of rear-posts, including ports, fortified cities and strongholds: Calais, Montreuil-sur-Mer, Abbeville, Doullens, Amiens, Bapaume, Péronne, Fort Ham, Saint-Quentin and Guise. So the Pré Carré was conceived in depth, like infantry battalions in a battle formation. If the enemy broke into the first line, the second and third lines would hold him until reinforcements could arrive.

Most of the Pré Carré towns were fortified by the Spaniards and reshaped by Vauban. However certain of them were built from scratch, such as the citadel of Lille or the fortifications of Maubeuge. The solidity and density of Vauban's Pré Carré was severely tested, and showed its value at the end of Louis's reign by resisting invasion in 1708–1712. The double line played an important deterrent role up to 1814, when France was invaded after the fall of Napoleon.

In Artois, Vauban was assisted by engineer Mesgrigny, in Flanders by engineers Cladech, Filley, Robelin and Choisy.

Thomas de Choisy, marquis de Mogneville (1632–1710), originating from a rich middle class family, was ennobled and became a cavalry officer. From 1668 on, he served under Vauban's command and participated to the conception and construction of Lille citadel, Longwy, Sarrelouis and Montroyal. Choisy was promoted to be governor of Sarrelouis in 1679; he was also a combatant who took part in the sieges of Maastricht, Liège, Dinant, Philippeville, Luxembourg, Bonn, Keiserswerth and Mayence. Another among Vauban's collaborators was François de La Motte-Villebert, viscount of Aspremont (1634–1678), who worked in Douai in 1667. D'Aspremont built the citadel of Arras and later the fortifications of Auxonne and Toulon. At Lille, Vauban could rely upon the talent of master mason Simon Vollant, who built the impressive citadel and the famous Gate of France.

MONTREUIL-SUR-MER

Montreuil, situated in Pas-de-Calais, was founded in the seventh century by the bishop of Amiens, Saint Saulve. Placed on a rocky ridge some 40 meters high, dominating the estu-

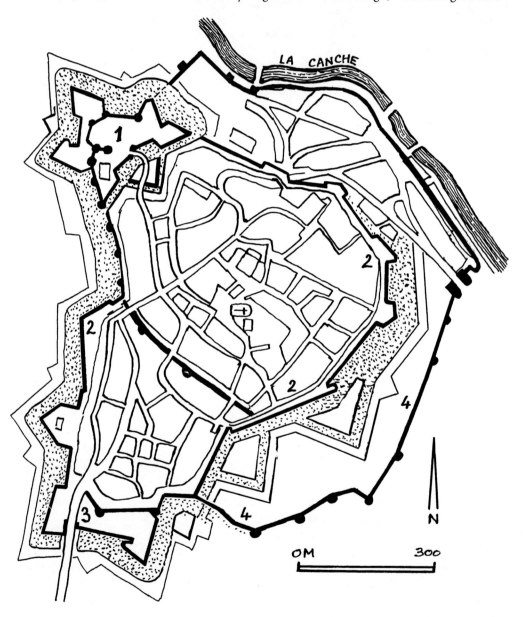

Groundplan, Montreuil-sur-Mer. (1) Citadel; (2) sixteenth-century bastioned enceinte; (3) gate of France; (4) remains of the thirteenth-century medieval enceinte.

ary of the River Canche, it lay on the land route connecting Normandy with Flanders and, as the Canche estuary was accessible to seagoing vessels, it grew to be a harbor in Charlemagne's time. It is also believed that the site would have been used in Roman times, and was known as Classis Sambrica, intended to serve as a port for the Roman fleet in the English Channel. This port, later named Quentovic, was destroyed by Viking raiders in the tenth century. A castle was erected about 900 by Count Helgaud de Ponthieu and during the thirteenth century, King Philippe Auguste of France had the walls considerably strengthened and flanked by towers. The city was then a major commercial port exporting grains, wine and cloth to Champagne, Italy and England. As the Canche became choked with sand, the role of the city as port diminished but it remained a key pawn in the defense of France. In 1537, Montreuil was taken, looted and burned by Carlos V of Spain. The reconstruction of the town and its fortifications, as well as the existing citadel (designed by Jean Errard), occurred in several stages between 1549 and 1634. Vauban executed two projects at the city in 1675. He redesigned the urban defenses in 1677 and reinforced the citadel with a hornwork and a demi-lune. The military role of Montreuil, however, started to decline from 1677, when the final conquest of the province of Artois had pushed back France's border some 100 km. to the north and east. Today, important and impressive parts of the fortifications are preserved, dating from the Middle Ages through to the nineteenth century.

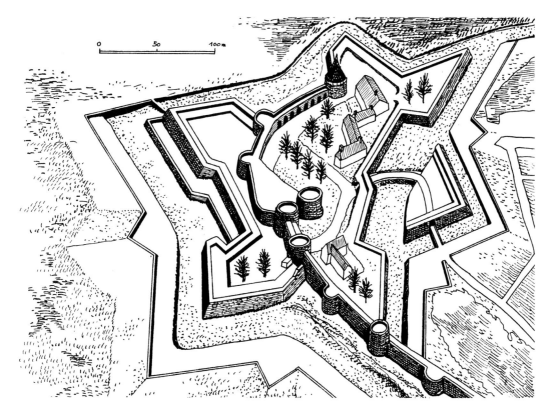

Montreuil citadel. Note the medieval defenses incorporated into the modern bastioned fortifications.

Fort Vauban, Ambleteuse

AMBLETEUSE

Located between Montreuil-sur-Mer and Boulogne-sur-Mer at the mouth of the River Slack facing England, this site had been a port since Roman times. In 1544, the British built a battery near the mouth of the estuary and a citadel dominating the port. These fortifications were dismantled by order of King Henri II, but the site was reactivated by Louis XIV. Vauban made an ambitious design for a large fortified port including sluices, citadel, bastioned enceinte and fortified jetties protecting the canal leading to the harbor. This project was not carried out, and only a coastal fort was constructed between 1684 and 1690. Typical of Vauban's coastal defenses, the fort consisted of a tower topped with an artillery and observation platform; a low, half-circular gun battery facing the sea with the capacity to house 20 artillery pieces; quarters for the gunner; a house for the officer and various service buildings. Fort Ambleteuse was restored during the reign of Napoléon I, when the emperor gathered a wide army at Boulogne to invade England. During World War II the fort was occupied by the Germans, who built a concrete observation post on top of the tower. Today the fort has become a museum.

CALAIS

The proximity of England (only 38 km.— in clear weather one can see the cliffs of Dover) foredooms Calais to be an embarkment harbor between the British Islands and the European Continent. The city started as a small fishing village, and became a port in the twelfth century. For centuries, the possession of the port was eagerly contested. In 1228, Count Philippe Hurepel, the son of King Philippe Auguste, built a castle and ringed the

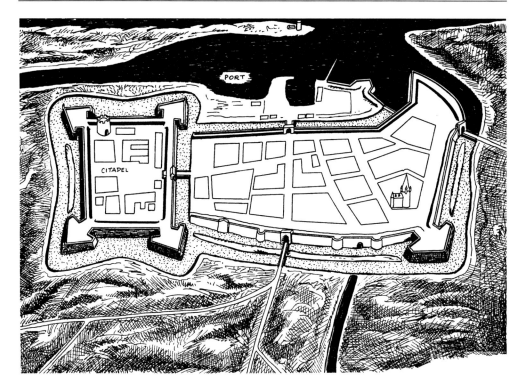

Calais, sixteenth century

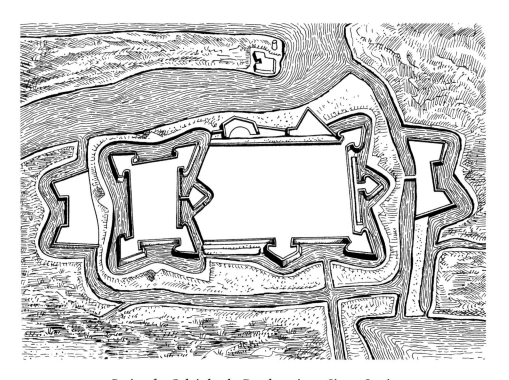

Project for Calais by the Dutch engineer Simon Stevin

town with a stone wall. After the victory of Crécy-en-Ponthieu on August 26, 1346, the English King Edward III besieged and took Calais in 1347 (the sculptor Rodin later immortalized the "six burghers" in bronze). The port proved an important asset to establish a firm grip upon the occupied territory and enabled easy access to the Continent. For 211 years the city was English and the occupiers made of Calais an administrative center, a foothold and a powerful fortress with fortified advance posts at Sangatte, Marck, Oye, Fretun, Hames, Guines and Balinghem. The medieval defenses were adapted to the increasing power of artillery with the construction of Italian-style bastions in the sixteenth century. Calais was besieged, taken and given back to France by Duke François de Guise in 1558. Henri IV and then Richelieu carried out considerable defensive works. The British fortifications were redesigned by the Italian engineer Castriotto in 1560 and a citadel was built by Jean Errard in 1564. The Dutch mathematician and military engineer Simon Stevin proposed water defenses in 1591 but his project was not built. In 1640, a fortress (called Fort Risban) was built to protect the entrance to the harbor. The fortifications of Calais were inspected and modified by Vauban in 1675, 1689 and 1694. He advocated construction of a stronghold in the west of the town, Fort Nieulay. Although its military role declined, Calais remained a key to France and a check against invasion. During the Second World War, Calais suffered heavy bombardment in 1940 and 1944, and almost the whole of the old town was destroyed. Fortunately, numerous vestiges of its defensive heritage remain, including sections of medieval walls, the citadel, the maritime fort, and Fort Nieulay, protecting the sluice-gate. Engineers of the Nazi building company Organisation Todt left behind a number of imposing artillery bunkers in the dunes around the city.

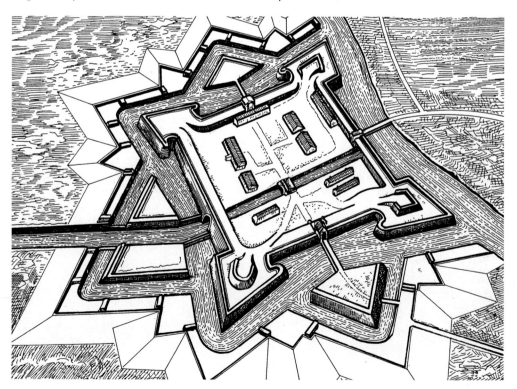

Fort Nieulay (Calais)

FORT NIEULAY

Fort Nieulay, situated west of Calais, was built in the sixteenth century by Flemish and English engineers to protect the bridge of Nieulay crossing the Hames River, and to control the defensive flooding of the western approach to Calais. Vauban drew up plans for it in 1675. It was his intention to improve the protection of the sluice-gate bridge across the River Hames, which enabled the regulation of large-scale flooding around the flat region, thereby making attack on Calais impossible. The fort was completed in 1679. Connected to Calais by a dike, it was a rectangle with four bastions and outworks. It included the sluice-gate bridge, barracks, an arsenal, a powder store, a cistern, and a house for the commanding officer. Fort Nieulay remained in military use until 1903. During the Second World War, the Germans built several concrete bunkers for the operation of a flak (anti-aircraft) battery.

SAINT-OMER

The city of Saint-Omer in the département of Pas-de-Calais, originated from a Benedictine abbey built in the seventh century on a small island on a marshy site. It was chosen by Vauban as a stronghold in the second line of the Pré Carré between Gravelines and Aire-sur-la-Lys. Vauban made only minor modifications to the existing sixteenth century

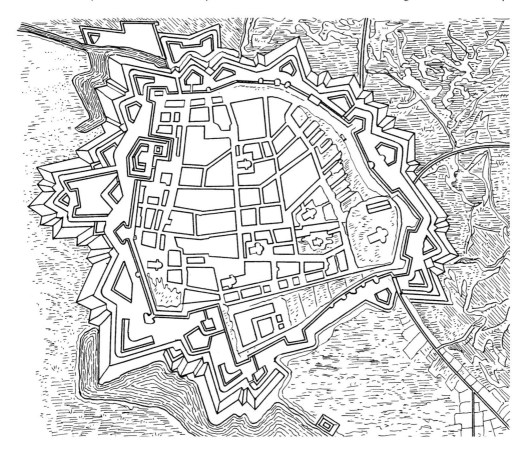

Saint-Omer, seventeenth century

Spanish fortifications. Today only a few ruined vestiges of the fortifications can be seen at the Boulevard Vauban near the swimming pool in the Jardin Public in the western part of the old town.

DUNKIRK

Dunkirk (Dunkerque in French, Duinkerken, "church in the dune," in Flemish) was founded in 1067 as a small fishermen's haven. In the sixteenth century, the city was occu-

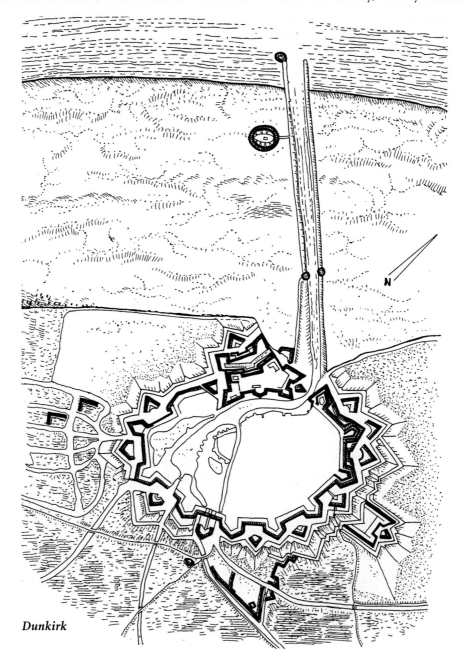

Dunkirk

pied by the Spaniards and yielded to the British in 1657. Louis XIV purchased it back for 5 million pounds from King Charles II of England in 1662. Dunkirk was fortified by Vauban and Benjamin Descombes from 1668 on. On the land front they installed a bastioned enceinte, several outworks and an ingenious hydraulic system allowing the flooding of the countryside. The harbor was enlarged and deepened (so as to be suitable for ocean-going ships) and dominated by a powerful citadel; the entrance of the harbor was defended by batteries placed on two long piers. An oval fort armed with 66 guns called Fort Risban was built in 1671. Erected on an unstable sandbank, the fort required complex pilings and special curved walls intended to lessen the power of the waves washing over it. Vauban conceived a complex and ingenious arrangement, allowing it to hold back high tide waters and release them at low tide in order to flush the harbor and ditches, thereby avoiding silting up. Vauban devoted a lot of his energy, skills and time (between 1672 and 1680) to making Dunkirk a powerful naval base used by privateers such as Jean Bart. He was particularly proud of his achievements. In 1706, during the War of Spanish Succession, Vauban, then aged 73, defended the city, threatened by John Churchill, duke of Marlborough. However at the end of this disastrous war, Louis XIV was obliged to dismantle Vauban's ingenious *chef-d'œuvre*: Calais was such a thorn in the English side that they demanded the demolition of its defense at the Treaty of Utrecht in 1713. Marshal Vauban (who died in 1707) did not witness this humiliation.

GRAVELINES

Gravelines, called Gravelingen in Flemish, is the gate to Flanders. The site's strategic importance on the mouth of the River Aa between Calais and Dunkirk was noticed as early

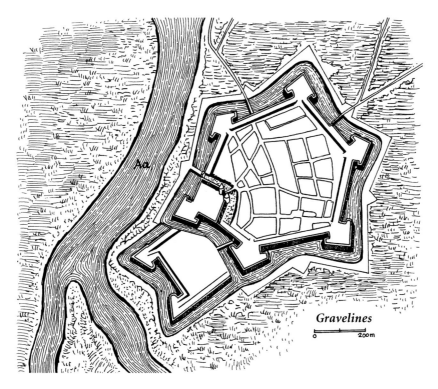

Gravelines

as 1150 by a count of Flanders, Thierry of Alsace. The medieval defenses were reinforced between 1513 and 1528 by Carlos V of Spain, who ordered the construction of six Italian-style bastions. In 1654 a large part of the citadel was destroyed by the accidental explosion of the powder house. Annexed to France in 1658 after a successful siege led by Chevalier de Clerville and the young Vauban, Gravelines was later modified by the latter, who made three designs, in 1683, 1696 and 1699. A detached work (Fort Philippe), several outworks, a hornwork, sluices allowing flooding of the flat and marshy surrounding countryside, an entrenched bastion with a powder house and an arsenal forming a reduit called the *Château* on the River Aa transformed the modest city into a powerful stronghold incorporated in the second line of the Pré Carré. In June 1706, the sick and old Vauban was promoted to the rank of governor of the cities of Western Flanders including Dunkirk, Bergues, Furnes and Gravelines. Completed and partly rebuilt by Director of Fortifications François Damoiseau between 1733 and 1751, and restored in the twentieth century, the fortifications of Gravelines are today well preserved. They display an interesting mixed style showing Italian/Spanish and French influences, using both fortifications and water as defense systems.

FURNES

The city of Furnes (Veurne in Flemish) originated from a small village named Furnae in 877. The city developed around an earthen castle built about 1040 by the counts of Flan-

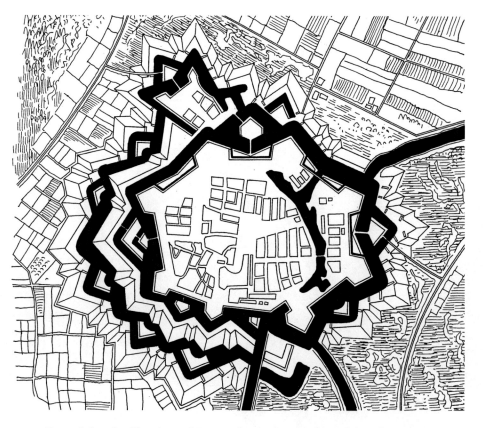

Groundplan fortifications of Furnes (beginning in the eighteenth century)

ders. Fortifications, comprising a broad moat and an earth rampart were built during the French-Flemish war of 1213–1214. These were replaced by a stone wall with gates and 33 towers between 1388 and 1414. By 1578, the four gates were adapted to the increasing power of firearms by the addition of artillery bulwarks. During the Nine Years' War (1688–1697), Furnes was incorporated into Vauban's Pré Carré to help protect the strategically important port of Dunkirk. New, modern, bastioned defenses designed by Vauban included a bastioned enceinte, outworks and wet ditches. Pressures of time and limited finances meant that the new works were built in several stages between 1693 and 1713. When the fortifications were barely completed, Furnes came under the control of the Austrian Empire as a consequence of the Treaty of Utrecht in 1713, and became a border fortress against the French.

The fortifications were totally demolished in 1781 by order of Emperor Joseph II of Austria.

Fort de la Kénoque

Situated on a marshy island on the River Yser southeast of Furnes, Fort de la Kénoque (Knocke in Flemish) was for a short while a part of Vauban's first "Pré Carré" line. The fort, inspected by Vauban in December 1683, was eventually decommissioned and dismantled when the completion of the neighboring fortifications of Furnes, Ypres and Bergues rendered it redundant.

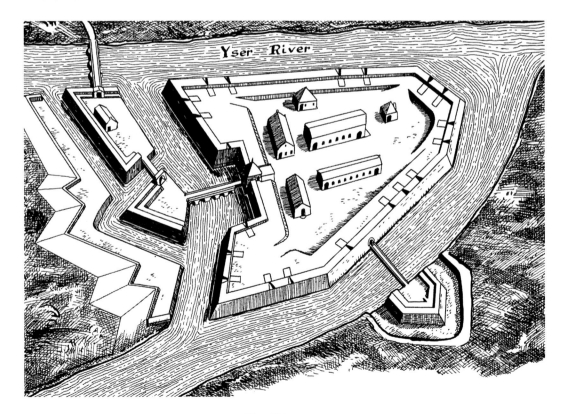

Fort Kénoque

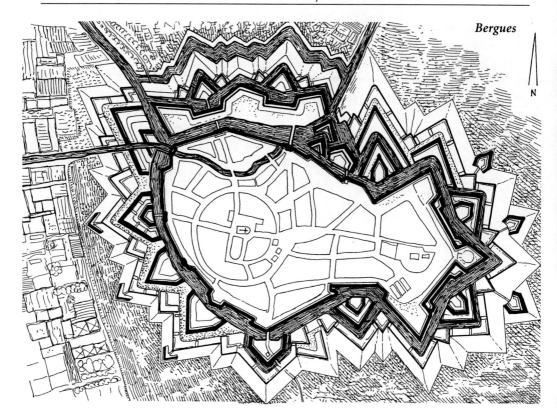

Bergues

BERGUES

Situated south of Dunkirk, Bergues (called Sint-Winochberg in Flemish) was founded by Saint Winoch as a Benedictine abbey in the tenth century. The town soon consisted of two centers with a small settlement established west of the monastery. Count Baudouin II of Flanders ordered the construction of an earth-wall enclosure to protect against Viking raids. Later this was strengthened with a yellow-brick wall with towers. During the reign of Philippe II of Spain, about 1558, the medieval wall was partially modernized owing to the addition of Italian-style bastions. Taken by the French in 1667, and officially yielded to France by the Treaty of Aix-la-Chapelle a year later, Vauban included the city in the first Pré-Carré line. Between 1674 and 1679, he reconstructed the sixteenth-century Spanish fortifications by establishing a detached work (Fort Français), various outworks, two crown-works and a flooding system supplied by the waters of the River Colme. After the demolition of Dunkirk in 1713, Bergues's importance increased and the fortifications were maintained and improved until the nineteenth century. Bergues was partly spared in the 1914–1918 war, and despite heavy damage in 1940, the little Flemish city has retained its ancient character and interesting elements of its fortifications.

MENIN

Menin, situated between Tourcoing (now in France) and Kortrijk (Courtai, now in Belgium), grew from 1087 as a crossroads over the River Leie. Because of its strategic position on the roads connecting Lille to Bruges and Ypres to Kortrijk, Menin was besieged no

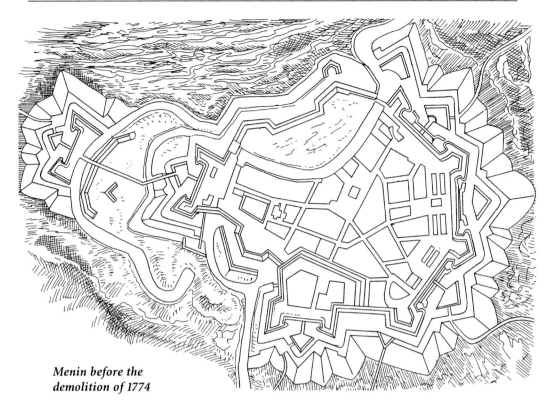

Menin before the demolition of 1774

less than 22 times between 1579 and 1830. In the twelfth century, the lords of Menin constructed a fortified residence and the town developed into an important medieval center of the cloth industry. The small city was further fortified in 1578 during the Wars of Religion with six Italian-style bastions. In 1678, Menin was captured by the French and included in the Pré-Carré when Vauban rebuilt the fortifications which had been pulled down some twenty years before. Completed by 1689, the defenses included eleven bastions, four gates, a wet moat, tenailles, ravelins, a hornwork, a glacis, and a flooding area along the Leie plain. For political reasons, the fortifications were totally demolished in 1774 under the reign of Louis XV. After the fall of Napoléon I in 1817, the defense was rebuilt by the Dutch, following the French design, but with significant changes including casemates and bomb-proof shelters. Completed in 1830, the fortifications were again dismantled in 1852. Fortunately this was only partly carried out and Menin has preserved interesting vestiges of Dutch-style fortifications.

LILLE

Situated on the River Deule, Lille (Rijsel in Flemish) was protected by fortifications as early as 1030. Count Baldwin V of Flanders built a castle in 1066. The medieval history of the city and its region was complicated because, although under French feudal domination, the Flemish drapery and cloth industry relied upon English wool supplies. Between 1603 and 1617, the town was enlarged and included the suburbs Saint-Maurice and Notre-Dame. The Spaniards improved the fifteenth-century walls by adding gun towers and Italian bastions. Lille was annexed to France in 1667 and immediately underwent immense

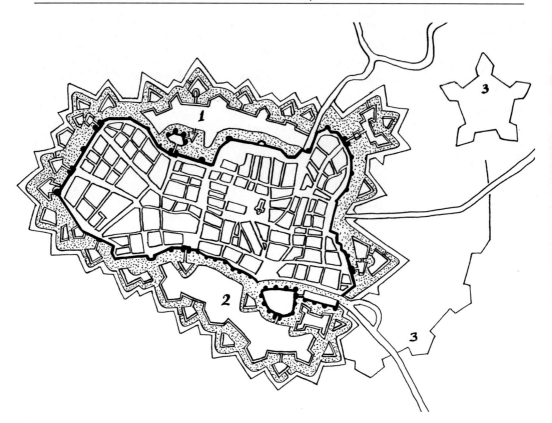

Lille in 1665. The old medieval town was enlarged by the addition of the suburbs Notre-Dame (1) and Saint-Maurice (2). New bastioned walls and a citadel (3) were planned by Vauban.

transformation with the construction of the citadel and the building of a new district. Louis XIV himself entrusted Vauban to fortify the capital of the northern provinces. Supported by Louvois, Vauban's first great project was Lille. The town was enlarged. Vauban installed modern bastions (with an entrenched one south of the enceinte called Fort Saint-Sauveur forming a reduit), a broad wet ditch with outworks, four hornworks in front of the most vulnerable points, a wide glacis with outposts and a vast system of water defense. Northeast of the town, Vauban built his first *chef-d'œuvre* between 1667 and 1670: a magnificent regular pentagonal citadel with two lines of ditches, outworks and esplanade; Vauban was inspired by the citadel of Antwerp built by Paciotto for the Spaniards in 1567. The citadel was built in a marshy site preventing any attack from that side as trenches could not be dug and artillery not brought into position. It was only from the other side of the city that the citadel could be besieged, thus only after a first siege to take it. One Spanish expert in fortification, Don Francisco d'Arguto, predicted that Lille, and more particularly Vauban's citadel, would remain impregnable "as long as French women bear children." The fortifications of Lille were dismantled in 1896. Fortunately the citadel is totally preserved. Since 1871 it has been the headquarters of the 43rd Infantry Regiment. The Gate of Paris, an imposing arch of triumph in Baroque style designed and built between 1682 and 1695 by architect Simon Vollant, is also preserved.

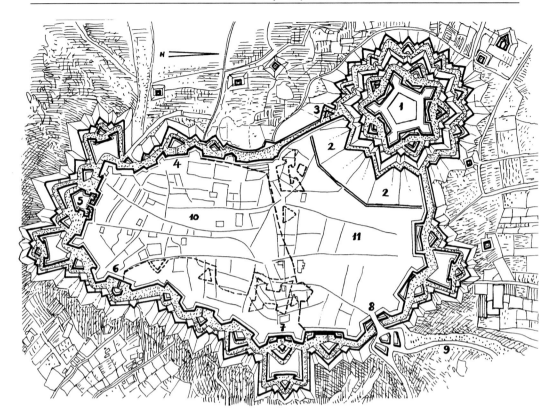

Lille after 1667. (1) Citadel; (2) esplanade; (3) La Blaze gate; (4) Notre-Dame gate; (5) Fort Saint-sauveur; (6) Saint-Maurice gate; (7) Dauphine gate with hornwork; (8) watergate; (9) River Deule; (10) old city; (11) town extension after 1668.

ATH

Situated on the River Dender in Belgium, Ath has always been an important crossroad. The city was annexed by France in 1668 after the Treaty of Aix-la-Chapelle and fortified the same year by Vauban. The fortifications included a regular octagon flanked by eight bastions, eight demi-lunes and a hornwork. In 1671, Vauban considered Ath too far in front of the Pré Carré and wished either to demolish its fortifications or to exchange the town. The city was yielded back to Spain after the Treaty of Nimegue in 1678.

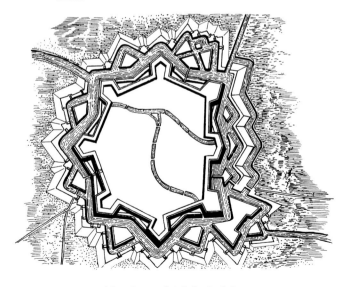

Fortifications of Ath in Belgium

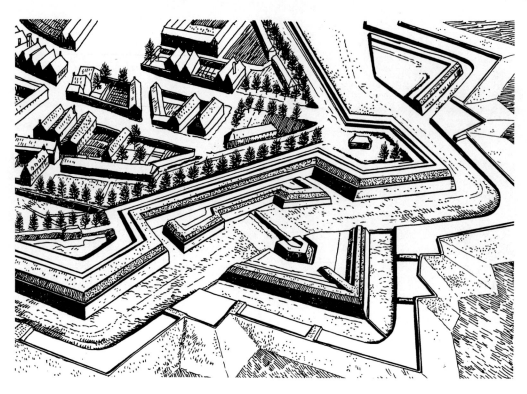

Ath (Belgium)

However Ath was retaken by Marshal Catinat and Vauban in 1697. During the siege Vauban successfully experimented with his "ricochet" firing technique. Ath was re-conquered in 1706 by Marlborough; the Dutch and Austrians reshaped the fortifications in the beginning of the eighteenth century.

Condé-sur-l'Escaut

Condé was strategically situated at the junction of the rivers Hayne and Scheldt. Holding Condé protected the Scheldt Valley and the towns of Valencienne, Bouchain and Cambrai. It seems that the site was occupied as early as A.D. 880 by Viking raiders. Condé was taken in 1655 by Turenne's army, in which the young Vauban served as a military engineer. The city was re-taken by Spain the following year. In April 1676, Vauban and Louis XIV personally conquered it again. Between 1680 and 1695, the ancient medieval and Spanish fortifications were profoundly transformed by the construction of eleven bastions, outworks and demi-lunes in wet ditches, detached redoubts in the glacis and a vast flooded zone of 2.450 hectares using the waters from the neighboring marshes. Within the town Vauban built two barracks, a cavalry barrack with stalls and a powder-store. Condé was integrated into the first Pré Carré line between Lille and Maubeuge.

Valenciennes

The merchant city of Valenciennes on the Escaut River was besieged and taken in March 1677. The town became permanently French after the Treaty of Nimegue in 1678, and soon was incorporated in the Pré Carré's first line between Condé-sur-l'Escaut and Le

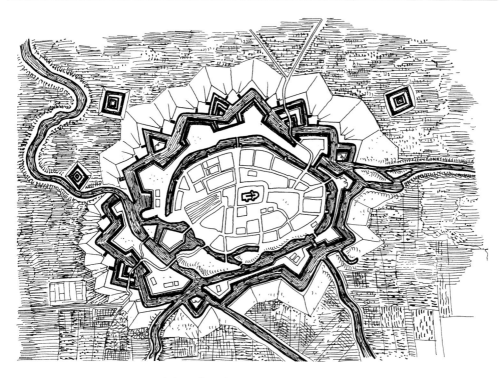

Groundplan, fortification of Condé-sur-l'Escaut

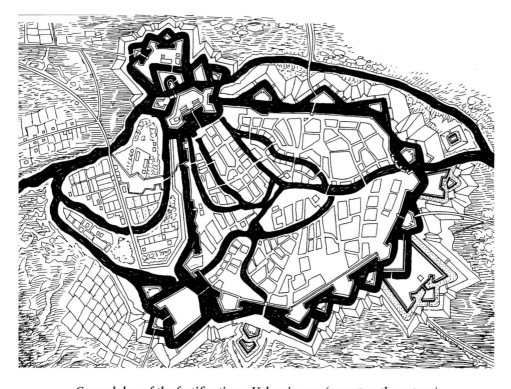

Groundplan of the fortifications, Valenciennes (seventeenth century)

Quesnoy. To the medieval walls and to the sixteenth-century Italian-style bastions built by the Spaniards, Vauban added several demi-lunes, hornworks at the most important accesses, a traverse covered way, and a system of inundation in the low ground around the river banks. Nothing is left of the old urban fortifications. Valenciennes was heavily damaged during the Second World War. What had survived the combats of 1940 was destroyed in 1944.

LE QUESNOY

In the eleventh century, Le Quesnoy was only a small village with a castle and stone wall erected about 1160 on Count Baldwin IV of Hainaut's order. In 1556, Carlos V of Spain ordered the construction of an enceinte with seven Italian-style bastions and demi-lunes in the ditch. Le Quesnoy was taken by Turenne in 1657 and officially yielded to France by the Treaty of the Pyrenees in 1659. Strategically situated between Valenciennes and Maubeuge and closing the access between the Cambrésis and Picardie regions, it was incorporated in the first Pré-Carré line. Vauban modernized the defenses in 1676 by remodeling the southern front, by establishing a strong bastion defended by a hornwork, by constructing various outworks in the wet moat and by establishing a large flooding zone in the approaches to the town using the waters of the Pont Rouge lake and the Ecaillon canal. A hornwork, set up southeast in front of the Fauroeulx-gate, completed the fortifications, which are today totally preserved.

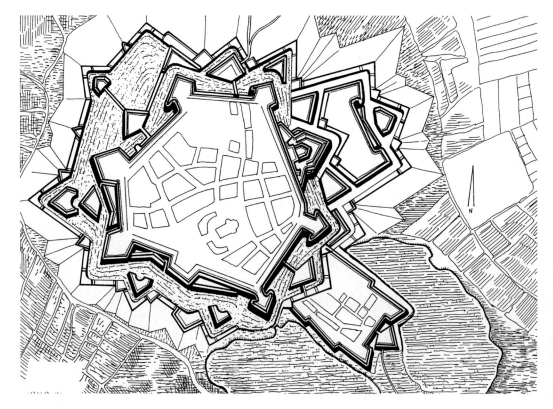

Le Quesnoy

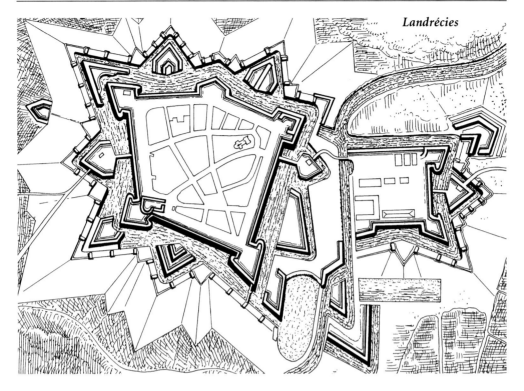

Landrécies

LANDRÉCIES

The small fortress Landrécies is situated on the River Sambre. The sixteenth-century fortifications were built by the Spaniards on older medieval defenses. The place was besieged and taken in 1665 and united with France in 1668. Vauban renovated the defenses and incorporated the town into the second Pré Carré line between Cambrai and Avesnes. The fortifications were dismantled in 1889.

MAUBEUGE

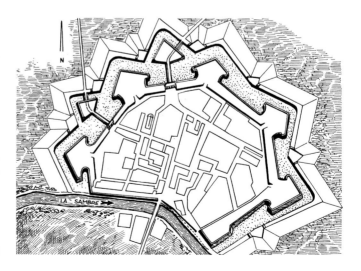

Maubeuge, situated on the River Sambre, was founded in the seventh century around a monastery. The city was acquired by France after the Treaty of Nimegue in 1678. To consolidate the position between Philippeville, Le Quesnoy and Valencienne, Vauban incorporated Maubeuge in the first Pré Carré line. In November 1678, he made a design in-

Maubeuge

cluding a regular heptagonal wall including a nine-meter-high enceinte, seven bastions fitted with ears and cavaliers, demi-lunes in the ditch, one hornwork west of the city, a covered way and a system of flooding supplied by the waters of the River Sambre. In 1680, Louis XIV visited the construction site, directed by engineer Jean Mesgrigny. The regular fortifications of Maubeuge, built between 1679 and 1685, were used by the French army until 1914. Having suffered heavily from destruction during the First World War, the fortifications were scheduled for demolition. The demolition went very slowly from the 1920s to the 1940s, due to a lack of funds. Today a part is still preserved.

AVESNES-SUR-HELPE

Avesnes on the River Helpe is situated south of Maubeuge. In the tenth century, the site was fortified by the local lord, Wedric the Hairy, who had a tower built. Two centuries later the small city was enclosed by a stone wall. In the sixteenth century, the duke of Croy commissioned an Italian engineer, Jacopo da Modena, to adapt the fortifications to the use of artillery by adding six bastions with ears. The Treaty of the Pyrenees gave the city to France, and Vauban incorporated it into the second Pré-Carré line. Tasked in 1673 to modernize its defenses, he designed outworks and advance works, reinforced the powder houses, created barracks for the garrison, built new gates and established a flooding zone in the valley of the Helpe. Avesnes was decommissioned as a military border city in 1873, but has retained several interesting vestiges, such the bastion Saint-Jean and some eighteenth-century barracks.

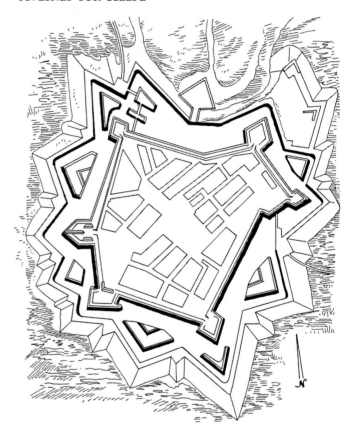

Avesnes-sur-Helpe

PHILIPPEVILLE

The military town of Philippeville was created by King Charles Quint (Carlos V of Spain) in 1555 to compensate the loss of Marienburg, taken by the French King Henri II in 1554. Carlos named the place after his son Philip II. Designed by the Dutch engineer

Sebastien van Noyen, the fortifications were fully in the Italian tradition with a radial urban groundplan and five casemated bastions with ears. Philippeville was occupied by the French from 1660 to 1695. The fortifications were slightly improved by Vauban and incorporated into the first Pré Carré line between Maubeuge and Dinant. The fortifications were dismantled in 1860. Only an underground network of countermines and a powder house (now transformed into the chapel Notre-Dame des Ramparts) are preserved today.

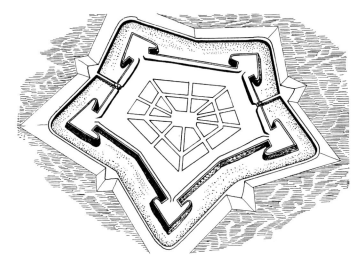

Philippeville (sixteenth century)

CHARLEROI

Situated at an important crossroads on the River Sambre, the small village of Charnoy was fortified by the Spaniards in 1666 and rebaptized Charleroi in honor of the king of Spain. A year later, Charleroi was taken by France and Vauban continued the

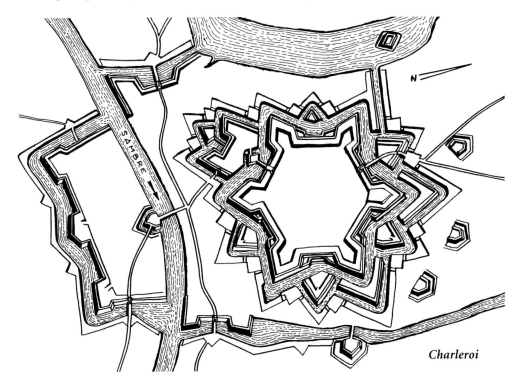

Charleroi

Spanish engineers' work. The fortifications, which counted among his first accomplishments, were of a beautiful regularity, with five curtains, six bastions with cavaliers, five demi-lunes in a dry ditch, two counterguards and one hornwork. In the northern glacis Vauban installed three detached lunettes and a countermine network; in the south, on the opposite Sambre bank, he built a large crownwork as a defense for the town. Charleroi was yielded back to Spain (together with Courtai, Audenarde, Ghent, Ath, and Binche) after the Treaty of Nimegue in 1678. Unfortunately the fortifications were completely demolished in 1868.

ARRAS

Arras (in Flemish, Atrecht), situated on the River Scarpe in the département of Pas-de-Calais, is the ancient Nemetacum, capital of the Gallic tribe Atrebates. Arras developed around the Benedictine abbey Saint-Vaast, and grew to be a rich medieval town which became capital of the province Artois. The province was officially united with France in 1659 and the city was incorporated in the second Pré Carré line between Béthune and Douai.

The ancient Spanish fortifications were modified by Vauban by the installation of two hornworks and outworks. The citadel was built in the southwestern part of the city from 1668 to 1672 by chevalier François d'Aspremont, after Vauban's design of the citadel of Lille. The citadel was threatened with demolition in 1862, but owing to the bishop of Arras and Napoléon III, only partially destroyed. Today it houses the 601st Régiment de Sécurité Routière.

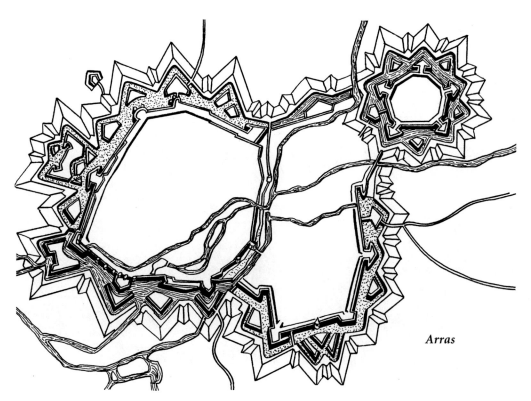

Arras

AUDENARDE

Audenarde (in Flemish, Oudenaarde, meaning "old earth") is situated on the River Scarpe in East Flanders. In the eleventh century, Count Baldwin IV of Flanders built a castle. Audenarde was fortified in 1521 by King Carlos V of Spain. The city was taken by the duke of Parma in 1581, and conquered and given to France by Turenne in 1658. In 1668, Vauban designed a project but considered the place, just like Ath, Mons and Charleroi, too far into Belgium to be incorporated into the Pré Carré. In 1674, Audenarde was besieged by the famous Dutch stadhouder Willem of Orange and victoriously defended by Condé and Vauban. The place was yielded back to Spain in 1679 and re-taken by the French in 1701. After Marlborough's victory at Ramillies in 1706, Louvain, Brussels, Antwerp, Ghent, Bruges and Audenarde passed under Austrian domination. The city's irregular bastioned fortifications, including Spanish and French features, were dismantled in 1745.

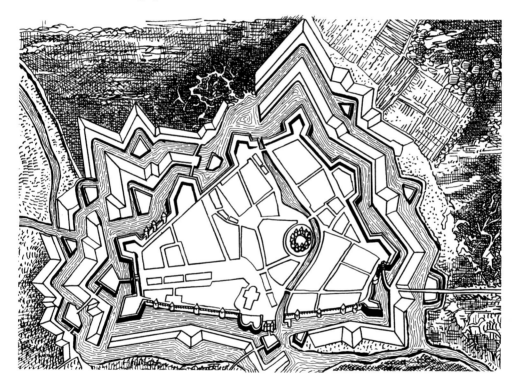

Audenarde

MAASTRICHT

Strategically situated on the River Meuse in the south of the Netherlands (province of Limbourg) Maastricht (then called Traiectum ad Mosam) was from Roman times an important crossroad on the way from Liege to Cologne. Two main medieval walls were successively erected in the Middle Ages. During the Dutch War in 1673, the city was successfully besieged by Vauban, who experimented in that action with his systematic approaches and parallels. During the siege, on June 25, Charles de Batz de Castelmore, lord of Montesquiou and count d'Artagnan (1620–1673), was killed. It is he who inspired Alexandre Dumas's

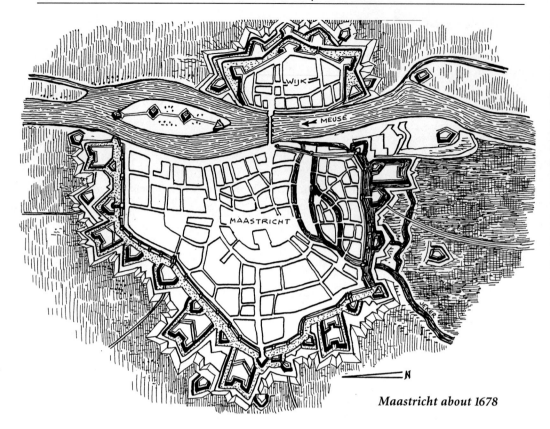

Maastricht about 1678

romantic hero in the famous novel *The Three Musketeers*. The French occupation of Maastricht, from 1673 to 1678, was marked by repair and improvement of the fortifications with the construction of outworks and hornworks. The suburb Wijk, forming a bridgehead on the opposite river bank, was also fortified. Using the waters of the River Meuse and its small tributary Jeker, Vauban established a wide flooding zone south of the town. Maastricht was yielded back to the Dutch after the Treaty of Nimegue in 1678. The fortifications were dismantled between 1871 and 1878 but many vestiges are fortunately preserved today.

LUXEMBOURG

Luxembourg, the capital of the principality with the same name, is situated on a rocky ridge with steep slopes at the junction of the rivers Alzette and Pétrusse. Inhabited since the Iron Age by Celtic tribes, Luxembourg was conquered by the Romans, who built a camp controlling the axis between Trèves-Arlon-Reims and Metz-Aix-la-Chapelle. The first stone wall was erected by Count Siegfried in 965 and a larger second one by Count Giselbert in 1050. The growth of the town necessitated the construction of a third stone enceinte with 37 towers and gates set up by the king of Bohemia, Wenceslas II, in 1393. In 1597, Baron Jean de Beck constructed for the king of Spain eight Italian-style bastions and a ditch. In 1684, Vauban and the marshal of Créquy besieged and took the town. After the Peace of Ryswick in 1697, Vauban was charged with restructuring the fortifications. He reinforced the bastioned ramparts, built outworks and installed detached lunettes, and crown- and

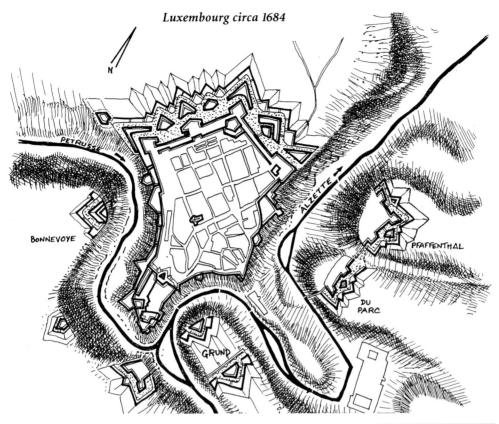

Luxembourg circa 1684

Luxembourg

hornworks on the hills surrounding the city (Pfaffenthal, Grund, du Parc and Bonnevoye). After the Treaty of Utrecht in 1713, Luxembourg passed under Austria's domination.

Ardennes and Lorraine

The French province Lorraine is a remnant of the ancient kingdom of Lotharingia created between France and Germany after the partition of Charlemagne's empire in A.D. 843. The (German-speaking) province was constituted as a duchy which was successively dominated by the lords of Alsace and Anjou, then by the German Empire. Carlos V gave the duchy its independence in 1542. When Louis XIV began his personal rule in 1661, the frontier between France and the free Duchy presented a confusing and disorganized outline. The dukes of Lorraine were under heavy French pressure and their duchy was a patchwork of lands overlapped by French possessions (Toul, Metz and Verdun, annexed by France in 1552, as well as Thionville and Longwy). Unclear borders and enclaves provoked numerous conflicts between France and Lorraine. The whole province became officially French only in 1766. One of Vauban's main collaborators in Lorraine was the lord of Saint-Lô.

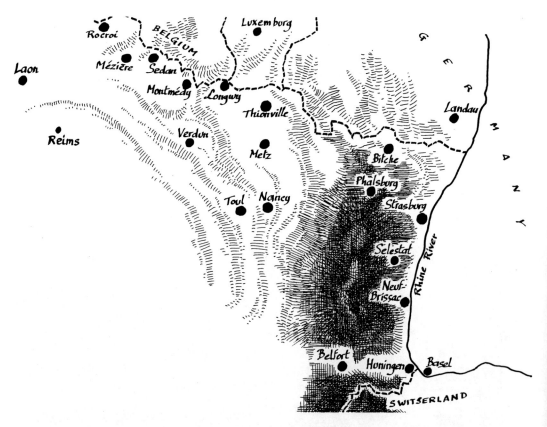

Map of Lorraine and Alsace. Although the Ardennes Mountains in the north, and the Vosges Mountains and the Rhine River in the east could frustrate enemy attacks, Vauban did not leave this border with Germany defenseless. Besides, he knew the province very well, having fought there as a young soldier.

ROCROI

Situated near Mézières in the Ardennes, the military city of Rocroi was created in 1554 by King Henri II of France in order to defend the border facing the Spanish town of Charlemont and control the road between Charleroi and Mézières. The fortifications of Rocroi were directly influenced by the Italian style, with a radial groundplan, a pentagonal outline and five bastions. In May 1643, Rocroi was besieged by Spanish troops commanded by Francisco de Melo. Then the young Louis II, prince of Condé and duke of Enghien,

Rocroi. (1) Bastion of Nevers; (2) Bastion of Dauphin; (3) King's Bastion; (4) Bastion of Petit Fort; (5) Bastion of Montmorency.

aged twenty-two, came to rescue the besieged and won an important battle, saving Paris from invasion. In 1676, Vauban incorporated Rocroi into the second Pré Carré line and strengthened the old-fashioned fortifications by the addition of outworks and a traverse covered way. Today Rocroi's defenses are well preserved.

MÉZIÈRES

Situated on a bend of the River Meuse, the city of Mézières was created in the ninth century near a castle whose walls (*maceria* in Latin) gave it its name. A possession of the counts of Rethel in the eleventh century, Mézières developed into a rich merchant city owing to the traffic on the Meuse River. A stone wall with towers and gatehouses was built about 1233. The defenses were adapted to the use of firearms at the end

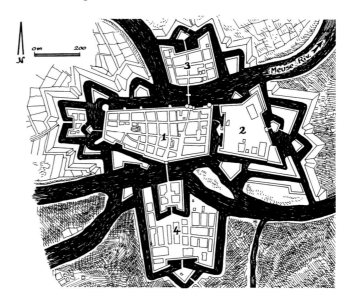

Fortifications of Mézières at the end of the seventeenth century. (1) Old medieval city; (2) military citadel built between 1590 and 1593; (3) northern suburb of Arches enclosed by hornwork; (4) southern suburb of Pont-de-Pierre enclosed by hornwork.

of the sixteenth century by the addition of artillery emplacements and bulwarks, as well as a citadel with Italian-style bastions built between 1590 and 1593. The defenses were improved between 1620 and 1655 by the addition of demi-lunes and counterguards in the wet ditches. By 1687, powder houses and barracks were built. The role played by Vauban and chevalier de Clerville are not clear but by the end of the seventeenth century, vast hornworks were added to defend the new suburbs of Pont-de-Pierre and Arches. Mézières remained a fortified city until 1870, but between 1883 and 1886 large-scale demolitions were undertaken. However some parts have been spared; in the west of the city are three medieval walls and towers, a gatehouse, and three bastions and curtains from the sixteenth-century citadel.

SEDAN

Sedan is situated on a curve of the River Meuse in the département of Ardennes. Its name comes from an ancient Celtic king called Sedanus. An important strategic crossing on the river, Sedan appeared about A.D. 997 as a possession of the monks of Mouzon until the fifteenth century. The city then passed under the domination of the bishops of Liège, then under the lords of La Marck and then under the lords of La Tour d'Auvergne, before being united to France in 1642. Sedan Castle with its surface of 35 hectares is a huge stronghold built on a hill dominating the town; its construction was begun in 1424 by the lords of La Marck. Between 1550 and 1570, engineer Marin Fourre added a bastioned enceinte. The urban fortifications were modified in 1651 and then transformed by Vauban from 1682 to 1689. They were dismantled in 1875. The castle was preserved and used as a citadel and a prison from 1642 to 1962.

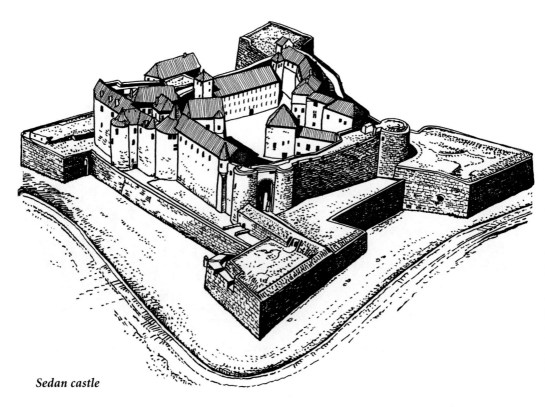

Sedan castle

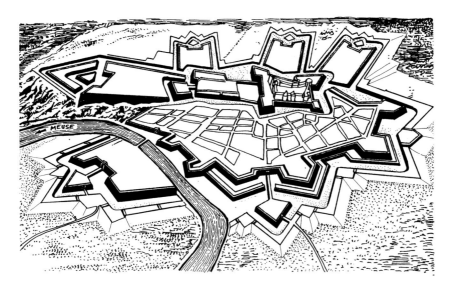

Fortifications of Sedan (seventeenth century)

Sedan is associated with two major French historical disasters. Napoléon III's defeat in September 1870 put an end to the Second Empire. On May 13, 1940, the Germans launched a decisive offensive which hastened the French army's unraveling. Sedan — though badly damaged during World War II — has kept many vestiges of its ancient fortifications.

MONTMÉDY

Montmédy was the capital of the count of Chiny. Count Arnould III built a castle on a hill dominating the River Chiers. Spanish fortifications were erected in the 1550s by

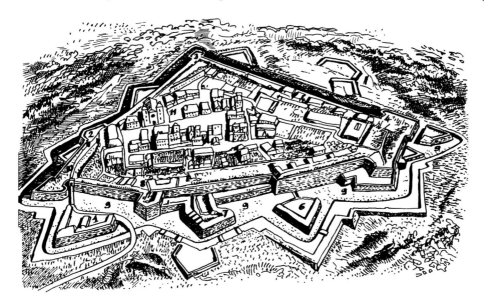

Citadel, Montmédy. (1) Main gate demi-lune; (2) Saint-Martin bastion; (3) Notre-Dame bastion; (4) Des Connils bastion; (5) Saint-André half-bastion; (6) Des Porcs demi-lune; (7) Bas bastion; (8) Boulevard bastion; (9) main ditch; (10) Charles V gate; (11) Saint-Martin church.

Carlos V and completed under his son Phillip II. In 1657, the young Louis XIV attended his first siege here and Vauban got one of his first wounds. Montmédy became officially French after the Treaty of the Pyrenees in 1659. Vauban undertook two modernization projects in 1679 and 1698: he increased the flanking possibilities by adding demi-lunes and improved the covered way. The irregular fortifications are well preserved today and house a military architecture museum.

LONGWY

Longwy, situated on the River Chiers in the département of Meurthe-et-Moselle, successively belonged to the dukes of Luxembourg, the counts of Bar and the dukes of Lorraine. The city was yielded to France after the Treaty of Nimegue in 1678. A year later, on Louis XIV's order, Longwy was completely modified and given an urban chess-board pattern, developed around a wide central square. In fact the shape of the town was dictated by the outline of the fortifications. These were entirely created by Vauban and Choisy, who built a regular hexagonal enceinte reinforced by six bastions with ears, five demi-lunes, one hornwork, a traverse covered way with places of arms and a glacis. In 1698, Vauban proposed the construction of a vast entrenched camp at the south of the city but this project was not carried out. The fortifications of Longwy were maintained and modernized until 1880. Today about one-third of the ramparts and the majestic Gate of France are preserved.

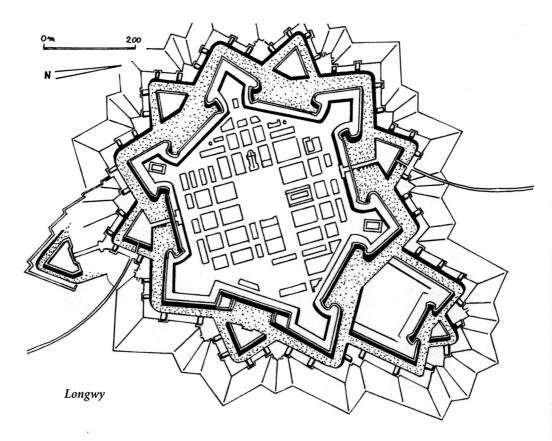

Longwy

SARRELOUIS

Sarrelouis is situated northwest of Sarrebruck in Germany. Just like Phalsburg, it was a military city entirely newly created by Vauban. Sarrelouis, erected between 1679 and 1685, was intended to defend the road to Metz and Lorraine. Vauban gave the city a regular chessboard pattern organized around a central square, regrouping all military buildings. The hexagonal fortifications also displayed a beautiful regularity, with six bastions, five demilunes and two decorated gateways (Gate of France facing south and Gate of Germany facing the river). On the right bank of the River Sarre, Vauban installed a hornwork and a demi-lune connected to the place by a sluice-bridge. Since 1815, due to frontier modification, Sarrelouis (rechristened as Saarlouis) has been in Germany. The place was occupied and reshaped by Prussia between 1816 and 1854. The urban fortifications were declared obsolete in 1887 and totally demolished about 1889. Today, only the original street layout can be seen.

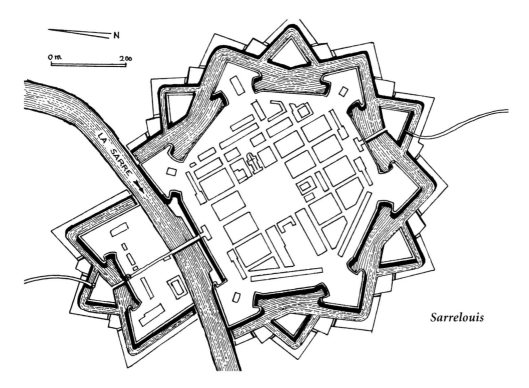

Sarrelouis

THIONVILLE

Theodonis Villa originated as a residence and a castle built by Charlemagne on the River Moselle. Thionville (Diedenhofen in German) was fortified in 1567 on Philip II of Spain's order by engineers Jacques van Noyen and Francesco de Marchi, in order to protect the roads leading to Metz, Luxembourg, Arlon and Namur. The city's defenses, set up on the left bank of the Moselle, included six Italian bastions with ears and a ditch. Thionville was annexed to France in 1643. Vauban re-structured the Spanish enceinte, installed a bridge over the River Moselle and built entrenched hornworks.

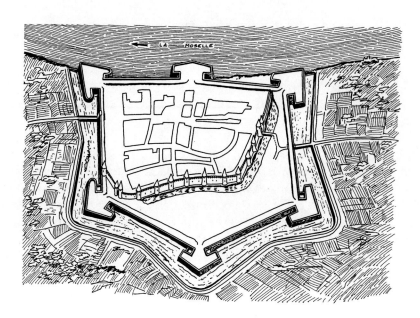

Thionville in 1596

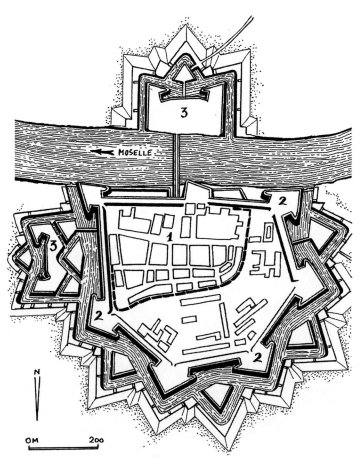

Thionville in 1673. (1) Ancient medieval town; (2) Spanish works built between 1568 and 1643; (3) hornworks established by Vauban about 1673.

Toul

The ancient Gallo-Roman city of Toul, situated in the département of Meurthe-et-Moselle, formed with Verdun and Metz the "Trois Evéchés" (three bishoprics) which were annexed by King Henri II of France in 1552 and officially yielded to France by the Treaty of Münster in 1648. Between 1698 and 1700, Vauban replaced the old medieval walls with regular fortifications, including nine bastions, demi-lunes in a floodable ditch, two gate-houses and a covered way.

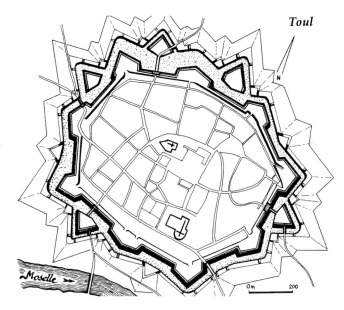

Toul

Verdun

Strategically placed on the River Meuse, Verdun was successively a Gallic town, a Roman camp (called Virodunum) and an important medieval bishop's seat. In 843, the

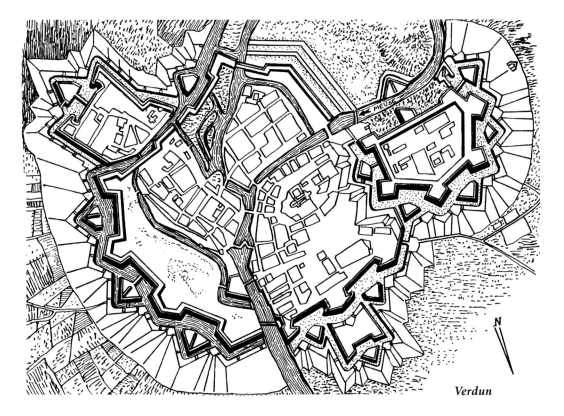

Verdun

treaty signed in the city divided Charlemagne's empire. Verdun, one of "Trois Evéchés," has been French since 1552. Under Louis XIII's reign in 1640, Jean Errard built the citadel on a high spur commanding town and river. From 1664 to 1692, Vauban and his collaborators reinforced the citadel with demi-lunes, built barracks, installed a bastioned enceinte around the city and established a large flooding zone on the southern front. Today Errard's citadel is preserved, as well as many end-of-nineteenth-century Séré de Rivières's detached forts, which played an important role during the battle of Verdun in 1916.

METZ

Metz is situated at the junction of the rivers Moselle and Seille. Occupied by the Gauls and the Romans, the city was the capital of the Frankish kingdom of Autrasia and one of Charlemagne's favorite residences. In the twelfth century, Metz became a free city. In the following centuries, the rich bishop's town was protected by a six-kilometer stone wall, 38 towers and strong gate-houses.

Metz was the third Evéché annexed by King Henri II in 1552. Besieged the very same year by Carlos V of Spain, Duke François de Guise ordered the construction of new fortifications adapted to firearms and a square citadel with four bastions in 1560. Vauban was particularly devoted to the defense of the town and worked on it in 1675, 1680 and 1698. He

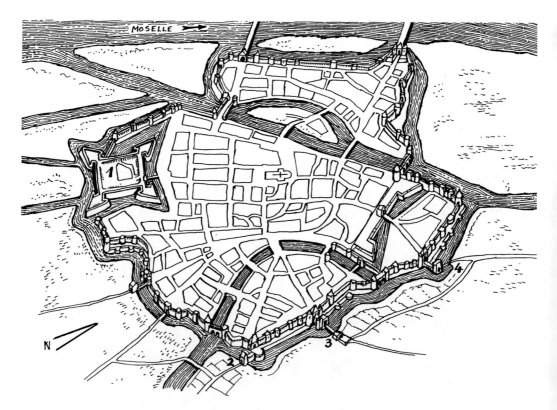

Groundplan, Metz, circa 1560. (1) Citadel built by Duke François de Guise in 1560; (2) Mazelle gate; (3) Gate of Germany; (4) Saint Barbara gate.

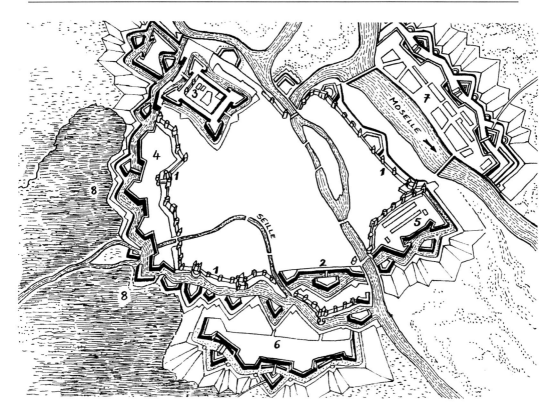

Metz in 1752. (1) Medieval walls with towers and gates; (2) entrenchment built by the duke of Guise in 1552; (3) citadel erected in 1560; (4) Saint-Thiebault and (5) chambière fronts commenced by Vauban in 1676 and finished in 1752; (6) double crownwork Bellecroix, and (7) double crownwork Front de Moselle, both built by Cormontaigne between 1728 and 1740; (8) water defenses.

designed a cunning system of flooding and planned the establishment of a huge entrenched camp. However his ambitious projects were only realized in the eighteenth century by his follower, Louis de Cormontaigne. From 1728 to 1752, Metz's fortifications were greatly reinforced by the construction of the Moselle double-crownwork (erected between 1728 and 1732) and the Bellecroix double-crownwork (built from 1736 to 1740), which both are good examples of Cormontaigne's modern bastioned front. With medieval and bastioned fortifications, polygonal French forts, German Festen and Maginot line bunkers, Metz displays today the whole evolution of military architecture.

MONTROYAL

Situated northeast of Trève (in German Trier), in Rhineland (Germany), Montroyal was created on Louis XIV's order in 1687 on a steep hill surrounded by a curve of the River Moselle, facing the small village of Starkenburg. The fortress was meant to close the Moselle valley between Coblence and Trier as well as to defend the access to Luxembourg. Vauban, charged with planning the place, showed little enthusiasm because he considered Montroyal one of those fortresses that scattered funds and troops, like Fort-Louis-du-Rhin and

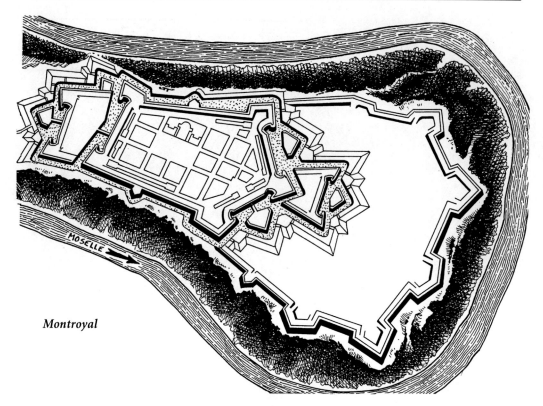

Montroyal

Landau. Montroyal was composed, in the north, of a bastioned stronghold with two horn-works and, in the south, of a vast entrenched bastioned camp, able to house an army of 4,000. The fortress was given back to the Germans in 1698 and all the fortifications were immediately and completely demolished.

Alsace

The province Alsace is the ancient barbarian Alamans's territory, which was conquered by Clovis's Franks in A.D. 496. After Charlemagne's empire was partitioned in 843, Alsace belonged to the kingdom of Lotharingia, then to the German Empire. During the Middle Ages, the main cities were emancipated from the empire's domination. After the Peace of Münster in 1648, France got some rights to the province, which officially became French after the Treaty of Nimegue in 1678. The main city, Strasburg, was "reunited" (that was conquered by force) in 1681. Vauban's principal collaborators in Alsace were the engineers Fiers and Tarade. Jacques Tarade (1645–1720), a member of the Parisian bourgeoisie, was a talented civilian architect who got involved in military architecture; from 1672 he worked with Vauban in Flanders, then in Alsace from 1676 to 1681. Tarade, promoted to provincial inspector of the fortifications of Alsace, participated in the conception and construction of Sélestat, Neuf-Brisach, Haguenau, Saverne, Freiburg, Strasburg, Kehl, Landau, Huningen and Belfort. The province of Alsace, rich in cultural and linguistic distinctive features, was constantly disputed between France and Germany and alternatively occupied by both lands until 1945.

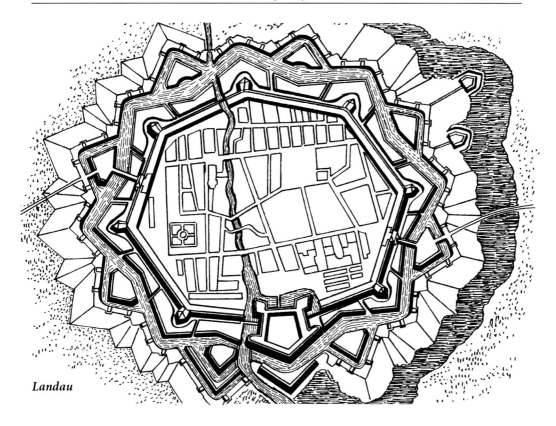

Landau

LANDAU

Landau, on the River Guisch, is situated in the German province of Palatinat. The city was fortified in order to protect the northern part of Alsace. It was there where Vauban developed his "second system" in 1687. Landau's regular fortifications, finished about 1691, prefigured Neuf-Brisach. Built by Jacques Tarade, they included a regular polygon with seven bastioned towers, counterguards, curtains with tenailles, demi-lunes in a wet ditch, a traverse covered way with places of arms, a glacis and a fore-ditch. East of the main enceinte, a bastion was entrenched and fitted with its own ditch to form a citadel. In the northwest, Vauban established a vast crownwork with three demi-lunes; in the south two hornworks were planned but not built. Landau was taken by the Germans in 1704. Today, Vauban's creation has disappeared and only two gate-houses and a few military buildings remain.

PHALSBURG

Phalsburg, situated between Sarreburg and Saverne, was newly created and established by Vauban from 1679 to 1685. The military town was destined, together with Brisach, Freiburg and Strasburg, to defend the middle part of Alsace. Phalsburg was a regular hexagon flanked by six bastions with ears, six demi-lunes, a ditch and a covered way. Access was given by the France-gate and the Germany-gate. The city interior was divided into a chessboard pattern and a central square.

Phalsburg. (1) Royal bastion with arsenal; (2) Royal demi-lune with Germany-gate; (3) Château bastion; (4) Château demi-lune; (5) Dauphin bastion; (6) Dauphin demi-lune; (7) La Reine bastion with military hospital; (8) La Reine demi-lune with France-gate; (9) Saint-Louis bastion; (10) Saint-Louis demi-lune; (11) Sainte-Thérèse bastion; (12) Sainte-Thérèse demi-lune.

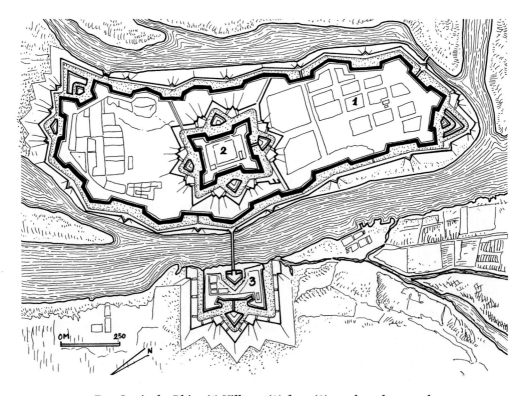

Fort-Louis-du-Rhin. (1) Village; (2) fort; (3) northern hornwork.

FORT-LOUIS-DU-RHIN

Fort-Louis-du-Rhin was created by Vauban in 1687 in northern Alsace, on the small island of Giesenheim between two arms of the Rhine (Bras d'Alsace and Bras d'Empire). Vauban was very reluctant to design the place, which he considered a waste of funds and an unnecessary scattering of troops, but on Louis XIV's insistence he had to give in. The fortifications were composed of an irregular bastioned enceinte following the outline of the island's banks. The interior of the fortress was occupied by a small village and a rectangular fort with four bastions, four demi-lunes and a ditch. Each of the two bridges giving access to the island was fortified by a hornwork. After the Treaty of Ryswick, the southern hornwork and bridge giving access to Germany were dismantled. The fortifications of Fort-Louis were completed in 1698 and demolished in 1794.

STRASBURG

Strasburg is situated on several arms of the River Ill near the Rhine. The site occupies an important strategic position (Strasburg in German means "castle on the road"). The town, called Argentoratum, was founded by the Romans about 15 B.C., and grew to be a wealthy commercial center and a fortified stronghold facing barbaric German tribes.

Devastated during fourth- and fifth-century invasions, Strasburg grew again to be a prosperous city belonging to the kingdom of Lotharingy and then to the German Empire

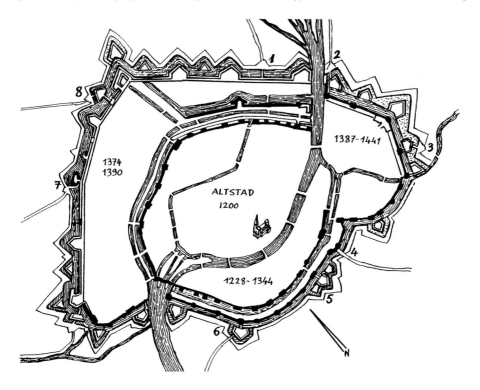

Groundplan, fortifications, Strasburg before 1681. (1) Jewish gate; (2) Fishermen's gate; (3) New gate; (4) Metz gate; (5) Hospital gate; (6) Elisabeth gate; (7) Kronenburg gate; (8) Steinstrasse gate.

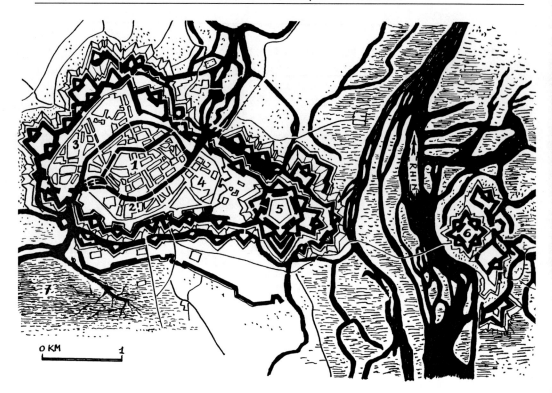

Strasbourg (1690). (1) Ancient city or Altstadt up to 1200; (2) medieval extension between 1228 and 1344; (3) second medieval extension from 1375 to 1390 on which Daniel Specklin built bastions (4) between 1577 and 1589; (5) Vauban's citadel; (6) Fort Kehl in Germany; (7) water defenses.

(870). From 1201 on, Strasburg was enlarged, and emancipated from German tutelage and became a free town surrounded by stone walls, towers and gates. During the Wars of Religion, Strasburg was a Protestant artistic, cultural and economic center. From 1577 to 1589, the Strasburg military engineer Daniel Specklin established modern bastioned fortifications which were remodeled in 1633.

Strasburg was brutally annexed by Louis XIV in 1681. Vauban, assisted by engineer Jacques Tarade, undertook a vast program of modernization from 1682 to 1690, including new bastions, demi-lunes, hornworks, detached lunettes and flooding; gate-houses were particularly monumental and decorated to show the Germans Louis XIV's power, richness and magnificence. East of the town, dominating the Rhine and facing Germany, Vauban and Tarade built a powerful pentagonal citadel with two hornworks; on the right Rhine bank, they established a stronghold named Fort Kehl, acting as a bridgehead. Seventeenth century Strasburg fortifications are no more.

SÉLESTAT

Sélestat (in Alsatian, Schletstadt) is situated north of Colmar on the left bank of the River Ill. Fortified in the fifteenth century, the city was destroyed in 1632 during the Thirty Years' War. Sélestat was renovated by Vauban and Tarade in 1675. The new fortifications were composed of six bastions, outworks in a wet ditch, a covered way, detached lunettes in the glacis and a wide flooding east and south of the town. Sélestat has preserved the ancient arsenal Sainte-Barbe, one curtain and two bastions, today Boulevard Vauban and Quai de l'Ill.

ANCIEN AND NEUF-BRISACH

Brisach in Germany is situated on several marshy islands on the right bank of the River Rhine. A bridge, the only one in the whole region, afforded a crossing of the wild river; this explains the strategic importance of the city. Brisach was occupied by France from 1648 to 1697. About 1667, Vauban fortified the town by designing twelve bastions, seven demi-lunes, a ditch and two detached works: Fort Saint-Jacques and Fort Mortier. During the construction, Vauban was involved in a misappropriation of funds scandal; his innocence was recognized in 1671. After Louis

Sélestat (Alsace) circa 1675

XIV's visit in 1673, urban development brought an extension on the near island and the creation of a new town, Saint-Louis, fortified by Jacques Tarade in 1678.

After the Treaty of Ryswick in 1697, Louis XIV was allowed to keep Strasburg but had to give back Kehl, Freiburg-im-Breisgau and Brisach. The loss of Brisach constituted a serious weakness in southern Alsace. Therefore, the king ordered Vauban to create a new fortress on the French left Rhine bank. Vauban inspected the region, selected several sites and finally chose a bare plain near the village of Volgensheim, facing Brisach. Vauban made three designs; Louis XIV chose the best and the most expensive of them. The new place was baptized Neuf Brisach, the existing Brisach in Germany thus becoming Vieux Brisach (in German, Alt-Breisach-am-Rhein).

The direction of the work was entrusted to Jacques Tarade and construction was undertaken by contractor Jean-Baptiste Regemorte. To bring materials from the stone-quarry at Pfaffenheim, Vauban had the Rouffach canal dug. Construction started in 1698 and only three years later, Neuf Brisach was completed. A unique example of Vauban's "third system," the fortifications form a perfect octagon with eight casemated bastioned towers, reinforced curtains 300 meters long and 9 meters high, detached bastions (actually large counterguards), broad tenailles, demi-lunes with reduits, a dry ditch, a traverse covered

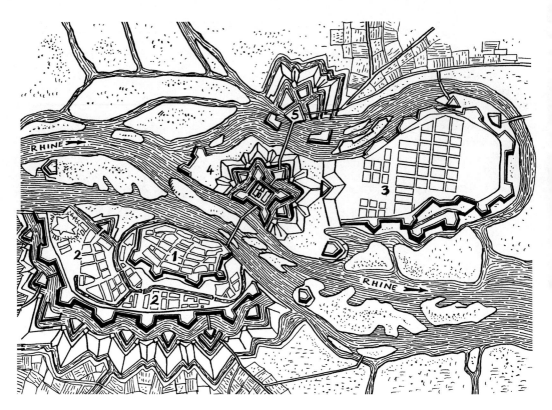

Ancient Brisach. (1) Upper city; (2) lower city; (3) new town, Saint-Louis, also called Stroh-stadt; (4) Fort Saint-Jacques; (5) Fort Mortier.

way with places of arms and a wide glacis. Four monumental and majestic gate-houses designed by architect Jules Hardouin Mansart give access to the city: Colmar-gate (west), Strasburg-gate (north), Bâle-gate (east) and Belfort-gate (south). Vauban had planned a huge crownwork, but this was never built. The internal urban space was organized in a chessboard pattern divided into 48 square habitation quarters, allowing for a population of 3,500. The city center was arranged with a spacious place of arms surrounded by the Saint-Louis church, the governor's palace, the steward's residence, the king's lieutenant's

Groundplan, Neuf-Brisach. (1) Belfort gate; (2) Bale gate; (3) Strasbourg gate; (4) Colmar gate.

house, the city hall and the arsenal. Four barracks, officers' pavilions, hospital, powder houses and various military buildings were placed near the combat emplacements, bastions and curtains. The fortress was not troubled by war until 1870, when it was besieged and taken by the Prussians. Neuf-Brisach was occupied by the German army and bombarded by the Allies in 1945. Today the fortifications are perfectly preserved and beautifully display Vauban's genius as a builder and an urbanist.

HUNINGEN

Situated near Basel, Hunigen (Huningue, in French) is a strategic crossroad in southern Alsace near Switzerland. In spite of Swiss protestations, Louvois gave orders to Vauban and Tarade to construct a fortress to control the passage to Germany and Switzerland. The beautifully well-ordered fortifications were erected from 1679 to 1682 and included five bastions with ears, outworks, two covered ways, two hornworks advanced in wide glacis and a bridgehead on the opposite Rhine bank; they gave a fine example of Vauban's "first system."

The area of the fortifications represented seven times that of the city, which made Huningen more a large fort than a fortified town. Huningen played a dissuasive role and acted as a support position for Marshal Villars during the Battle of Friedlingen in 1702. After the Second Treaty of Paris in 1815, the Swiss at last were allowed to dismantle the menacing French fortifications.

Huningen

Franche-Comté

The province Franche-Comté corresponds today to the départements of Doubs, Haute-Saône and Jura. The region was occupied by the Celtic tribe of Séquanes, by the Romans, by the barbaric Burgunds and then by the Franks. In 1032, the territory passed into the German empire. Governed by independent counts since the fourteenth century (whence its name "Free County"), the region was annexed by the dukes of Burgundy in 1384. By means of marriage and heritage, Franche-Comté became an Austrian Habsburg possession and then Spanish. After two military campaigns in 1668 and in 1674, the Treaty of Nimegue in 1678 permanently gave Franche-Comté to France.

BELFORT

Belfort is situated on an important strategic passage called the Gate of Burgundy, between the Vosges and Jura mountains, which allows communication between the Rhône and Rhine valleys. Belfort was originally a Gallo-Roman town. In the Middle Ages, it developed around a castle set on the hill dominating the city. Belfort was taken by the French count of Suze's troops in 1638 and united to France after the Treaty of Wesphalia in 1648. The Treaty of Nimegue in 1678, by which Franche-Comté became French, increased the importance of Belfort. On Louis XIV's orders, Vauban designed an ambitious project in 1687. All the ancient urban fortifications were demolished, the town was enlarged westwards down to the bank of the River Savoureuse and organized in a chessboard pattern. Vauban established three bastioned towers, counterguards, a ditch, three demi-lunes and a covered way according to his so-called "second system." The medieval castle was transformed into a powerful citadel which was reinforced by a hornwork, a demi-lune, and underground installations and barracks. North of the city, on La Miotte Hill, Vauban erected a detached fort. Due to the mountainous conditions, most of the works were furnished with traverses. The fortifications of Belfort were completed in 1705 and re-adapted in the nine-

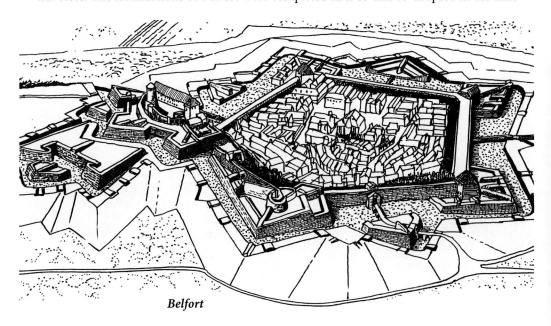

Belfort

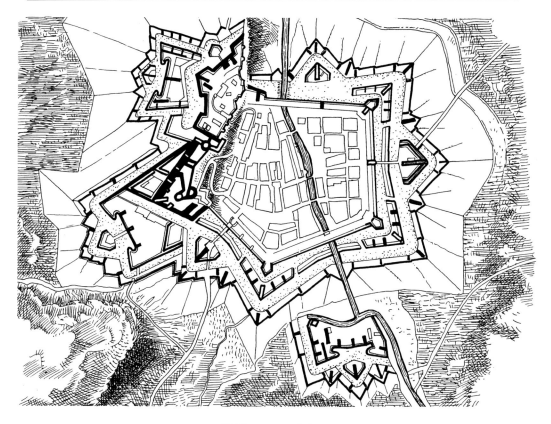

Belfort groundplan

teenth century with a girdle of detached forts. The city and its garrison led by Colonel Denfert-Rochereau successfully resisted a siege by the Prussians in the winter of 1870–1871. A part of the fortifications is partially preserved today, as well as the huge statue, the Lion, made by the sculptor Bartholdi from 1875 to 1880 to commemorate the 1870 siege.

BESANÇON

The capital of Franche-Comté, situated on a bend of the River Doubs, occupies a strategic position allowing communication among France, Italy and Switzerland. The site was already inhabited by the Gallic tribe Séquanes, who were conquered by Julius Caesar in 58 B.C. The Gallo-Roman town, called Vesontio, was destroyed by barbarian invasions and regained importance and wealth in the eleventh century under the inspired leadership of Archbishop Hugues de Salins. Although under the guardianship of the German emperor, the city enjoyed freedom in the Middle Ages. In 1667, Besançon was occupied by France, and Vauban designed a fortification project. However work had hardly started when the city was given back to Spain under the Treaty of Aix-la-Chapelle in 1668. Taking over Vauban's plan, the Italian engineer Precipiano began the fortifications of the city and started to build the citadel. Work was, again, suddenly interrupted when Besançon was re-conquered by Condé in 1674 and officially united to France after the Treaty of Nimegue in 1678. For thirty years, Vauban made of the city a first-class stronghold. Between

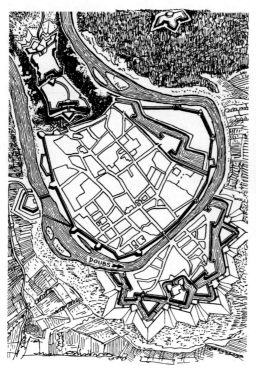

Besançon   *Besançon citadel*

1674 and 1688, attention was given to the citadel because Franche-Comté's integration to France was shaky. Many inhabitants harbored nostalgic regret for their medieval freedom and the autonomy under Spain. Vauban completed Precipiano's work by building a demi-lune in front of the northern wall (front Saint-Etienne), by establishing a second bastioned front in front of the citadel (front Royal) and by finishing the southern defense (front de Secours). On both sides of the citadel, slopes being very steep and inaccessible, a single stone wall was sufficient. From 1689 to 1695, Vauban fortified the urban enceinte by building three bastions and five bastioned towers. On the right bank, in the north of the town on the bridgehead (a neighborhood called Le Battant), Vauban constructed a bastioned enceinte; one of the bastions was entrenched in order to form a small citadel called Fort Griffon. Simultaneously, Vauban arranged the inside of the citadel with the Saint-Etienne chapel, a 132-meter well, barracks, powder houses, various stores, and a King's Cadets School. Today, the citadel is perfectly preserved and houses several museums, gardens and a zoo.

FORT SAINT-ANDRÉ

Fort Saint-André is situated on a hill dominating Salins-les-Bains in the Jura Mountains. Salins owes its name to its saline waters used for bathing and drinking. Salins is situated in the narrow valley of the Furieuse River, between three high hills. The site has been occupied since Gallic and Roman times. It is sometimes believed to be the famous Alesia, where Vercingetorix was defeated by Julius Ceasar in 52 B.C. The territory was enfiefed in the tenth century by the Abbey of Saint-Maurice-en-Valais to the counts of Mâcon. It remained in the possession of their descendants until 1175, when Maurette de Salins, heiress

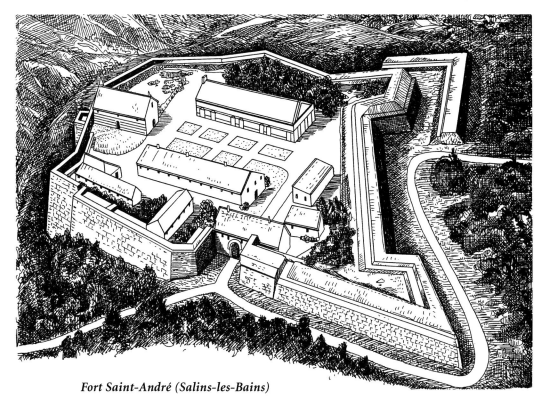

Fort Saint-André (Salins-les-Bains)

of this dynasty, brought the lordship to the house of Vienne. Salins was sold in 1225 to Hugues IV, duke of Burgundy, who ceded it in 1237 to Count Jean de Chalon. In 1477, during the reign of Louis XI, Salins was taken by the French. In 1668 and 1674 it was retaken and thenceforward remained in French power. Work on Fort Saint-André started in 1638 but had to be stopped because of an epidemic of plague. Work was resumed, but the fort was not complete when Franche-Comté became French. Louis XIV ordered the completion and Vauban made a design for the most exposed part of the fort. Salin-les-Bains successfully resisted German troops in the Franco-Prussian war of 1870. During World War I the fort was used as a home for the wounded and convalescents.

FORT JOUX

Fort Joux is strategically situated on a narrow rocky ridge named Cluse-et-Mijoux in the upper valley of the River Doubs near Pontarlier. Originally a castle set up by the dukes of Burgundy, it was adapted to the use of firearms under Carlos V of Spain by a massive semi-circular artillery bulwark. Fort Joux became French in 1674. Vauban reinforced the fort in 1690 by installing a 135-meter well, and by constructing a bastioned front and a ditch in front of the sixteenth century bulwark. Fort Joux was also used as a state prison; the most famous prisoners were the revolutionary politician Honoré Gabriel Count of Mirabeau (1749–1791) and the Haitian slave abolitionist Toussaint-Louverture (1743–1803). Fort Joux also played a military role during the Franco-Prussian War of 1870 by allowing the regroupment of General Bourbaki's army. A polygonal fort, designed by the future Marshal Joseph Joffre (1852–1931), was added in 1880. The fort today is well preserved and displays a very

Joux Castle. (1) Original castle; (2) medieval enceinte; (3) sixteenth-century bulwark; (4) seventeenth-century bastioned front; (5) end-of-the-nineteenth-century polygonal fort.

interesting summary of French military architecture history in an imposing, mountainous landscape.

AUXONNE

Auxonne (Côte-d'Or) is strategically situated on the River Saône on the road between Dijon and Dole. A medieval enceinte composed of stone curtains, towers and gate-houses was built by the dukes of Burgundy about 1345. Auxonne became French in 1477 and Louis XI ordered the reshaping of the urban walls. The king also decided to construct a castle-citadel in a typical end-of-fifteenth-century transitional style. Adapted to firearms, the citadel was composed of thick curtains flanked by five, low, circular artillery towers fitted with casemates, round breastworks and embrasures. A border city until the union of Franche-Comté to France, the fortifications of Auxonne were maintained and rebuilt under Louis XII and François I. In 1673, Louis XIV charged Marshal François de la Motte-Villebert, viscount of Aspremont (1634–1678), with building a bastioned enceinte and an arsenal. These works, improved and finished by Vauban in 1675, were completed in the eighteenth century by barracks, a powder-magazine and an artillery school, where the young Napoléon Bonaparte was a cadet from 1788 to 1791. The fortifications of Auxonne were partially demolished between 1900 and 1914. However a few vestiges are kept.

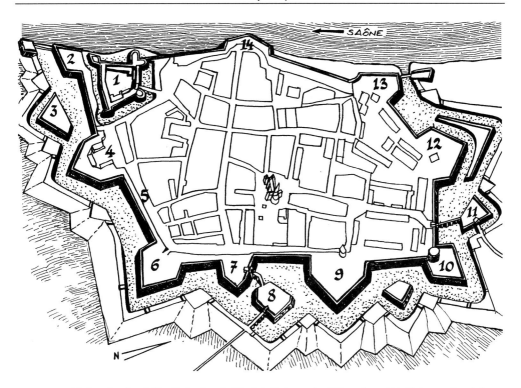

Auxonne. (1) Castle-citadel built by Louis XI; (2) Château half-bastion; (3) Château demi-lune; (4) Moineau bastion; (5) Ursulines curtain, casemated in 1826; (6) Notre-Dame bastion; (7) porte du Comté bastion; (8) porte du Comté demi-lune; (9) Gouverneur bastion; (10) Signe tower and bastion; (11) Royale gate and demi-lune; (12) Royal bastion; (13) Béchaux bastion; (14) porte de France bastion.

Dauphiné and Savoy

The old province of Dauphiné today is formed by the départements of Isère and Hautes-Alpes, as well as parts of Drôme and Ain. King Philippe VI of France purchased the region with its capital Grenoble in 1349 from the count of Viennois, Humbert II. From 1364 until 1830, the province was traditionally the apanage granted to the heir to the throne of France; the king's eldest son was called the "Dauphin." An apanage or appanage is the grant of an estate, titles, offices, or other things of value to the puisne sons, younger male children of a sovereign, who under the system of primogeniture would otherwise have no inheritance. The apanage returned to the crown at the recipient's death. The system, intended to avoid civil war among throne contenders or the division of the kingdom among princes of royal blood, was widespread in much of Europe. During the wars in Italy (from 1494 to 1515) the Dauphiné played an important role as a passage to the peninsula. The province was officially re-united to the French royal domain in 1560.

The province of Savoy, situated between France, Switzerland and Italy, was occupied by the Gallic tribe of the Allobroges and by the Romans (118 B.C.). Burgundian barbarians conquered it about 443 and Clovis's Franks took the region in 534. Savoy was a part of Burgundy (888) and of the German Empire (1032). From the twelfth to the fourteenth cen-

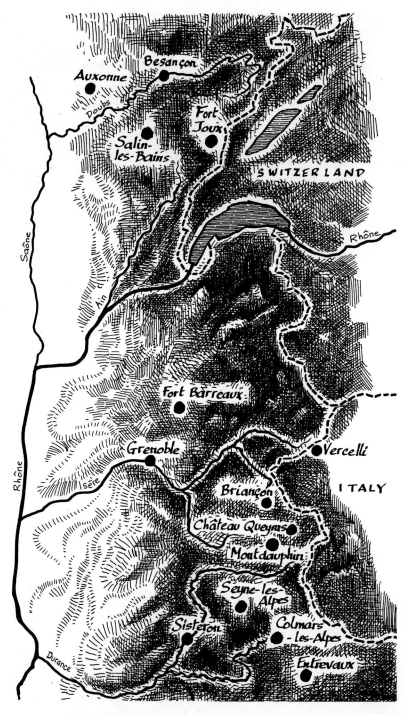

Map of the Alps. The Alps formed a high and difficult barrier between France, Switzerland and Italy. Although a hostile environment, particularly in winter, the Alps are not impassible. They include passes (e.g., Petit Saint Bernard, Iseran, Mont-Cenis, Fréjus, Galibier, Mont Genèvre and Tende), and river valleys (e.g., Isère, Arc, Romanche, Drac, Drôme, Durance, Guil, Ubaye, and Verdon, all emptying into the Rhône River) opening onto Savoy and Italy.

turies, the lords of Savoy emancipated themselves from the German Empire and led an expansionist policy in Switzerland and Italy. Savoy was instituted as a duchy in 1416 and its capital was removed from Chambéry to Turin. Throughout history, relations between Savoy and France were marked by peaceful diplomacy and marriages but also by violence because the dukes played a political, diplomatic and military role as guardian of the important passes in the Alps. Savoy was occupied between 1536 and 1544 and, in 1601, a part of the duchy situated on the French side of the Alps (Bresse, Bugey, Valromey and Gex) was annexed by King Henri IV of France. Under Louis XIII's reign the duchy was again occupied from 1628 until 1631. Franco-Savoyard relationships deteriorated by the end of Louis XIV's reign, when Duke Victor-Amédée joined the anti–French coalition (League of Augsbourg). The duke launched a devastating raid in Dauphiné in 1692, and therefore Louis XIV ordered Vauban to reinforce the Alps frontier. Savoy was again occupied by France in Louis XIV's time, from 1690 to 1696 and later between 1792 and 1815. The duchy and the county of Nice became permanently French after a referendum in 1860 during Napoleon III's Second Empire. The definitive line of the Franco-Italian frontier was set in 1947.

In the Alps, Vauban was assisted by engineers Beauregard, Niquet, Guy de Creuzet de Richerand and Beauvoisin.

Given the mountainous terrain, the enemy was likely to be less concentrated, so only the passes were fortified. In steep, rocky mountains there was often no space to build bastions and outworks. Besides, heavy siege artillery was difficult to transport to mountainous sites, so old medieval fortifications kept a part of their military value (e.g. Sisteron, Castle Queyras, Briançon). According to the basic principle of command, mountain fortifications were always placed on positions dominating the passes and vital roads. So in the Alps the French enjoyed a significant advantage, but this should not blind us to the impressive scale of the effort deployed by Vauban and his assistants.

GRENOBLE

Grenoble, the capital of the province of Dauphiné, is situated at an altitude of about 214 meters at the foot of the Alps, surrounded by the Chartreuses to the north, the Vercors to the west and the Belledonne to the east. Strategically placed at the confluence of Drac into the Isère River, it has been the capital and fortified town of the Allobroge Gallic tribe (then named Cularo), and became Gratianopolis under Roman rule. After the collapse of the Roman Empire it was part of the first Burgundian kingdom, until it passed under domination of Clotaire I, king of the Franks and a son of Clovis I. Later the city was a possession of the Carolingian dynasty, then a part of the kingdom of Arles, and finally a possession of the counts of Vienne, whose title "dauphin" gave the region its traditional name of Dauphiné. This region and Grenoble became French in July 1349 when the last dauphin of Vienne, Humbert II, sold the region to the king of France, Philippe VI, on condition that the heir to the French crown use the title of dauphin. The last heir to carry this title was Louis-Antoine of Bourbon, duke of Angoulême and son of Charles X.

Vauban made a first tour of inspection in Grenoble in 1660 and found the ancient fortifications in a poor state, particularly the Bastille, the citadel situated north of the city. He undertook renovations in September 1692, including a reinforcement of the existing enceinte, the establishment of a new bastioned wall for the suburb of Île Verte, and the strengthening of the citadel, the key position dominating the whole town. Between 1832

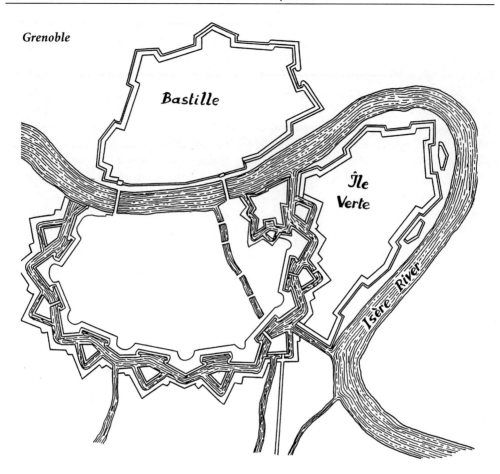

Grenoble

and 1848, the fortifications of Grenoble were greatly reinforced by General Haxo, who brought significant changes to the bastioned enceinte, reshaped the Bastille citadel, and built several detached forts on the hills surrounding the city. By the end of the nineteenth century Grenoble had become an important administrative, university and industrial city (its population was 45,000 in 1875), and the ancient fortifications stood in the way of development. It was only in 1920 that all the defensive works were dismantled. Today Grenoble has retained the Bastille citadel, accessible via a cable car. It is one of its most visited tourist attractions, and a good vantage point for viewing the town below and the grandeur of the surrounding mountain landscape.

Fort Barraux

Fort Barraux is situated south of Chambéry and dominates the valley of the River Isère leading to Grenoble. The construction of the fort started in August 1597 after a design by the Italian engineer Ercole Negro, on the duke of Savoy's order. Almost completed, the fort was taken in March 1598 by Constable Lesdiguières, in King Henri IV's service. The fort was redesigned between 1608 and 1635 by the king's engineer Jean de Beins. In 1692, Vauban reshaped it by reinforcing the forefront, by deepening the ditch, by strengthening the bastions and by building an arsenal, two powder houses and a well.

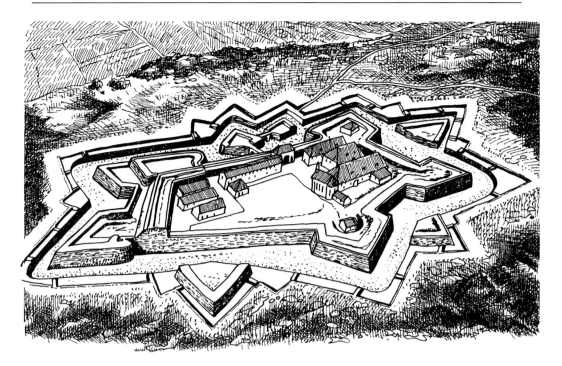

Fort Barraux

MONTMÉLIAN

Situated at the crossroads between the valley of Combes de Savoie, Grésivaudan Ridge, and Isère Valley between Chambéry and Albertville, the small town of Montmélian has been a strategic passage through the Alps since Roman times, when it was called *Montis Meliani.*

In 1030 for the first time, a castle, named *Pierre-Forte* ("Strong Stone"), was men-

Citadel of Montmélian

tioned. In the Middle Ages, the town was an important administrative and economical center depending from the Duchy of Savoy. Montmélian did not escape the struggle between France and Savoy, and was several times besieged by the French, namely by king François I in 1536, Henri IV in 1600, Louis XIII in 1630, and Louis XIV in 1691 and 1705. Between 1560 and 1570, the castle on the ridge dominating the city was transformed into a powerful bastioned citadel in the Italian style. Constantly modified, modernized and enlarged by the Dukes of Savoy, Montmélian had a reputation as one of the best fortresses of Europe in the 17th century. After the siege of 1705, Louis XIV, following Vauban's advice, ordered the destruction of the citadel.

BRIANÇON

Briançon, the highest French town (altitude 1,326 meters), is situated in the valley of the River Durance on a very important crossroads in the Alps. This exceptional situation foredoomed the city to be a fortress. Inhabited since about 800 B.C. and called Brigantio, the village grew to a Roman stronghold about A.D. 64 called Castellum Virgantia. Successively occupied and devastated by the Burgunds, Ostrogoths, Lombards, Sarrasins and Hungarians, Briançon belonged to Dauphiné in the eleventh century. The counts built a castle on the spur dominating the town, including a square, 24-meter high keep and a stone wall with three towers. The Dauphiné and the Briançonnais were annexed by France in 1349 under Philippe VI. During the Italians Wars (from 1495 to 1559) and the Wars of Religion (from 1562 to 1598) the city was looted several times. In 1580, Constable Lesdiguières added two bastions to the castle and built a hornwork on the existing Champ de Mars. In 1624,

Briançon

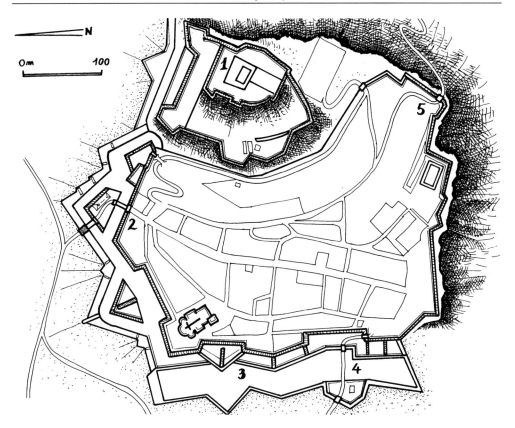

Briançon groundplan. (1) Château citadel; (2) Pignerol gate; (3) Embrun front; (4) Embrun gate; (5) Durance gate.

Briançon was destroyed by fire and king's engineer Persens re-built and enlarged the town. In 1692, the duke of Savoy, Victor-Amédée, joined the anti–French coalition (League of Augsbourg) and took the cities of Embrun and Gap. Briançon, menaced by invasion, was then hastily fortified by engineer d'Angrogne and defended by Dauphiné's governor, Marshal Catinat. Unfortunately, another fire damaged the town again. When Vauban came on inspection tour in January 1692, he found Briançon in a pitiful state. Vauban immediately made a new design. On the gentle slope of the northern Champs de Mars, he protected the Pignerol-gate by a strong curtain, two casemated redans and a demi-lune; on the northwest front, he built two bastions, one traverse demi-lune and the Notre-Dame-et-Saint-Nicolas church. On the western Embrun front, he created a terraced position including bastions and curtains, a traverse fausse-braie and a covered way. In front of the southwestern Embrun-gate, Vauban set up a place of arms and a chicane. On the abrupt and inaccessible southern front plunging into the canyon of the Durance, a single stone wall was sufficient. On the eastern front, Vauban proposed to dismantle the Middle Ages castle and to erect a bastioned citadel, but due to lack of funds, this part of his project could not be realized. Vauban completed the ensemble by constructing a barrack and two powder houses. In 1700 he made another plan for Briançon, including detached forts on the Salettes and Trois Têtes mountains which dominate the town. After Vauban's death in 1707, his successors continued this project. During the three following centuries, Briançon was transformed into an exceptionally strong fortified site. Today the city and its surrounding mountains have numerous detached forts, entrenched camps, batteries and Maginot Line concrete casemates.

CASTLE QUEYRAS

Castle Queyras is situated in the Guil River valley. The fortress, built in the fourteenth century, victoriously resisted the duke of Savoy's attack in 1692. The very same year, Vauban decided to redesign it by installing bastioned batteries. On an inspection tour in 1700, Vauban was very unsatisfied with the execution of his design and ordered the modification and the destruction of the offending parts. Today, Castle Queyras is well preserved in a magnificent mountain landscape.

Castle Queyras

VERCEIL

Verceil (Vercelli in Italian), situated northeast of Turin in Piemont, belonged to the duke of Savoy and formed a border stronghold with the duchy of Milan. The city was fortified in 1372 by master builder Perrino Selvatico. To convince the duke of Savoy to ally France against the Dutch, Louis XIV sent Louvois as ambassador in July 1670. Louvois was accompanied by Vauban, who participated in the modernization of the defenses of Turin, La Verruca and Verceil. Verceil's fortifications partly designed by Vauban included fourteen bastions with cavaliers, nine demi-lunes in a wet ditch supplied by the waters of the River Cervo, two accesses (the Turin-gate and Milan-gate), a covered way with places of arms, a glacis and a triangular citadel.

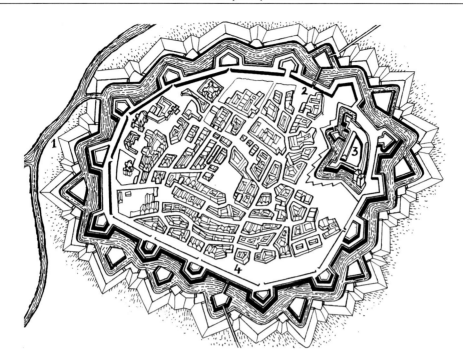

Vercelli (Italy). (1) Cervo River; (2) Turin Gate; (3) citadel; (4) Milan Gate.

PIGNEROL

Pignerol (Pinerolo in Italian) is situated in the valley of the River Chisone on the Piemontese side of the Alps, west of Turin. Pignerol was yielded to France by the Treaty of Westphalia (1648). Pignerol (with Casal and Fenestrelle) enabled control of the duke of Savoy's province of Piémont and menaced the region of Milan, held by Spain. Vauban designed defenses in February 1669. The fortifications, completed in 1682, were composed of an irregular enceinte including ten bastions, six demi-lunes in a dry ditch, a covered way and a glacis. Dominating the town, a rectangular bastioned citadel with outwork and ditch was constructed. Vauban inspected Pignerol in 1692, and added a few

Pignerol (Italy)

improvements, but recommended a compromise with the duke of Savoy. By the Treaty of Turin (August 29, 1696), France gave back Pignerol, Casal and Suse.

MONTDAUPHIN

Invaded by Duke Victor-Amédée of Savoy in 1692, the province of Dauphiné appeared to be a vulnerable region. Vauban convinced Louis XIV to create a new fortress near Embrun

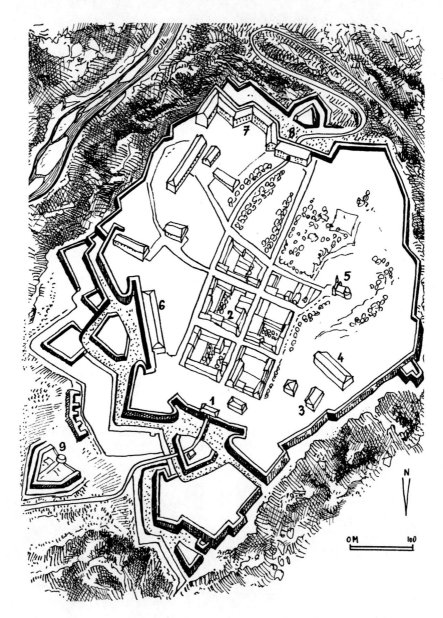

Montdauphin. (1) Briançon gate-house; (2) village; (3) powder house; (4) arsenal; (5) church; (6) Campana barrack; (7) Rochambeau barrack; (8) Embrun gate-house; (9) Napoleonic lunette built by Le Michaud d'Arçon.

in the Upper Alps. Advised by his friend Marshal de Catinat, Vauban chose a rocky ridge (altitude 1,030 meters) dominating the junction of the rivers Guil and Durance. The new fortress, situated 31 km. south of Briançon, enabled defense of the Queyras mountains, the Vars pass and the Durance valley. Montdauphin's construction began in 1693. Because of the steep ridge, Vauban was obliged to adapt to the natural site. The irregular outline of the fortress was particularly fortified on the gentle northern slope with a double bastioned front with outworks. The other slopes being inaccessible only demanded simple stone walls. To prevent the garrison from feeling lonesome and isolated, Vauban wanted to create a village within the fortress. Because of the poor density of population and the raw, mountainous weather of the region, the urbanization of Montdauphin was a total failure. Few civilians ever showed up and the large area (16 hectares) planned for the village has remained empty until today. Vauban inspected Montdauphin in 1700 and was very displeased with the execution of his plan. The fortress was modified in 1765 and 1783, and again during the Napoleonic period. Transformed into a prison in the nineteenth century, Montdauphin today displays its fortifications in a majestic mountain landscape.

Seyne-les-Alpes

An important crossroad between Digne and Provence, Seyne in the Alpes-de-Haute-Provence (Upper Alps), was fortified in the Middle Ages by a tower set up about 1220. The village, then called Seyne-la-Grande-Tour, grew to be a border town with Savoy after the annexation of Provence to France in 1481. In 1690, engineer Niquet constructed an enceinte with nine bastions. Vauban, in 1692, charged engineers Richerand and Beauregard to design the existing citadel and urban fortifications. With the annexation to France of the Ubaye Valley in 1713, the Franco-Italian frontier was fixed at the Larche pass, therefore Seyne lost a great part of its strategic importance and only garrisoned a few soldiers until its decommissioning in 1907. The abandoned fortifications today are well restored.

Colmars-les-Alpes

Situated at 1,250 meters on the left bank of the River Verdon between Barcelonnette and Entrevaux, Colmars has for centuries been a border town between French Provence and the duchy of Savoy. The name comes from Collis Martis (a hill dedicated to the Roman god Mars). The urban fortifications dating from the twelfth and fourteenth centuries were restructured during François I's reign. In 1690, engineer Niquet arranged five bastions on the ancient walls and designed two detached works.

The Fort de France (also called Fort du Calvaire) was built by engineer Richerand south of the city between 1693 and 1695. The fort is a square redoubt, 25 meters in length, surrounded by a dry ditch and connected to Colmars by a communication wall fitted with loopholes; the redoubt sheltered a battery, a guardhouse, two stores and a water tank.

The Fort Savoy (also named Fort Saint-Martin), built on the hill Saint-Martin dominating the River Verdon in the north, was composed of a trapezoidal enceinte with a half-bastion, a tower and a redan. The fort was connected to the town by means of a zigzag communication way. The fort includes a barrack, a powder house and a water tank. Vauban, on inspection tour in 1700, sharply criticized Colmars-les-Alpes's fortifications and proposed a new design which, due to lack of funds, could not be carried out. After the Treaty

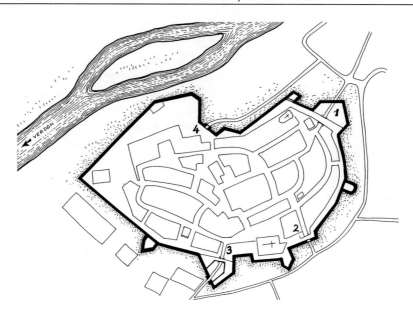

Colmars-les-Alpes. (1) Savoy gate; (2) Boulangerie gate; (3) France gate; (4) des Tennis gate.

Fort de Savoie at Colmars-les-Alpes

of Utrecht in 1713, the Ubaye Valley was given to France, and the frontier with Savoy was displaced to the Larche pass. Colmars, just like Seyne-les-Alpes, lost its strategic value. Today the fortifications are well preserved.

Right: *Groundplan, Fort de Savoie (Colmars-les-Alpes). The dotted line shows Vauban's bastioned design from 1700 (not completed).*

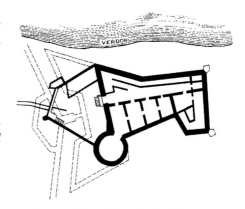

ENTREVAUX

Entrevaux, situated in the valley of the River Var, northeast of Castellane in the département of Alpes de Haute Provence, was a French stronghold defending the border with the

Bastioned tower at Entrevaux

Northern side of the citadel of Entrevaux

County of Nice and Savoy. The town was attacked by the duke of Savoy in 1692. Louis XIV then ordered the organization of defenses in this vulnerable part of the southern Alps. After a design by Vauban in 1692, engineer Niquet reinforced the urban walls by installing two bastioned casemated towers; he also fortified the cathedral and constructed a hornwork (named Corne du Puget) in front of the gate of France. The old medieval castle dominating the small city was reinforced with the addition of a barrack and two artillery-platforms; it became a citadel connected to Entrevaux by a Z-shaped traversed communication passage. In the eighteenth century the communication was reinforced by two gun emplacements placed halfway on the steep sloping hill: Battery Langrune on the left and Battery Pandol on the right. Entrevaux remained a frontier stronghold until Savoy's union to France in 1860 during the reign of Emperor Napoléon III. Today, the city fortifications, the passage and the fort are well preserved.

Mediterranean Coast

Vauban's work along the Mediterranean coast (Provence and Languedoc provinces) was rather limited for many reasons. The region of Provence was French for a long time (since 1481), and was relatively well fortified beginning with the reigns of François I and Henri IV — notably by engineers Raymond and Jean de Bonnefons. Besides, coastal and harbor fortifications were planned and constructed by the Navy, directed by Colbert and not by Louvois, to whom Vauban was attached. Indeed Vauban's engineering corps was placed under Louvois's War Department, which meant that when working on a naval site, Vauban passed under another authority, that of Colbert's Navy Ministry. Another reason was that this part of France was not directly threatened, owing to the comparative strong French

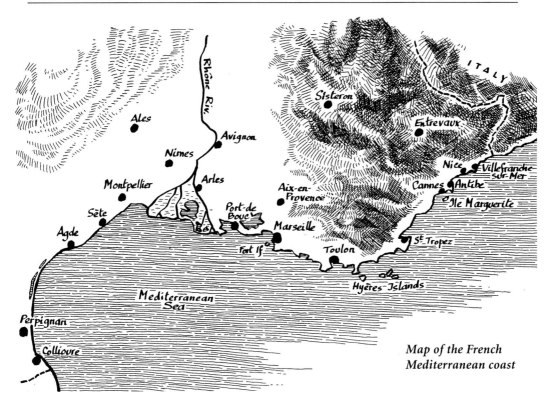

Map of the French Mediterranean coast

fleet. The Mediterranean Sea was, however, unsafe because of Spanish and Turkish raiders, Algerian and Genoese pirates as well as British and Dutch fleets. Finally, the maritime nature of the threat meant that naval fortifications could be relatively simple affairs defending only beaches where landing could occur, anchorages and main ports. For all these reasons, Vauban's principal contribution in this region was the securing of the two main French harbors: Toulon and Marseille.

In Languedoc (today corresponding to the department of Gard, and part of Lozère and Hérault), the military engineers François Ferry and Jean-Baptiste Minet re-shaped old-fashioned fortifications dating from preceding reigns: Saint-Hippolyte-du-Fort, a citadel and forts in Alès and Nîmes, the citadel of Montpellier, Fort Richelieu and Fort Saint-Pierre in Sète and Fort Cap d'Agde.

It should be noted that in Louis XIV's time, Corsica belonged to Genoa; the island was purchased by France in 1768.

ANTIBES

The much-frequented resort town of Antibes lies on the far side of the Baie des Anges facing Nice. The city originates from the ancient Antipolis, a trading-post created and fortified by Greek merchants from Marseilles in the fifth century B.C. For centuries—actually until 1860—Antibes was a border town between France and Savoy. As a result, each reign brought improvement and enlargement to Antibes's fortifications. Fort Carré on the Saint-Roch cape and an urban enceinte were erected in the sixteenth century. Vauban hated the outdated, Italian-style Fort Carré from 1580, with its acute-angled bastions, narrow

Antibes. The fortifications connecting the ancient Fort Carré to the city were planned by Vauban, but this project was never completed.

gorges, short walls, and almost non-existent counterscarp defense. He therefore added a modern bastioned enceinte around it. He also planned an ambitious project to link the town, its harbor and the Saint-Roch cape by a large bastioned enceinte, but this design was not carried out. The fortifications of Antibes were dismantled from 1895 to 1900. Fortunately, Fort Carré and the sea-front ramparts (Promenade du Front de Mer, Avenue Amiral De Grasse) have been preserved.

SAINTE-MARGUERITE ISLAND

Sainte-Marguerite is the largest island belonging to the Lérins archipelago off Cannes. The island was already occupied and fortified in Roman times. About A.D. 410,

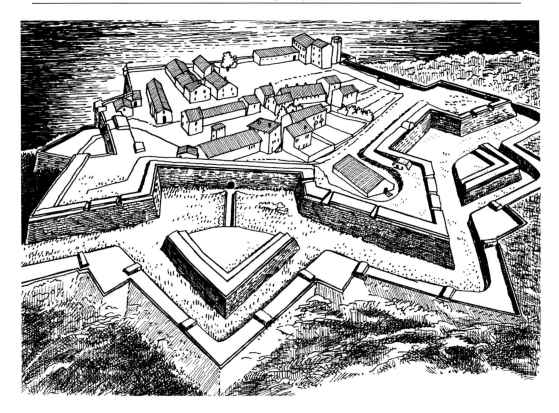

Fort Royal, Sainte-Marguerite Island

Saint Honorat founded a monastery which was fortified against pirates' raids. In 1634 Richelieu ordered the occupation of Saint-Marguerite and the construction of a stronghold, called Fort Royal, designed by engineer Jean de Bellon. In 1635 the island was taken by the Spaniards, who continued working on the fort. Finally, Sainte-Marguerite was re-conquered by the French in 1637. Vauban completed the defenses by installing several outworks and a covered way. Fort Royal became a state prison from 1685 on, in which were detained a number of French Protestants after the revocation of the Edict of Nantes. One of the most famous prisoners was the mysterious Man with the Iron Mask (who actually wore only a simple velvet mask), whose identity has never been established with any certainty.

Toulon

Neither the Greeks nor the Romans paid attention to the exceptional site of Toulon, and today France's chief naval port lies behind its anchorage, one of the safest and most beautiful harbors of the Mediterranean, surrounded as it is by sunny slopes and high hills crowned by forts. In the Middle Ages, Toulon remained a modest fishing village. The annexation of Provence by France in 1481 marked the beginning of a new destiny. Toulon grew to a military and commercial harbor used during the Italian Wars. In 1514, under Louis XII's reign, a circular gun tower was set up to defend the eastern entrance to the harbor. The enormous Royale Tower (known also as the Grosse Tour de la Mitre), with a diameter of 55 meters and walls 7 meters thick, was completed ten years later under François I's

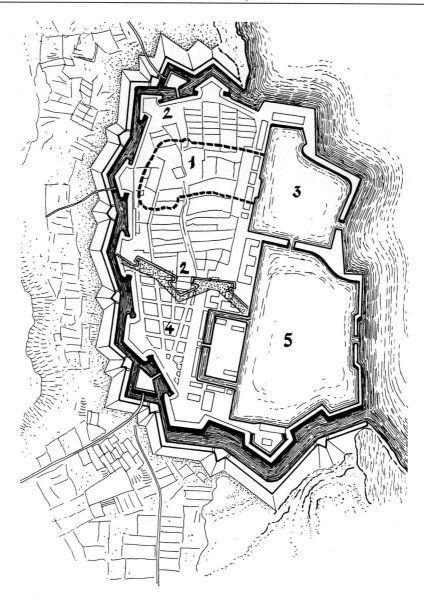

Groundplan, Toulon. (1) Medieval village; (2) fortifications about 1600; (3) old harbor; (4) city and arsenal extension under Louis XIV; (5) new harbor.

Opposite bottom, *Tour Royale (Toulon). The Royal Tower was intended to defend the bay of Toulon. Designed by the Italian engineer De Laporta, its diameter is 55 meters. The tower, completed in 1524, includes a lower casemated battery with eight embrasures, an open top terreplein, a barrack, a cistern, a powder house and a storeroom. The Tour Royale was part of the defense of Toulon during the attack of the British-Spanish coalition in 1707, but when Fort Lamalgue was built in 1770, its role diminished. During the Franco-Prussian War of 1870, it was secretly used to store gold for the Bank of France. In 1942, the German occupiers established a flak battery on the tower's platform. Damaged during the liberation of Toulon in 1944, the tower was classed as an historical monument in 1947. Since 1951, it has housed a Museum of the French Navy.*

Fort Saint-Louis (Toulon). West of the Tour Royale, the Tour des Vignettes was designed by Vauban in 1696 to aid the defense of the bay of Toulon. Destroyed in 1707, it was rebuilt a year later with a new name: Fort Saint-Louis. It is a typical Vauban-style sea fort: a lower semicircular gun battery faces the sea, and a tower in the gorge accommodates the garrison.

reign. The tower proved its efficiency by repulsing two Spanish attacks in 1524 and in 1536. The future of Toulon was assured by the naval arsenal created by King Henri IV. From 1589 onwards, on orders of the duke of Epernon, governor of Provence, the harbor and the town were enlarged and surrounded by an enceinte with five Italian-style bastions whose design was attributed to the Piemontese architect Ercole Negro. About 1600, the fortifications were reshaped by engineer Raymond de Bonnefons. In 1635, Richelieu created a military arsenal to build and repair warships, making Toulon the strategic center of the French Mediterranean (mostly galley) fleet. The western harbor defenses were completed by the construction of the Balaguier Tower, facing the Royale Tower. In 1680, Colbert decided to reinforce the important military city. The harbor was widened; shipyards, a new wet dock and an enlarged arsenal were built. Around the arsenal and the town, Vauban built a strong bastioned enceinte and two detached bastioned works: Fort des Pommets and Fort Saint-Louis. In 1707 an entrenched camp was built (Camp Sainte-Anne). Today, of Toulon's fortifications, there still exist the Royal Tower, and three bastions arranged as public park with the Salle Omega Zenith (concert hall) and the Espace Culturel des Lices (culture hall). Another bastion still exists near the ancient Porte d'Italie (Italy Gate). Several detached forts built in the eighteenth and nineteenth centuries (e.g. Fort Lamalgue, Fort Sainte-Catherine), as well as French concrete coastal batteries established in the 1930s and German World War II bunkers make of Toulon an open-air museum of the history of fortification.

PORT-MAN

The fort of Port-Man was part of a chain of posts, watchtowers and forts built on the order of Louis XIII's minister, Cardinal Richelieu, in the archipelago south of Giens, including the islands of Grand Ribaud, Porquerolles, Bagaud, Port-Cros and Levant. The fort was intended to protect the Strait of Grottes between the island of Port-Cros and the island of Levant, and to defend the green amphitheater of Port-Man Bay against a Spanish threat. The small fort of Port-Man was built in 1634 on a narrow, rocky cape in the eastern part of Port-Cros island. Originally the position included a circular watchtower and a low gun battery. Port-Man was enlarged in 1750 by the addition of a barrack and a crenellated

Fort of Port-Man
(Port-Cros Island)

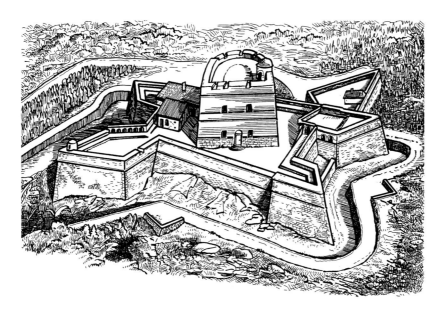

Fort Estissac (Port-Cros Island). Built between 1634 and 1640 under Richelieu and Louis XIII, Fort Estissac comprised a massive artillery tower enclosed by a bastioned enceinte.

caponier, forming together a tenailled front in order to resist a land attack from the rear. The fort of Port-Man remained a military post until 1881. The island of Port-Cros included other coastal strongholds, notably Fort Estissac.

FORT ALYCASTRE

Situated on a rocky cape in the island of Porquerolles, Fort Alycastre was intended to defend the Bay of Hyères and the two beaches of the island (Grande Plage and Plage Notre-

Fort Alycastre (Porquerolles Island)

Dame). Built between 1634 and 1640, it testifies to Cardinal Richelieu's efforts to fortify the islands off the peninsula of Giens. The fort is quite typical of the time. It is composed of a massive central square tower (16 meters × 16 meters) accommodating quarters for the garrison, a cistern, a powder-store, a bread oven and supply stores. The top of the building was arranged as an open terreplein for observation and artillery. The tower is enclosed with a rectangular enceinte with four redans forming an eight-pointed star; a bastion was added later.

MARSEILLE

Marseille owes everything to the sea and its admirable situation in a wide bay sheltered by two limestone mountains, Estaque and Etoile. Twenty-five centuries of history make Marseille the oldest of the great cities of France. It originates from a trading post founded about 600 B.C. by a group of Phocean merchants (Greeks from Asia Minor). Called Massalia, the town was for centuries a free, rich, merchant republic, until it was conquered by Julius Caesar in 43 B.C. Ravaged by barbarian invasions, Marseilles regained importance and wealth during the Crusades as a port of embarkation to the Holy Land. In 1481, Provence and Marseille became French, however relationships between the boisterous and proud population and the French monarchs were always stormy and therefore led to the construction of citadels. The first citadel was set up on François I's order on the hill

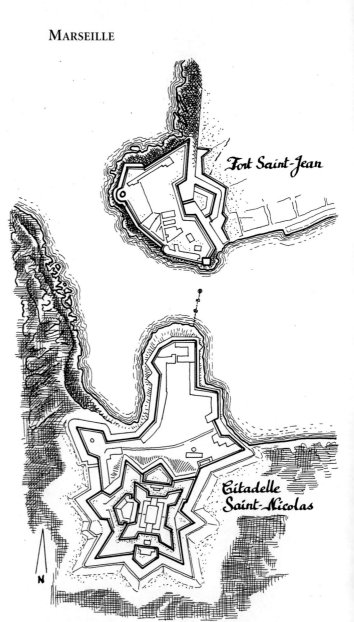

Entrance port of Marseille. The groundplan shows Fort Saint-Jean (top) and Citadel Saint-Nicolas (bottom) defending the entrance of Marseilles harbor.

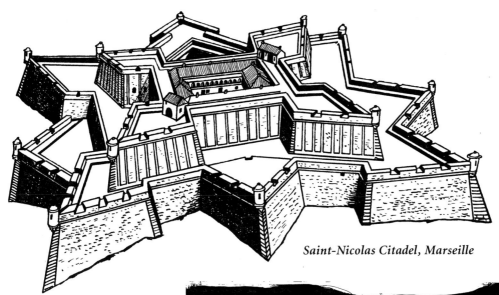

Saint-Nicolas Citadel, Marseille

Notre-Dame-de-la-Garde. It was an irregular bastioned triangle defending the harbor, the road to Toulon and the road to Italy, but also was meant to control the population. The fort was used as a foundation for the existing church Notre-Dame-de-la-Garde, completed in 1864. During the Wars of Religion, the Catholic Marseillais were opposed to the Huguenot King Henri IV and allied with the Spanish enemy. After the Peace of Vervins and the Spaniards' departure in 1597, Henri IV ordered his engineer Raymond de Bonnefons to fortify the islands of Ratonneau and Pomègues as well as Fort Port-de-Bouc. During the Fronde civil war, Marseille was in armed rebellion against royal authority. Louis XIV's troops occupied the city in 1660. The

Fort Saint-Jean, Marseille

king ordered the demolition of the medieval fortifications, the enlargement of the city, the widening of the harbor, the creation of a galley arsenal and the installation of two citadels.

The first one, called Citadel Saint-Nicolas, was designed by Chevalier de Clerville south of the harbor mouth. Completed in 1664, Citadel Saint-Nicolas was composed of two parts: a lower fort (Bas-Fort Ganteaume) and an upper fort (Haut-Fort Entrecastraux), including two superposed bastioned enceintes. The second citadel, called Citadel or Fort Saint-Jean, was erected north of the harbor entrance; it was built by Clerville between 1668 and 1671 on the ruins of an ancient Greek acropolis, and vestiges of a twelfth-century command post built by the Knights of Saint-John of the Hospital of Jerusalem (the Hospitallers). In 1679, Vauban sharply criticized Clerville's designs and redesigned both citadels. He also pleaded for the construction of a strong bastioned enceinte to defend the city, but this was never carried out for political reasons. Louis XIV mistrusted the rebellious citizens, and Marseille was to remain a defenseless city, in fact having the same fate as Paris.

Port-de-Bouc, Martigues. Fort Port-de-Bouc at Martigues near Marseille was built by engineer Raymond de Bonnefons under Henri IV. The fort was improved by Vauban in 1664 by the addition of a demi-lune and a covered way. During the Second World War (1939–1945), the fort was used by the Germans as an anti-aircraft artillery position.

CASTLE IF

The small rocky island If is situated off Marseille. If Castle was set up from 1524 to 1529, on King François I's order, as an advanced defensive work but also as a citadel controlling navigation to the harbor. Castle If was a 28 meter square which was flanked with three towers; one of them, tower Saint-Christophe, was higher than the others and acted as a keep and a lighthouse. The fort was fully adapted to firearm weaponry with artillery casemates and port-holes, gun platforms, and thick and roundish breastworks fitted with embrasures.

In 1536, the castle proved its effectiveness by deterring King Carlos V of Spain from attacking Marseille by sea. The fort was briefly taken and occupied by the grand-duke of

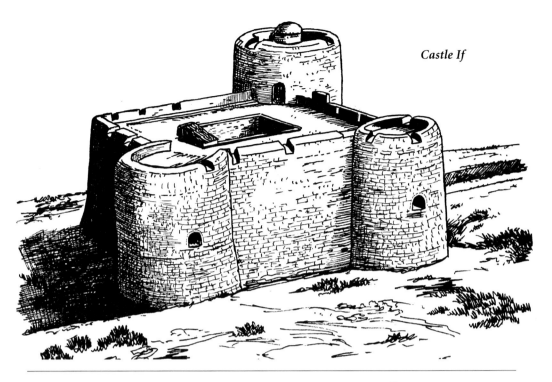

Castle If

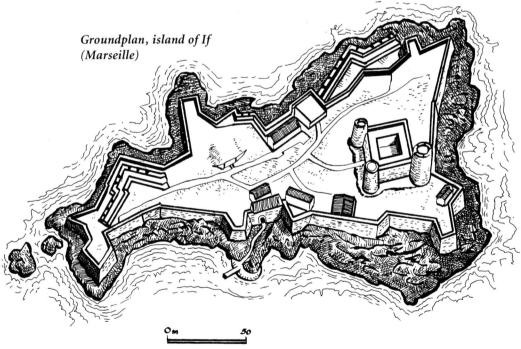

Groundplan, island of If (Marseille)

0m ____ 50

Tuscany in 1698. In 1701, Vauban established batteries and an irregular bastioned enceinte following the island coastline. Castle If later became the prison where the Man with the Iron Mask and many other political prisoners were locked away. Alexandre Dumas brought literary fame to the fortress by imprisoning two of his heroes within it, the count of Monte Cristo and Abbot Faria.

Rousillon

The ancient province of Rousillon today corresponds to the départements of Aude and Pyrénées-Orientales. The Pyrenees Mountains form a natural barrier between France and Spain. The high ridge is only crossable, for an army with artillery, at its ends in the Roussillon (at the Mediterranean Sea side) and in the Basque land (at the Atlantic Ocean side). This border zone and its capital, Perpignan, obviously have an unsettled history. Roussillon was dominated by King Alphonso II of Aragon in 1172, then by the kings of the realm of Majorca in 1272. France occupied the region from 1463 to 1473, then again between 1475 and 1493 under Louis XI, but King Charles VIII gave it back to Spain. Perpignan was vainly besieged by François I in 1542. Richelieu and Louis XIII took the province back again in 1641. Roussillon became officially and permanently French by the Treaty of the Pyrenees in 1659, but many inhabitants were still Spanish at heart. Fortifications in the Rousillon are, of course, to be found principally around Perpignan and in the few passes between France and Spain, as well as along the valleys of the rivers (e.g. the Tech) flowing down the Pyrenees Mountains: Villefranche-de-Conflent, Prats-de-Mollo, Amélie-les-Bains, Fort Bellegarde, Port-Vende and Collioure. Designs and work for the defense of Rousillon only started after Vauban's tour in that region in the spring of 1679, with the emphasis on the especially newly-created fortress of Montlouis. Vauban's main collaborators in this region were engineers Saint-Hillaire, Jean-Baptiste Joblot, Jean de La Vergne, and Christophe Rousselot.

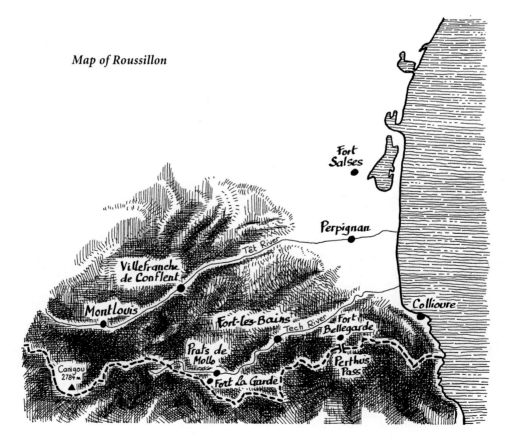

Map of Roussillon

PERPIGNAN

Perpignan, situated in the middle of the Roussillon plain, grew in importance when chosen as a count's residency in the tenth century. From the eleventh to the seventeenth centuries, the fortifications of Perpignan were marked by successive occupiers. At first a wall

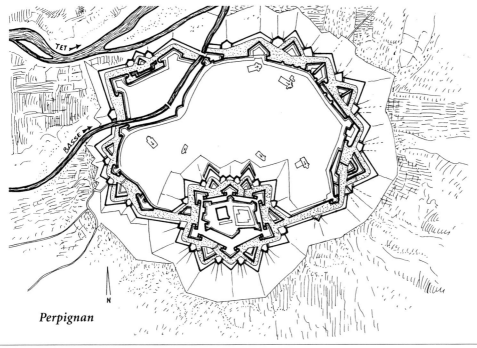

Perpignan

Citadel of Perpignan

was erected around the original village, then a second one was built about 1225. The kings of Majorca constructed a third one in 1330 and the Spanish kings completed the defense between 1535 and 1635. The fortifications of Perpignan were modified by Vauban in 1679 according to a design made in 1669 by engineer Saint-Hillaire. The urban area was enlarged, and seven bastions and five demi-lunes were installed. The work, directed by engineer Christophe Rousselot, lasted from 1679 to 1686. Vauban inspected Perpignan in 1679, again in 1680 accompanied by Louvois, and another time in 1686. The fortifications were dismantled between 1900 and 1930 but fortunately large parts as well as the citadel are preserved.

The citadel had a similar evolution to the urban enceintes. Its core was the castle built about 1277 by King Jaime I. Louis XI of France and Carlos V of Spain added bulwarks enabling the use of firearms. In 1560, Philip II of Spain gave orders to protect the citadel with six massive Italian-style bastions. Finally Vauban completed the fortifications by arranging six demi-lunes, a covered way, an esplanade and a glacis in 1669.

FORT SALSES

Fort Salses has nothing to do with Vauban's work in Roussillon, but it is worth notice as it gives an excellent example of transitional, pre-bastioned fortification totally adapted to the use of firearms. The Spanish Fort Salses is situated sixteen kilometers north of Perpignan in Pyrénées-Orientales. Built by King Ferdinando of Aragon to protect his territory in Roussillon against the French, the fort was designed by engineer Francisco Ramirez, and built between 1497 and 1504. Salses, at the time of its construction, was a remarkable attempt to cope with ballistic weapons, as it was especially designed to use and withstand artillery fire. It is an imposing rectangular fortress 110 meters × 84 meters, including four, low, cylindrical corner towers, outworks placed in the moat (20 meters wide and 7 meters

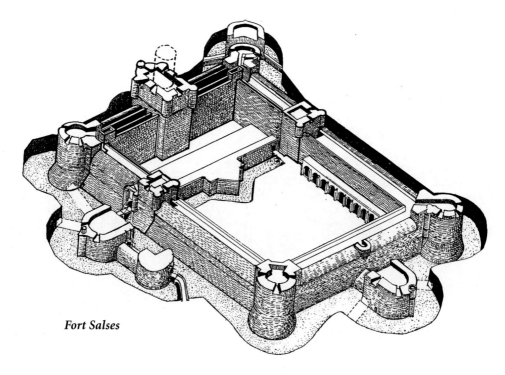

Fort Salses

deep), a double barbican in front of the main gate-house, a reduit with a 20-meter-high dungeon, a large central place of arms and various service buildings (supply-stores, barracks, stables, a chapel and others). Parapets are round to deflect enemy projectiles and fitted with embrasures. Walls and towers are casemated and particularly thick: 10 meters, and after the siege of 1503, their base was enlarged to no less than 14 meters. No doubt Vauban visited Fort Salses, but it is not known what he thought of it. The province of Roussillon became French in 1642, and the impressive fort lost its military border function. Salses was used as a prison and as a powder supply until 1889.

COLLIOURE

The small harbor of Collioure was founded by the Romans and called Cauco Illiberis. It was a stronghold defending the coastal road (Via Domitian) leading to Spain. A strategic site since then and a Mediterranean port of some importance, the town was fortified and a castle (called Château Royal or Château des Templiers) was erected in the twelfth century. The castle was enlarged and re-designed by order of the king of Aragon in 1344. During Carlos V of Spain's reign, the French invasion of 1463 resulted in a reinforcement of the defense. An ancient medieval watchtower situated on a surrounding hill was enlarged and transformed into a detached work named Fort Saint-Elmo. At the same time, Fort Miradou (in the form of a powerful hornwork with short wings) was erected on the north-

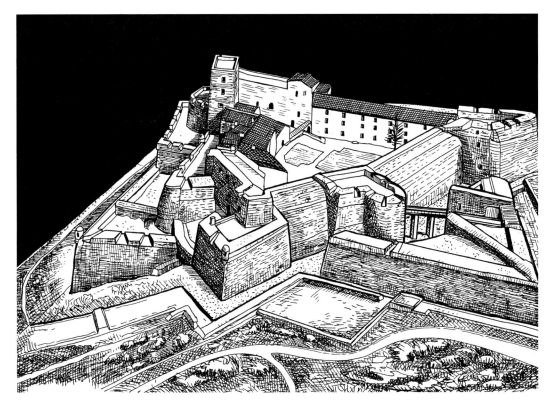

Collioure Castle. The Templar Castle is seen here from the land side, with the demi-lune protecting the entrance.

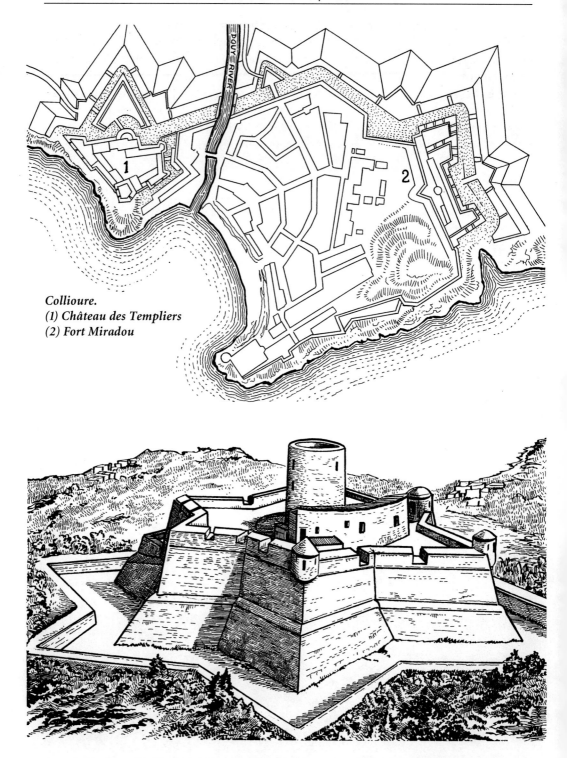

Collioure.
(1) Château des Templiers
(2) Fort Miradou

Fort Saint-Elmo (Collioure). Fort Saint-Elmo, originating from a medieval watchtower, was built by the Spaniards under the reign of King Philip II (1527–1598). Placed on a hill dominating the port of Collioure, it is a tenailled work in the shape of a star.

ern hill dominating the city. Collioure was captured in 1642 and became permanently French after 1659. Originally Vauban had in mind to dismantle Collioure and create a new fortress at Port-Vendres. But due to Louis XIV's and Louvois's insistence, Collioure remained fortified. Between 1668 and 1674, engineer Saint-Hillaire, carrying out a design by Vauban, brought some improvements to the Templar Castle. The curtains of the castle were enlarged, and a demi-lune was built; in addition all the buildings around the château were demolished in order to create a vast glacis. The Notre-Dame-des-Anges parish church having been destroyed by this new arrangement, Louis XIV gave the ground around the lighthouse to the inhabitants, who built a new church. South of Collioure, Vauban ordered the construction of a detached fort on Cape Béar in 1680. Today the city walls have been long dismantled but the Templar Château and the curious lighthouse/church-tower are preserved. Fort Miradou is now a working military fort where commando instructors for the French army, air force and gendarmerie are trained. Fort Saint-Elmo, now private property, sits five hundred feet above the eastern arm of the bay. Beautifully and pleasantly lit at night, it is visible from several miles away.

VILLEFRANCHE-DE-CONFLENT

Situated at the junction of the rivers Cady and Têt, Villefranche occupies a surprising position in a narrow valley giving access to the Cerdagne region. Inhabited by Celtic tribes,

Villefranche-de-Conflent. (1) Cornella bastion; (2) Bastion de La Montagne; (3) Tower du Diable; (4) Bastion de La Reine; (5) Saint-Jean gate; (6) Bastion du Roy; (7) Bastion de La Boucherie; (8) Bastion du Dauphin; (9) Saint-Jacques gate.

the site was occupied by the Romans, the Visigoths, the Muslim Moors from Spain and the Franks. At the end of the ninth century, the counts of Conflent enclosed the small town with a stone wall and in the following two centuries, towers were set up. About 1454, the Spaniards adapted some of these towers to firearms. After 1659, Villefranche became a French outpost facing Spain. In 1679, Vauban re-designed the fortifications by installing six bastions and gate-houses. The town being hopelessly commanded from all heights around it, Vauban decided to occupy one of the hills. On the mountain of Belloch, dominating the town from a 160-meter height, Vauban established a detached work called Fort Libéria. Villefranche remained a military city until 1925. Today all the fortifications are well preserved.

MONTLOUIS

Fortress Montlouis is situated east of Prades. The Treaty of the Pyrenees in 1659 divided the Cerdagne region: Spain kept the Sègre valley with the city of Puycerda, and France obtained the upper River Têt valley. To protect this new acquisition, Louis XIV charged Vauban to create a new fortress. In 1679, Vauban inspected the region, selected several possible places and finally chose a steep, rocky ridge (altitude 1,600 meters), dominating the River Têt and La Perche pass near the Canigou Mountains. The fortress, baptized Montlouis in Louis XIV's honor, was conceived ex nihilo and rapidly completed. Montlouis testifies to Vauban's fantastic capacity to adapt to natural conditions. Due to a steep declivity, the fortress is composed of a square fort with four bastions with orillon, three demi-lunes and a dry ditch. The stronghold dominated a small village surrounded by a line of three bastions and one demi-lune. A third lower part was also planned but was never completed. Today Montlouis, perfectly maintained and preserved, is still occupied by the French army as a commando training base.

Montlouis

PRATS-DE-MOLLO

This small town is situated in the Vallespir region (the valley of the River Tech) dominated by the Costabonne ridge and the Canigou Mountains. It became French by the Treaty of the Pyrenees in 1659. During his tour of inspection in 1679, Vauban gave instructions to engineer Rousselot to reinforce the eastern part of the old Spanish enceinte by the addi-

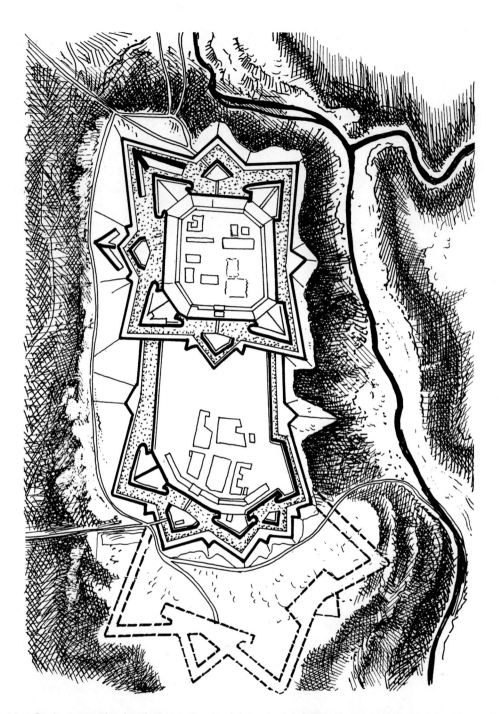

Montlouis, 1679. The sketch shows the citadel (top); the village (in the middle); and a planned extension of the fortress in the form of a crownwork (bottom), designed by Vauban but never built.

tion of three bastioned fronts and two demi-lunes, and by the improvement of the military buildings (the arsenal, watch-post, chapel, store-house and barracks). As an extra defense, he ordered reinforcement of Fort La Garde. Today only a section of rampart is preserved on the southern side of the city facing the Tech.

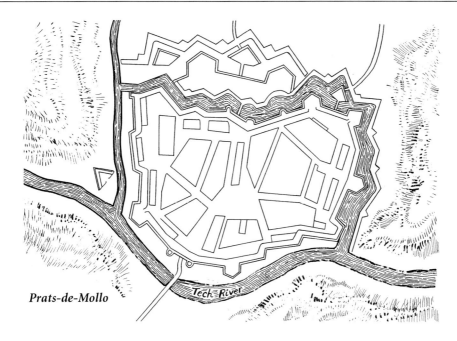

Prats-de-Mollo

FORT LA GARDE

Fort La Garde, east of Prats-de-Mollo, is situated on a narrow spur dominating the town and the valley of the River Tech, through which passes the road leading to the Ares

Fort La Garde, Prats-de-Mollo

pass and Barcelona. Vauban made a design in 1679 to reshape an ancient Spanish castle, adding a low, star-shaped enceinte. The new fort was completed about 1682. A protected communication path connecting it to the town below in the valley was built in 1851. The fort was abandoned by the army in June 1907. Today, Fort La Garde is well preserved.

FORT DES BAINS

The small stronghold of Fort des Bains, situated near the spa town of Amelie-les-Bains, was an ancient Spanish fort. Situated on the Montbolo road in the valley of the River Tech, the fort was reshaped by engineer Saint-Hilaire in 1670 by order of the count de Chamilly. It was composed of a central building for accommodating the garrison and a square enceinte with four bastions at the corners. During a tour of inspection in 1697, Vauban declared that the fort was no good at all, particularly the over-exposed barracks and the poor flanking capacity. As Vauban considered the place of little importance, the fort was left it as it was. The fort still exists today and is now private property.

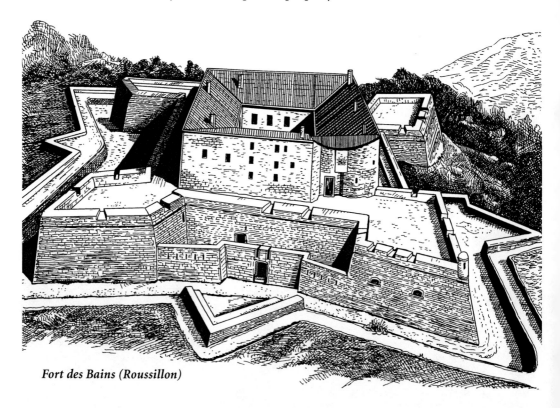

Fort des Bains (Roussillon)

FORT BELLEGARDE

Fort Bellegarde is situated near Le Perthus and enables control of the important Perthus pass. Bellegarde was originally a Spanish castle which was taken by the French in 1674 and which was re-designed in 1679 by engineer Rousselot. The ancient castle keep was destroyed and four bastions, three demi-lunes, and a covered way with places of arms were erected. Today Fort Bellegarde is well preserved.

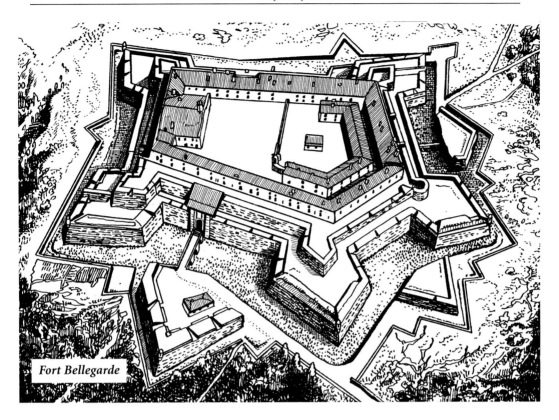

Fort Bellegarde

Western Pyrenees

The western part of the Pyrenees, near the Atlantic Ocean, formed a barrier between France and the Iberian Peninsula. That region was composed of several historically distinct territories.

Gascogne is the ancient land of the tribe of the Vasconii (Basques). The land grew to a duchy in the seventh century, which was annexed to Aquitaine in 1036. This huge part of southwestern France became the property of King Henry II (Plantagenêt) of England after his marriage with Duchess Eleanor in 1152. Aquitaine, better known in English as Guyenne, was eagerly disputed between England and France for centuries and finally became French in 1453.

Navarre is the small region around Saint-Jean-Pied-de-Port, at the foot of Roncevaux pass. The territory grew to a kingdom in the eleventh century with its capital Pamplona in Spain. King Henri de Bourbon of Navarre became King Henri IV of France in 1598. Henri IV was Louis XIV's grandfather and all Bourbon French sovereigns were called "king of France and Navarre."

Béarn, with its capital Pau, successively belonged to the lords of Foix, Albret and to the kingdom of Navarre. The small province became permanently French in 1620.

The numerous conflicts between France and Spain resulted in several fortified points on the passes along the Atlantic coast and in the Pyrenees. In this region, Vauban was assisted by engineer François Ferry (1649–1701). Ferry was knighted and promoted to the rank of ingénieur-général (general engineer) of the provinces Poitou, Saintonge, Aunis,

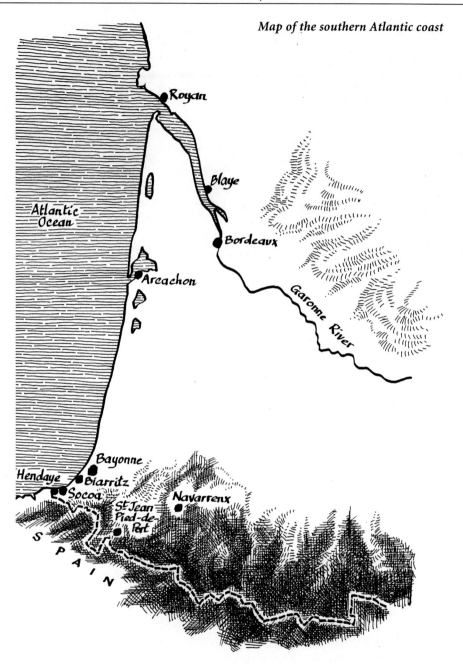

Map of the southern Atlantic coast

Guyenne and Béarn in 1683. The talented chevalier de Ferry carried out most of Vauban's plans on the Atlantic coast.

BAYONNE

Bayonne is situated at the junction of the Rivers Nive and Adour. In the first century B.C., the town was already fortified by the Romans. Successively invaded and occupied by the Visigoths, the Basques, the Moors (Spanish Muslims) and the Northmen (Vikings), the

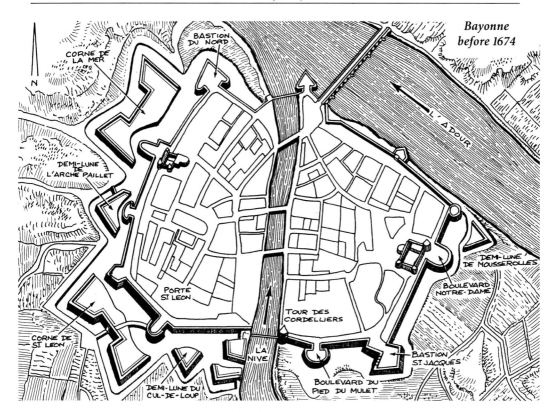

Bayonne before 1674

city gained in importance and wealth in the eleventh century. The ancient Roman fortifications were rebuilt and modernized in the Middle Ages by order of the Catholic bishops and by the viscounts of Labourd. After Eleanor of Aquitaine's marriage with Henry Plantagenêt, Bayonne passed under English domination until 1451. During the numerous Franco-Spanish wars that occurred in the sixteenth and seventeenth centuries, Bayonne was fortified on King François I's order between 1520 and 1530, and artillery-bulwarks and barbicans were set up. Under Henri IV's reign, engineer Jean Errard made a new bastioned design which was partly carried out. In 1636, Bayonne was menaced by a Spanish invasion and temporary forts were erected on the surrounding hills (Saint-Esprit, Saint-Jean and Castelnau). Once the danger was gone those works were dismantled. About 1650, engineer Dubois d'Avencour arranged two hornworks. Bayonne's fortifications were again improved by engineer Théodore Boucheron in 1672 and again reinforced in 1674 because of a threat by the Dutch fleet.

Between 1674 and 1676, the ingénieur-général of fortifications of provinces Aunis and Saintonge, Deshoulières, made new improvements, but an exceptionally violent flood of the River Nive in 1677 brought serious destruction. In early 1680, Vauban was on inspection tour and, assisted by François Ferry, decided to make Bayonne the central defensive point of the whole region. As a result, curtains and breastworks were thickened; bastions got foundations; fire fields were cleared; outworks, a covered way and a wide glacis were built; and the River Nive was channeled by batardeaus and sluices. On the opposite bank of the River Adour, on top of the Saint-Esprit hill, Vauban and Ferry built a powerful square citadel with four bastions and outworks. Bayonne's fortifications, completed in 1694, are partly preserved today.

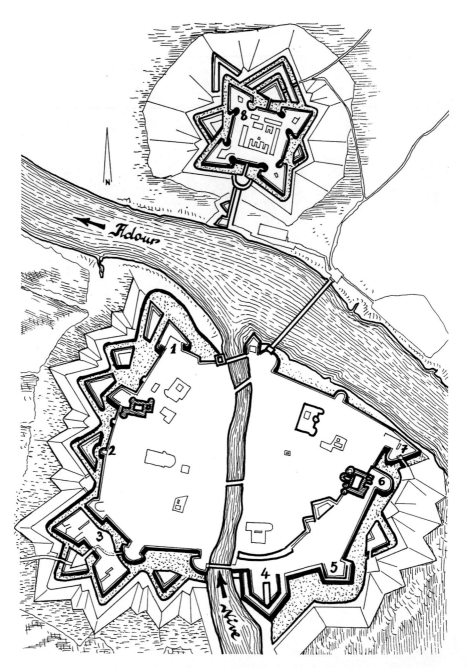

Bayonne after 1674. (1) Northern bastion; (2) L'Arche-Paillet demi-lune; (3) Saint-Leon gate and hornwork; (4) Pied-du-Mulet bastion; (5) Saint-Jacques bastion; (6) Notre-Dame bulwark; (7) Mousserolles gate and bastion; (8) Castelnau citadel on Saint-Esprit hill.

FORT SOCOA

Fort Socoa, situated on a rocky cape, protected the harbor of Cibourne in the bay of Saint-Jean-de-Luz. A defensive work on that place had already been planned at the time of Henri IV, but it was the Spaniards who built a stronghold with a watchtower, named the Fort of Castille, in 1636, during the Thirty Years' War. When the territory was retaken by the French, Vauban made a design in 1686 which was carried out by his assistant Fleury later in 1698. The ruins of the old work were transformed into a massive, circular, three-story tower crowned by an artillery platform and embrasures. The impressive tower formed the reduit of a fort composed of an enceinte, two low batteries, a barrack, a commander's house, a guardhouse and a chapel. Completed about 1723, Fort Socoa is a good example of the utilization of a medieval-style tower in classical bastioned fortification. The fort was taken by Spanish forces in 1793 and occupied by the British in 1814. It was repaired in 1816 and still exists today.

Socoa tower

Fort Socoa

HENDAYE

Hendaye is a border town between Spain and France located on the River Bidassoa. In 1618, the count of Gramont, on King Louis XIII's order, built a square tower dominating the bay, to which a gun battery was added in 1663 by engineer Poupart. In 1686 Vauban transformed the tower into a redoubt surrounded by thick curtains, a lower battery, a ditch defended by two caponiers and a covered way. In front of the gate, Vauban installed a guardhouse in a redan and a drawbridge. The fort of Hendaye was attacked and destroyed by the Spaniards in 1793. The ruins were dismantled and the site sold in February 1853 to a certain Pascault for the sum of 26,050 francs. Today only the name Place du Vieux Fort (ancient fort square) remains of the old city fortification.

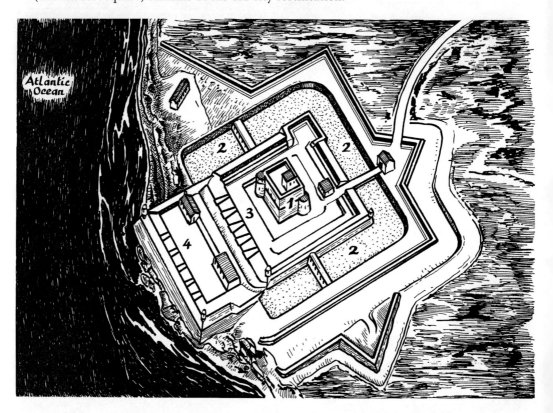

Possible layout of Fort Hendaye (from a drawing by Lomet in 1793 and a cadastral map of 1820). (1) Ancient tower; (2) ditch defended by two caponiers; (3) upper gun battery; (4) lower gun battery.

Defenses of Bordeaux

CHÂTEAU TROMPETTE

Bordeaux, situated in the Gironde, is the ancient fortified capital (oppidum) of the Gallic tribe Biturges. In the Middle Ages, the city was the capital of the rich province Aquitaine, which was under English domination for three centuries, from 1152 until the

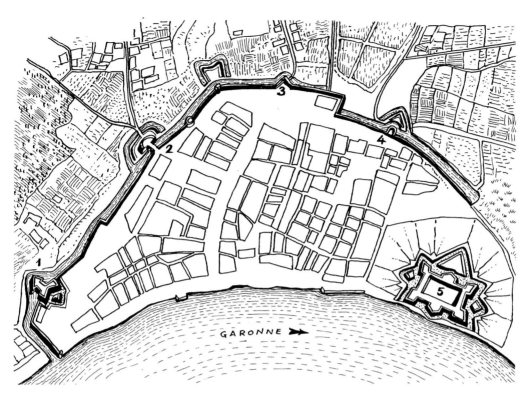

Bordeaux circa 1685. (1) Fort Sainte-Croix; (2) Aquitaine gate; (3) ancient castle; (4) Dijeaux-gate; (5) citadel Château-Trompette.

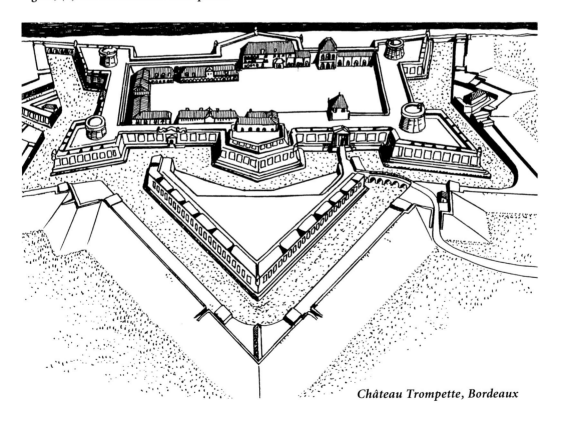

Château Trompette, Bordeaux

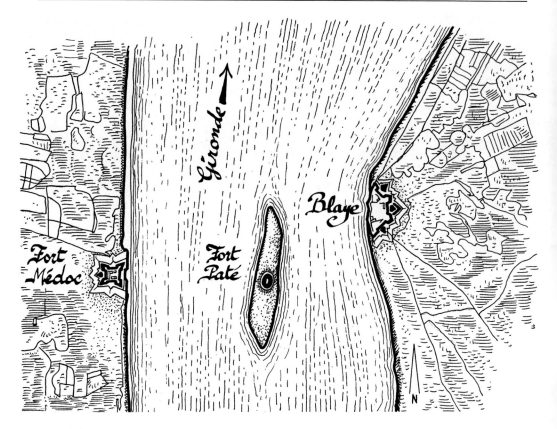

Defense of Bordeaux. The map shows the Gironde estuary with forts Médoc, Paté and Blaye.

end of the Hundred Years War in 1453. Medieval Bordeaux was defended by three successive stone walls and towers. During Louis XIV's reign, the rich city's defense was secured
by three forts built in the large mouth of the Gironde: Fort Médoc, on the left bank of the
Gironde; Fort Paté, in the middle of the estuary and Fortress Blaye, on the right bank. Louis
XIV, who distrusted the wealthy and anglophile population, ordered the establishment of
a citadel called Château Trompette inside the town. Built in 1660, and reshaped in 1671 and
1681 under engineers Poupart and Nicolas Payen, the citadel looked like a theater setting.
Highly decorated, Château Trompette was a regular rectangle with six bastions, to which
a vast counterguard, two demi-lunes and a ditch were added. The beautiful Château-
Trompette was alas demolished to make room for the existing square named Esplanade des
Quinconces. Today there remains only a remarkable relief map exhibited at the army
museum in the Hôtel des Invalides in Paris.

Blaye

    Situated on a rocky cape dominating the Gironde, the site of Blaye was already cho-
sen by the Romans in the fourth century to be a *castrum*, which they called Blavia. In the
Middle Ages, Blaye belonged to the county of Angoulême and became a halting-place for
pilgrims en route to Santiago de Compostella in Spain. In the twelfth century the lords of
Rudel built an irregular castle with four towers and a ditch. During the Hundred Years War,

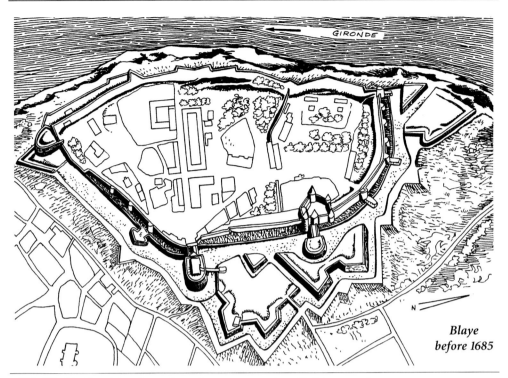

Blaye
before 1685

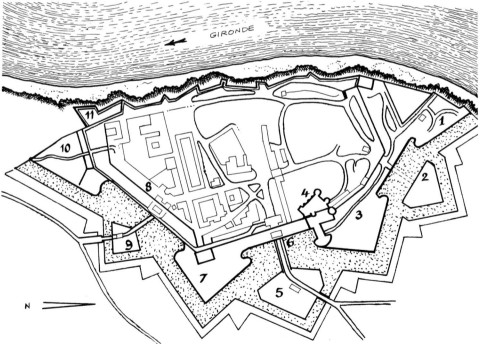

Blaye after 1685. (1) Bastion of Cônes; (2) demi-lune of château; (3) bastion of château; (4) ruins of Lord Rudel's castle; (5) Royal demi-lune; (6) Royal gate; (7) Bastion Saint-Romain; (8) Dauphine gate; (9) Dauphine demi-lune; (10) Bastion of Port; (11) artillery battery directed towards the Gironde.

Blaye was a disputed fortress belonging to the duke of Lancaster and King Edward I. Castle and city became French in 1451. During the Wars of Religion, Blaye was occupied by the Huguenots in 1568 and re-taken by the royal Catholic forces in 1592. The fortress, half destroyed and abandoned, was repaired and modernized between 1630 and 1652, on Louis XIII's order by governor Claude de Saint-Simon. The famous memorialist's father, Saint-Simon established two artillery bulwarks, two hornworks, a fausse-braie and a dry ditch flanked with five "moineaux" (sort of caponiers, small masonry works with firing ports extending across the ditch). Vauban made a design in November 1685. He installed a battery with artillery turned towards the Gironde and improved the land-front; both hornworks were dismantled and replaced by demi-lunes and a covered way; the main enceinte was reinforced by two bastions, two gate-houses and two half-bastions. Blaye was militarized, the civilian population was expelled, and barracks and an arsenal were constructed. Vauban's plan was carried out by engineer François Ferry from 1686 to 1689. Blaye remained in military use up to 1943 and is now well preserved.

Because of the limited artillery range of the time, Vauban decided to build two other strongholds in order to cover the wide Gironde: Fort Paté in the middle of the river and the trapeze-shaped Fort Médoc on the left bank. Fort Medoc had a powerful battery firing towards the river and four bastions to defend the land-front.

FORT PATÉ

The construction of Fort Paté was ordered by Vauban in 1691. Fort Paté is a massive, oval, masonry, casemated tower with a height of 12 meters, topped with a terrace protected

Fort Paté

by a thick breastwork fitted with embrasures. The fort could house about 30 guns, which could fire in all directions.

Together with forts Blaye and Médoc, Fort Paté completed the advance defensive position of Bordeaux, blocking by crossfire the access to the port. Fort Paté, with its pure roundish forms, does not conform at all to one of the "three systems" conventionally attributed to Vauban's style.

The fort was set up on a shifting sandbank in the middle of the Gironde, and because of the instability of the terrain, Vauban and Ferry were obliged to establish complicated and strong foundations requiring two layers of timber to be immersed in the water for a year before building could start. The construction was completed in 1695. Although the tower suddenly sank two meters down in the soft mud in 1707, Fort Paté is today well preserved.

FORT MÉDOC

Fort Médoc, together with Blaye and Fort Paté, formed a barrier to seal off the Gironde estuary in order to prevent an attack on Bordeaux via the river. Built in 1690, it was a rectangular fort with a bastion at each corner. The ditch could be flooded using sluices that connected to the Gironde. The main part of the fort was the battery looking out over the estuary.

Inside the fort there were barracks, supply stores, a bakery, and a chapel for the garrison of 300. Fort Médoc lost its military role in 1916. Abandoned for decades, it has been restored by a local association, and can be visited today.

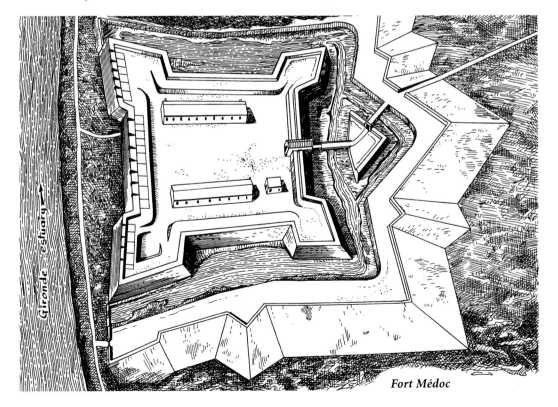

Fort Médoc

Defenses of the Pertuis

The pertuis are straits between the French Atlantic islands off La Rochelle and Rochefort. The pertuis of Antioche is situated between the isles of Ré and Oléron, the pertuis Breton between Ré and the mainland of Vendée. The defense of these islands was already a necessity in François I's time because of insecurity caused by raiders and pirates of all nationalities, especially English and Dutch. The islands had great strategic importance because of their closeness to the continent. If conquered and occupied by any enemy, they formed a

Map of the
Pertuis islands

threat to this part of the French kingdom. During the Wars of Religion and Louis XIII's reign, the important harbor of La Rochelle was dominated by the Protestants and their Anglo-Dutch allies. Besides, the rich haven of Brouage, owing its wealth to the exploitation of salt, had to be protected. Moreover, the military harbor and the maritime arsenal of Rochefort were created in 1666. All these reasons explain the particularly high number of fortifications in the region.

LA ROCHELLE

La Rochelle, capital of the small province Aunis (today department Charente-Maritime), was founded in 1130 by Duke Guillaume II of Aquitaine. After more than two

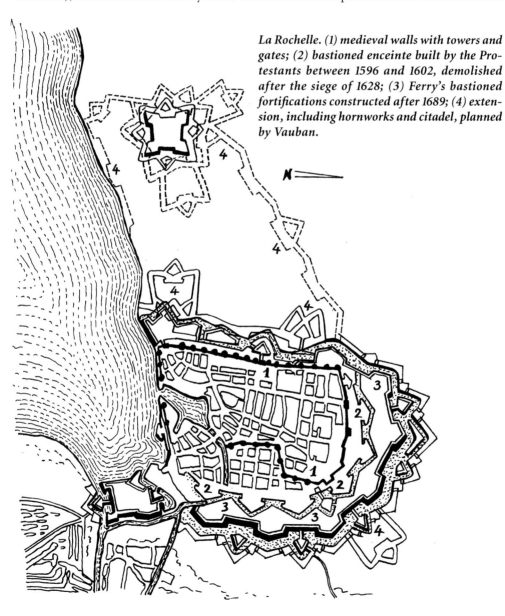

La Rochelle. (1) medieval walls with towers and gates; (2) bastioned enceinte built by the Protestants between 1596 and 1602, demolished after the siege of 1628; (3) Ferry's bastioned fortifications constructed after 1689; (4) extension, including hornworks and citadel, planned by Vauban.

centuries of English domination, La Rochelle became French in 1372. About 1500, artillery bulwarks were erected in front of the four medieval gate-houses. La Rochelle was the main Protestant center, nicknamed "French Geneva," and hastily fortified between 1558 and 1568 during the first Religious War. The promulgation of the Edict of Nantes in 1598 put an end to these civil wars and guaranteed the freedom of worship. However the edict preserved the status-quo rather than being a real peace treaty. The Protestants were allowed to maintain armed forces and fortified "places of security," notably Montpellier, Castres, Lunel, Bergerac and, of course, La Rochelle. In a background of civil war, La Rochelle's defenses were completely renewed between 1596 and 1602 by the construction of modern, Italian-style bastioned fortifications and two detached works: Fort Louis west of the town and Fort Tasdon in the south. During Louis XIII's reign, the independence of the Protestant center, supported by the Anglo-Dutch, was an unbearable thorn in Richelieu's side: "Satan's synagogue"—as the cardinal called it—was besieged and taken in 1628. For the purpose of permanently stopping Protestant military independence, Louis XIII and Richelieu ordered the demolition of all Huguenot strongholds, and the fortifications of La Rochelle were dismantled except the sea front and the gate-houses. In 1689, Louis XIV, fearing English raids, decided to rebuild the defenses of La Rochelle. The work was entrusted to the director of fortifications of the province Aunis, François Ferry. The project included a large bastioned enceinte, a ditch, outworks and a covered way. Vauban designed a city extension with defensive hornworks in front of the main gates, and planned the creation of a citadel, but this project was not retained. Today La Rochelle has preserved medieval works (Saint-Nicolas tower, La Chaîne tower and La Lanterne tower). As for Ferry's bastioned tracé, it is visible in the western part of the old city (Cherruyer Park). During the Second World War, La Rochelle was an important German submarine base, protected by a huge concrete bunker built by the Nazi building company Organisation Todt.

BROUAGE

The importance of Brouage was actually more economic than military because of its harbor, which enabled the transport of the precious salt collected in the surrounding salt-pans. In 1555, Jacques de Pons, baron of Mirambeau and lord of Hiers, founded a new city to which he gave his name: Jacopolis-sur-Brouage. During the Religious Wars, Catholics and Protestants eagerly fought for the economic, naval and military facilities offered by the small-but-rich town. Brouage was fortified in 1569 by Italian engineers Francesco Orologio, Bephano, Castriccio d'Urbino and Bernardino Riviero da Colle (nicknamed Bellamarto). In June 1570, the Protestant forces, commanded by Count La Rochefoucauld, besieged the town, which surrendered on 11 July. Fortifications were further constructed from 1570 to 1575 by engineer Robert de Chinon. Brouage was re-taken by the royal Catholic forces led by the duke of Mayenne in August 1577. At the beginning of the seventeenth century, Richelieu gave a vigorous boost to Brouage, and that was not without self-interest, as the cardinal was governor of the place and pocketed very substantial income from taxes on salt. In 1628, Pierre de Conty, lord of La Mothe d'Argencourt, the royal engineer for provinces Aunis, Poitou and Saintonge, assisted by master builder Jean Thiriot, designed the existing bastioned enceinte. Brouage's external perimeter, flanked by six bastions, is 2.5 km. in total length. In 1640, Richelieu's stronghold was reinforced by two hornworks. The fortifications of Brouage were improved by Vauban in 1685, who ordered the

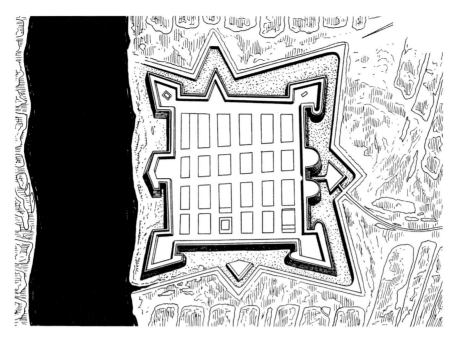

Brouage before 1628

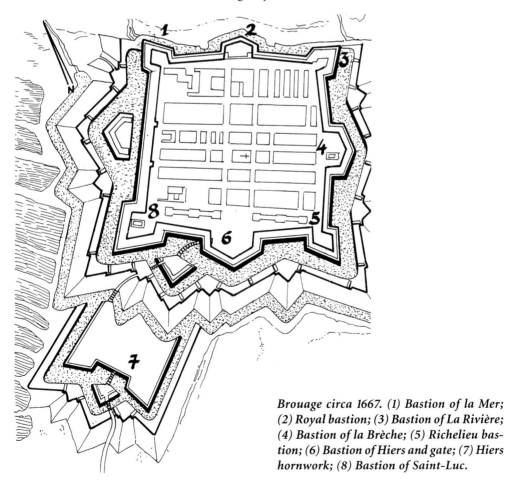

Brouage circa 1667. (1) Bastion of la Mer; (2) Royal bastion; (3) Bastion of La Rivière; (4) Bastion of la Brèche; (5) Richelieu bastion; (6) Bastion of Hiers and gate; (7) Hiers hornwork; (8) Bastion of Saint-Luc.

demolition of both hornworks (replaced by a demi-lune), the dredging of silted-up canals, the thickening of breastworks and the piercing of embrasures, the modifying of bastion slopes, the installation of beautiful echauguettes, the transformation of the powder house and the establishment of an ice-factory. Colbert considered creating a new military arsenal in Brouage but because of silting problems the site of Rochefort was preferred in 1666. That marked the start of Brouage's decline. Today Brouage is a tourist center in a unique, flat, salt-marsh landscape.

RÉ ISLAND

Ré is a 30 km.-long island off La Rochelle. Constantly disputed and invaded from the Middle Ages to the Napoleonic period, fortifications are particularly numerous.

The Fort de La Prée is the oldest work on the island. The fort was built in 1625, by order of Jean du Caylar de Saint-Bonnet, marshal of Toiras, and work was carried out by engineer Le Camus and Pierre de Conty, lord of la Mothe d'Argencourt, royal engineer for provinces Aunis, Poitou and Saintonge. The fort is situated on the northern shore, in a favorable anchorage 5 km. from the continent near the village of La Flotte-en-Ré. The fort was composed of four bastions linked by very curious round curtains, an envelope, a ditch and a small harbor. In 1672, chevalier de Clerville constructed counterguards and demi-lunes. Vauban sharply condemned the design of the fort with its ridiculous and inefficient curtains and above all the absence of a water supply. He ordered the demolition of the out-

Fort de la Prée in 1628

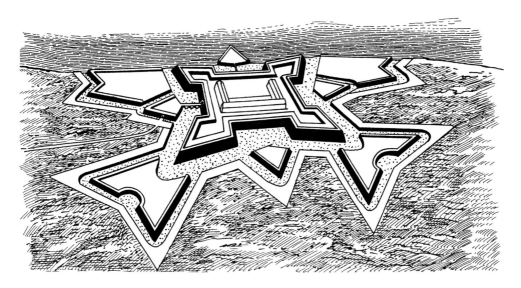

Saint-Martin-de-Ré citadel (circa 1629). The citadel was built in 1624 and demolished in 1629.

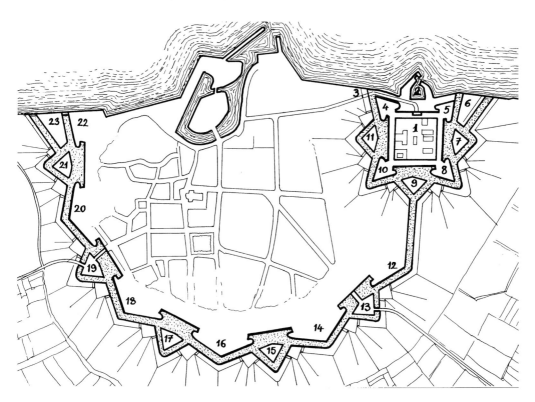

Groundplan, Saint-Martin-de-Ré. (1) Citadel; (2) citadel harbor; (3) city gate; (4) King's bastion; (5) Dauphin bastion; (6) Dauphin half-counterguard; (7) France demi-lune; (8) France bastion; (9) communication demi-lune; (10) La Reine bastion; (11) Saint-Martin demi-lune; (12) La Flotte bastion; (13) La Flotte demi-lune and Toiras gate; (14) Saint-Louis bastion with cavalier; (15) Saint-Louis demi-lune; (16) Sainte-Thérèse bastion; (17) Bourgogne demi-lune; (18) Bourgogne bastion with cavalier; (19) La Couarde demi-lune and Campani gate; (20) Bourbon bastion; (21) Bourbon demi-lune; (22) Ormeau or de la Mer bastion with cavalier; (23) Ormeau half-counterguard.

Redoute des Portes (Ré Island)

works in 1684. Today the fort is well preserved and displays a unique and peculiar form of military architecture.

The village of Saint-Martin-de-Ré is situated on the northern coast of the island, enabling communication with the continent. The small village and its harbor were already defended by a castle in the Middle Ages. In 1624, near the village, engineer d'Argencourt built a square bastioned fort surrounded by a fausse-braie, three demi-lunes, two swallow-tails and two bishop's miters. During Richelieu's campaign against the Protestants of La Rochelle in 1627, Saint-Martin was attacked by the British fleet commanded by Lord Buckingham. The fort was completely dismantled after La Rochelle's capitulation in 1629. With the creation of the new naval arsenal at Rochefort in 1666, Ré Island regained its strategic importance. Saint-Martin-de-Ré was re-fortified by Vauban and his collaborator Ferry from 1681 on. Vauban built a citadel because a part of the population was still Protestant and could be tempted to help the Anglo-Dutch. The citadel was a 280-meter square with four bastions, a half-counterguard, three demi-lunes, a ditch, a covered way and a fortified haven. A gate facing the sea gave access to the citadel, which contained a central place of arms, various service buildings, an officers' house, an arsenal and barracks for about 1,200 men.

The village Saint-Martin-de-Ré was defended as well by a vast enceinte. Prefiguring the concept of "entrenched camp," the fortifications enclosed a wide area intended to shelter the whole civilian population of the island with its cattle and goods in time of war. The bastioned enceinte still exists today. It forms a large bow with six bastions, five demi-lunes, a ditch, a covered way and a glacis. The enceinte has two similar monumental gatehouses

Redoute du Martray (Ré)

(Porte des Campani and Porte Toiras) fitted with portcullis and swing-back drawbridges. Citadel and urban enceinte, built together in a row and without site constraints, form a very harmonious ensemble and give a beautiful example of Vauban's "first system."

The redoubt of Portes, situated on the most northern point of Ré, was constructed in 1673. It was a 38-meter square battery surrounded by a ditch. The work has been abandoned since 1854.

The redoubt of Martray was set up in 1674 on a narrow sand bank, a passage controlling both parts of Ré Island. It was a 50-meter square work surrounded by a 10-meter broad and 3-meter deep ditch. The redoubt was fitted with a small barrack, a powder house and a drawbridge. It was surrounded by an enceinte reinforced by two hornworks and two redans; the advance works were dismantled by Vauban in 1685.

The redoubt of Sablanceaux is situated on the point of Sablanceaux, southeast of Ré, facing La Rochelle's harbor, called La Pallice. The site, being a favorable anchorage, was fortified in 1673 by a fortlet. The redoubt Sablanceaux was a 50-meter square masonry work surrounded by a ditch. The fortlet, armed with about twelve guns, contained a barrack, a powder house and a well. In 1701, the fire capacity of the redoubt was increased by a gun battery made of earth.

ROCHEFORT

The French Atlantic coasts being constantly threatened by Anglo-Dutch raiders, Colbert (Louis XIV's navy secretary) decided to create a completely new military harbor to

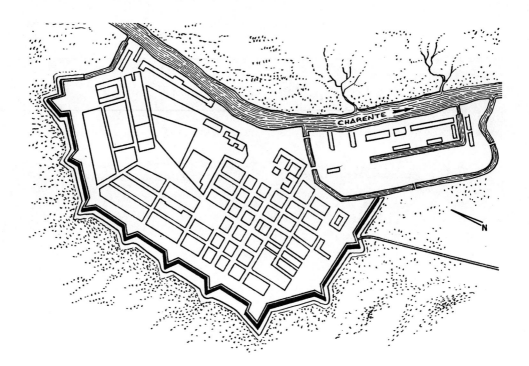

Groundplan, Rochefort 1677

Redoute de l'Aiguille. The redoubt of Aiguille, erected on the narrow point of the same name, was constructed in 1673 in order to defend the Aix road. It was a rectangular earthwork, 58 meters broad and 70 meters long, without bastions, surrounded by a ditch. The redoubt was reveted with masonry in the eighteenth century.

***Castle Fouras.** The Castle of Fouras, dating from the eleventh century, is placed on a small peninsula dominating the estuary of the River Charente. Its rectangular keep (30 meters high), rebuilt in 1480, was surrounded by a stone enceinte and towers. Fouras was used as a base for Richelieu's army during the siege of La Rochelle in 1628. In 1689, engineer Ferry repaired the medieval keep, thickened the walls and established gun embrasures as well as an outer low battery to command the Charente River. In 1705, engineer Girval built a barrack for 150 soldiers. Today the castle is completely preserved and houses a regional art museum.*

replace the silting-up Brouage. In 1666, he selected a place called Rochefort, situated 15 km. inland on the River Charente. Well protected against storms by the islands Ré, Aix and Oléron and by capes easy to fortify (Fouras and Le Chapus), the new harbor was designed by Colbert du Terron (the navy secretary's nephew), by architect François Blondel and by Director-General Louis Nicolas de Clerville. They gave the new city a regular chessboard pattern and built a huge naval complex on the Charente bank, including docks, an arsenal, shipyards, a foundry, a smithy, various smith workshops, saw-yards, a cooper's workshop, a vast rope factory and huge stores. In 1671, Rochefort already had 20,000 inhabitants, most of them working for the French royal navy. However the new port appeared to be a failure because of its location too far inland. Because the harbor lacked depth, big ships could not be armed there but had be tugged to the bay of Aix. A Dutch attack in 1674 prompted the decision to fortify the military town. The construction of the enceinte gave rise to a quarrel between Jean-Baptiste Colbert (navy) and François-Michel Le Tellier (War Department). Finally Rochefort's fortifications were designed by chevalier de Clerville and built by the army. Completed in 1690, they included half-bastions, redans and a long straight

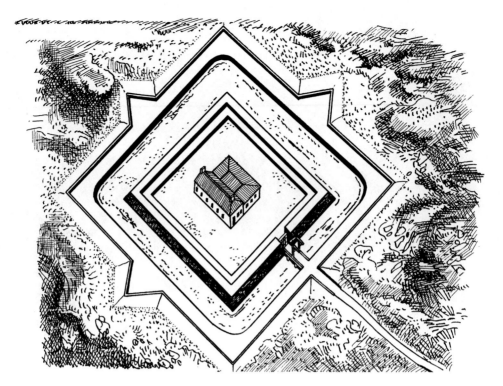

Redoute Île Madame. The fortlet of Île Madame, placed on an islet one kilometer off the mouth of the River Charente, was set up in 1703. The fort, actually a simple redoubt, was a 36-meter-square reveted stronghold surrounded by a ditch and a covered way. The terreplein was fitted with a barrack, a powder house and a cannonball oven.

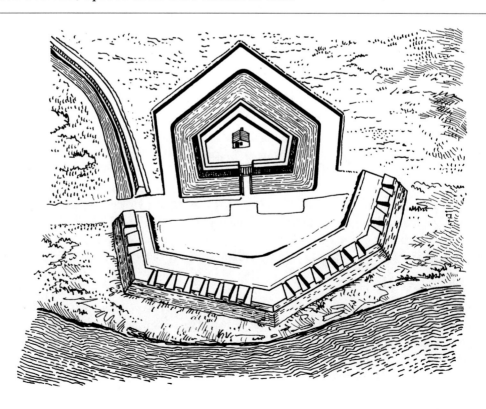

curtain surrounded by a 2.50-meter ditch. However the actual defense of town, harbor and arsenal was effected from detached works placed along the Charente's mouth, on the sea coast and on the islands. Rochefort remained in military use until 1927 and today many vestiges of its defenses are preserved.

AIX ISLAND

The small island Aix, situated between Oléron Island and the continent, dominates a narrow straight called the pertuis of Antioche. Aix formed an advance defense for the impor-

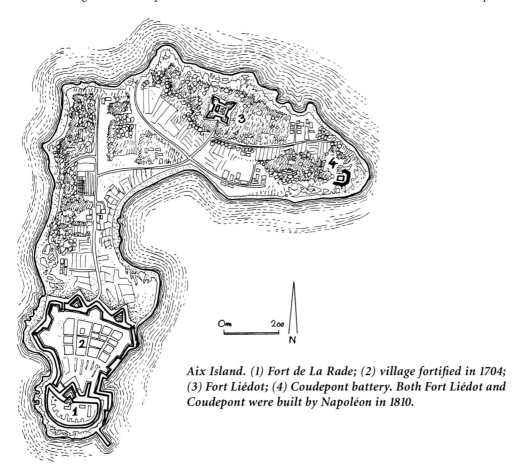

Aix Island. (1) Fort de La Rade; (2) village fortified in 1704; (3) Fort Liédot; (4) Coudepont battery. Both Fort Liédot and Coudepont were built by Napoléon in 1810.

Opposite: Fort de la Pointe. Fort de la Pointe was constructed in 1672 on the right bank of the River Charente. It was composed of a low, V-shaped battery defended by a demi-lune in the gorge. Fort Lupin (see the illustration in Chapter 4 regarding coastal forts) was erected on the left bank of the River Charente halfway between Rochefort and the Atlantic Ocean. Created in 1684 to defend the access to Rochefort, Fort Lupin still exists today. It is a typical Vauban coastal fort with a 72-meter-wide semi-circular battery with a parapet pierced with 22 embrasures. A square tower, placed in the gorge, constitutes a reduit and two contiguous small buildings give shelter to gunners and ammunition. The fort is surrounded by a wet ditch and a covered way. Fort Lupin was renovated in 1812 and 1838, then transformed into an ammunition store in 1881. Classified as an historical monument in 1950, the fort is now private property.

tant harbors of Brouage, La Rochelle and Rochefort. The southern Sainte-Catherine cape was the object of several plans by navy captain Descombes in 1690 and by engineer François Ferry in 1691. But it was finally Vauban in 1692 who designed the Fort de la Rade. This coastal work was composed of a wide, low, semi-circular battery armed with 75 cannons turned towards the sea and a 20 meter high tower built in the gorge. On the land-front, battery and tower were protected by a wet ditch and a demi-lune. Unfortunately the tower, probably ill-constructed, collapsed almost as soon as it was completed; it was then rebuilt in 1699. Fort de la Rade was completed in 1703. The following year, the small village contiguous to the fort was also fortified by a bastioned enceinte. In July 1815, the small village was the place where Napoléon I lived for a while. The destitute French emperor envisaged emigrating to the United States, but finally surrendered to the British, who detained him until his death in 1821 on the Atlantic island of Saint-Helena.

FORT BOYARD

After the foundation of the arsenal of Rochefort in 1666, Clerville advocated the construction of a fort in the middle of the sea to control Aix. He chose a rocky bank (called Banjaert or Boyard) situated halfway between Oléron and Aix islands. Descombes made a plan in 1692 but because of very high expenses and insurmountable technical difficulties, the project was abandoned. However Fort Boyard, an immovable masonry ship, would be built much later in 1857.

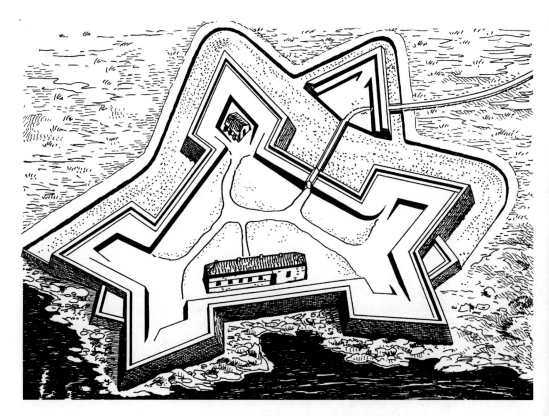

Citadel Château d'Oléron, built in 1633

Oléron Island

The island of Oléron (Charente-Maritime) is situated in the Atlantic Ocean off La Rochelle and off the mouth of the River Charente. The fortifications of Château d'Oléron,

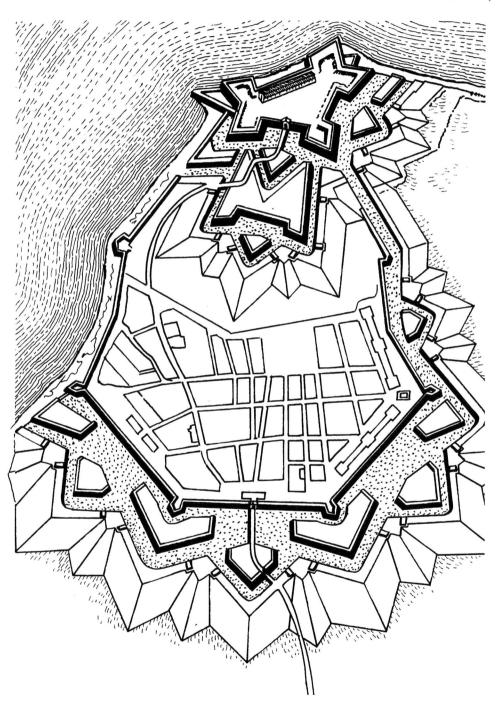

Château d'Oléron. Vauban's enceinte enclosing the village was never completed.

the main village on the island, were marked by misfortune and lack of skill. In 1633, engineer Pierre de Conty d'Argencourt was entrusted by Cardinal Richelieu to edify a citadel. D'Argencourt designed a fort with two bastioned fronts on the landside and two casemated half-bastions facing the sea. In 1673, Louis Nicolas de Clerville, Vauban's rival, was appointed governor of Oléron and added a bastioned envelope to d'Argencourt's citadel. Vauban designed two projects for Oléron in 1674 and in 1685. He modified certain bastions, constructed a hornwork in the surrounding marshes and built another hornwork on the landfront, which brought with it the destruction of a part of the village and the forced departure of the population. The work was done hastily and disorderly, leading to a costly failure. The hornworks built in the marsh sank in the mud and a part of the ill-constructed citadel was damaged by a storm in 1689. One year later, Vauban conceived a bastioned enceinte based on his "second system" to enclose the whole village with four bastioned towers and large counterguards. The expensive works began in 1699 but the construction was interrupted in 1704, leaving unfinished fortifications.

FORT CHAPUS

Fort Chapus, also called Fort Louvois, is situated on the continent on the Bourcefranc Cape facing the village and the citadel of Château d'Oléron. The work was constructed by François Ferry in 1691 and completed by engineer Henri-Albert Bouillet in 1694. Intended to defend the strait of Maumusson and the mouth of the River Seudre, Fort Chapus is

Fort Chapus

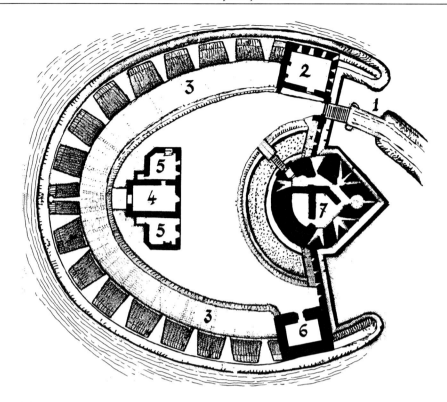

Groundplan, Fort Chapus. (1) Access passage submerged at high tide; (2) guardhouse and barrack; (3) artillery battery with parapet and embrasures; (4) arsenal and artillery-store; (5) gunners' quarters; (6) powder house; (7) keep tower with ditch.

placed on a rocky bank 400 meters in the sea and connected to the mainland by a passage, which can only be used at low tide. It is composed of an oval, low gun battery (78 meters in diameter), a three-story tower in the gorge and various service buildings on its semi-circular terreplein. The fort was renovated in 1875. Although damaged occurred as a result of combat in April 1945, Fort Chapus today is well preserved, and houses an oyster-farming museum.

Bretagne (Brittany) and Normandy

The Armorican peninsula became Bretagne (called Brittany in English) when the Gaelic population fled from Great Britain during the Danish invasions in the fifth century A.D. Culturally related and linguistically linked with Celtic Cornwall, Wales and Ireland, the duchy of Bretagne resisted the French penetration for centuries. Its annexation was prepared for by two successive marriages of Duchess Anne with two kings of France, Charles VIII in 1491 and Louis XII in 1498. The duchy of Bretagne was officially united to the French crown in 1532.

Vauban's work in Bretagne was characterized by the conservation and re-utilization of ancient fortifications as well as a few new creations adapted to the particularities of shore and harbor defense. Just as in mountainous sites, medieval coastal fortresses had not completely lost their military value. In Bretagne, Vauban was assisted by engineers Deshouillières and Traverse, as well as Garangeau. Jean-Simeon Garangeau (1647–1741) was born in Paris, the son of a master-carpenter. In 1672 he volunteered for the army and was wounded at the siege of Maastricht during the War of Holland. In 1667, he became an architect in Paris and was appointed controller of the buildings of Versailles and Fontainebleau, and a year later became royal engineer. Garangeau was posted as military architect at Marseille in 1679 and at Brest (Bretagne) in 1682. Vauban appointed him engineer-in-chief for the fortifications of Saint Malo, and for more than ten years Garangeau was involved in the building of fortifications in Bretagne; he designed Fort Taureau, Fort La Conchée, Fort La Latte, Fort Îles aux Moines, the tower at Cap Fréhel and several other sites.

Along the coasts of Normandy (French since 1204) and Picardie (French since 1477), Vauban fortified the main harbors which played an important role in the naval warfare against the Anglo-Dutch, but rivalry between Louvois (army) and Colbert and Seignelay (navy) thwarted his efforts to establish an efficient coastal defense. It should be noted that the great port of Cherbourg by the end of the seventeenth century was only an insignificant little coastal town; its development as military port came later under the reigns of Louis XVI and Napoléon. In Normandy, Vauban's principal assistant was engineer Benjamin Descombes (born in 1649), a sailor who had made it to the rank of lieutenant-de-Vaisseau and who had traveled to Canada and Africa. Appointed in 1693 to the post of director of fortifications in Normandy, Descombes lived at Saint-Vaast-la-Hougue, and until 1710 made designs and directed works. Specializing in hydraulics, he assisted Vauban at Dunkirk, Abbeville, Ambleteuse, Brest, Rouen, Dieppe, Honfleur, Fécamp and Le Havre.

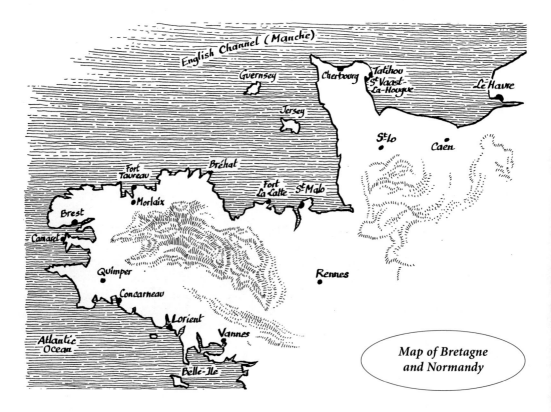

Map of Bretagne and Normandy

BELLE-ÎLE-EN-MER

Belle-Île, the "Beautiful Island in the Sea," is situated in the Atlantic Ocean in front of the Quiberon peninsula (the southern shores of Bretagne, called Morbihan). The most important village of Belle-Île, Le Palais, was first fortified by some monks of Quimperlé in the fourteenth century, as it belonged to the Abbey of Sainte-Croix in Quimperlé. On a hill dominating the small town and its harbor, King Henri II of France ordered the construction of a fort in 1549. Defense works were continued by the family Gondi, lords of Belle-Île, from 1574 to 1635. The ambitious and immensely wealthy Nicolas Fouquet, viscount of Vaux and Louis XIV's finance superintendent, purchased the island in 1650 and carried out its fortification, wishing to make the island a safe retreat in case of misfortune. But the king's jealousy and Colbert's hatred brought his disgrace in 1664. Fouquet was arrested by the famous d'Artagnan, and died in prison in 1680. Belle-Île had been attacked several times by the British and Dutch fleets. It had been occupied in 1572. Therefore Vauban designed a project in March 1683 including a large bastioned enceinte around the town, but this plan was not retained. However Vauban, assisted by Fortifications Director Jean-Anthenor Hue de Luc de Caligny and Guillaume Deshouillières, brought substantial modifications to Le Palais citadel in 1685 and established nineteen detached batteries on beaches where landings could occur.

The garrison of Belle-Île repulsed British raids in 1696 and in 1703. The island was besieged, taken and again occupied by the British between 1761 and 1763, when Belle-Île

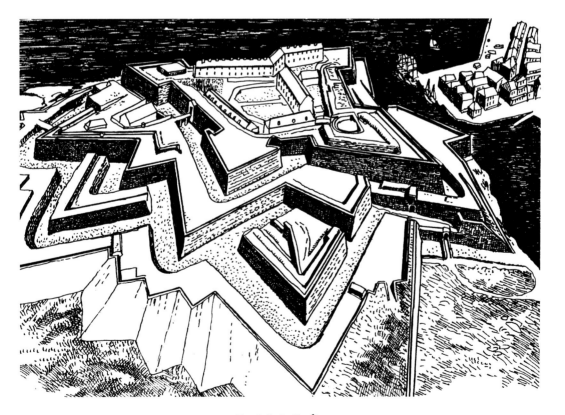

Citadel, Belle-Île

was exchanged for the Spanish island of Minorca. The citadel of Le Palais remained both a prison and a barracks until 1961. It houses now a museum devoted to the island's rich history.

NORD

Groundplan, Citadel of Le Palais at Belle-Île-en-Mer. Vauban's exterior defenses included a covered way with places of arms (1), a ditch (2), a counterguard (3), a traversed demi-lune (4) and an envelope (5). Henri II's citadel is a massive irregular square surrounded by a ditch (6). The main access is the Bourg gate (7) situated west; la porte de Secours or Rescue gate (8), situated north, leads to the second entrance, the Donjon gate (9). The citadel is composed of high and thick curtains, three bastions (10) and a half-bastion (11); the most important one is fitted with a cavalier and a circular powder house (12). The terreplein is occupied by the officers' pavilion (13), the arsenal (14), the governor's house (15) and three barracks (16). South of the fortress, steep slopes dominating the harbor are fortified by redans (17) and in the east facing the sea, the rocky shore forms a natural obstacle.

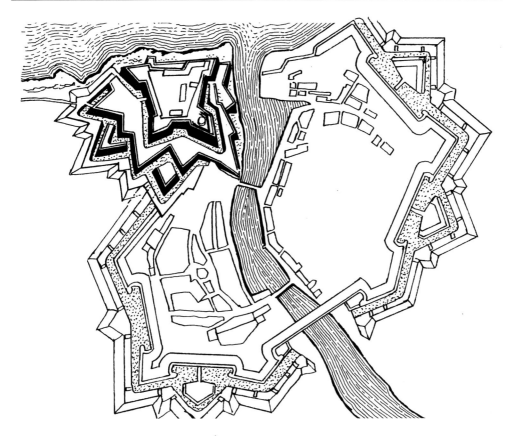

Vauban's design for Le Palais Belle-Île. This ambitious extension, designed in 1683, was intended to protect the port of Le Palais. The project was not accepted by King Louis XIV and thus never built.

CONCARNEAU

The so-called *Ville Close* (closed city) of Concarneau in the department of Finistère is located on a small rocky cape in the Bay of Moros. The walls and tower were built in the fifteenth century and during the Wars of Religion, the duke of Mercoeur adapted some of them to firearms by lowering and thickening them. In 1691, Vauban came to the city on inspection tour. Limited by financial constraints, he brought only a few small modifications, notably establishing lower batteries and a small demi-lune protecting the two small bridges linking the closed city to the mainland. The stronghold was slightly modified in 1823 but soon lost all military value. Today the Ville Close is perfectly preserved, and Concarneau is France's third largest fishing port, a big market for tuna, and also possesses many fish canneries.

LORIENT

The harbor of Lorient with its dockyard, commercial warehouse and dwellings was newly created by Colbert in 1664 for the Compagnie des Indes (India Company) for its far-East trade, mostly with India and China (l'Orient in French means the East). Situated on the right bank of the River Scorff in the Morbihan, Lorient was intended to replace Le

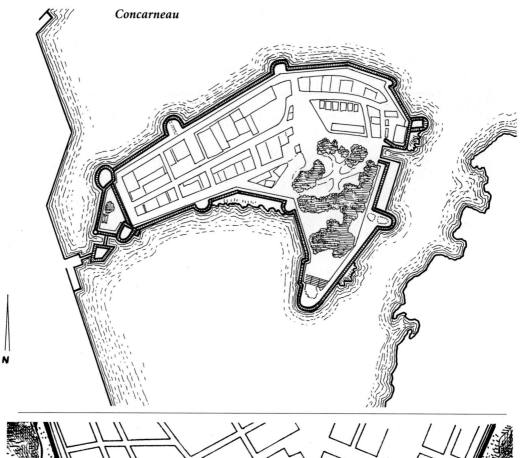

Concarneau

N

Lorient. The groundplan only shows the western part of the fortifications.

Havre because of the channel insecurity caused by Anglo-Dutch privateers. The city was enclosed by fortifications built by the Navy Department, which Vauban inspected in 1683. The bastioned enceinte was reshaped in 1747. In 1757, a detached work was constructed at Kerlin but the main harbor was defended from the entrance of the bay in Port-Louis. The French Indian colonies being lost in the eighteenth century, the company was ruined and commercial activities completely declined. From 1770 on, the harbor and its installations were taken over by the state and, under the reign of Napoléon, Lorient became a fortified military harbor and a naval arsenal. During World War II the port was an important German submarine base protected by a huge concrete bunker built by the Organisation Todt. The arsenal and the U-boat bunker are used by the French navy today.

PORT-LOUIS

The village of Port-Louis (called Blavet in the sixteenth century) is situated on a promontory facing Lorient. During the Wars of Religion, in 1590, the duke of Mercœur, governor in Bretagne for the Catholic League, allowed the Spaniards to erect a fort at Blavet. The Spanish fort, placed at the point of the cape, was designed by engineer Cristobal de Rojas. Called Fuerte del Aguila (Eagle fort) after the governor, Don Juan del Aguila, it is a rectangle with four Italian-style bastions with orillon. After the Treaty of Vervins in 1598, the Spaniards left and the fortress was partially dismantled by the French. Under Louis

Fuerte del Aguila (Port-Louis) 1591–1598. The citadel of Port Louis is shown here as it was in the period 1591–1598.

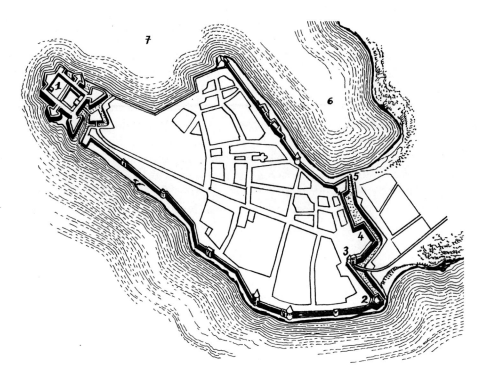

Port Louis. The groundplan shows the citadel and the enceinte enclosing the village of Port-Louis. (1) Citadel; (2) Bastion of Papegaut; (3) Locmalo gate; (4) Bastion of Pépinière Royale; (5) Saint-Pierre Bastion; (6) Bay of Driaker; (7) Bay of Lorient.

Citadel Port Louis (Morbihan)

XIII's reign, the fort was rebuilt and re-baptized Port-Louis (in Louis XIII's honor) by Richelieu. The cardinal also ordered fortification of the village and the small harbor of Blavet in 1618. Work was carried out between 1649 and 1653 by Marshal Meilleraye. In 1683, Vauban inspected Port-Louis and sharply criticized his predecessors' fortifications. However, because Lorient was so important a colonial harbor, he decided, helped by engineer Guillaume Deshouillières, to keep the fortress, and prescribed minor modifications and the construction of a powder house. The citadel later became a prison; among its occupants was Louis-Napoléon, the son of Emperor Napoléon III. Today the fortifications and the citadel of Port-Louis are well preserved and house a naval and historical museum.

BREST

Situated in the mouth of the River Penfeld, the site of Brest was occupied by a *castellum* in Roman times. In the thirteenth century, the dukes of Bretagne built a castle which was several times enlarged, strengthened, and then adapted to firearms with a barbican and gun-towers in the fifteenth century. Brest was chosen by Richelieu to become, with Le Havre and Brouage, one of the ports from which the French navy would operate in the Atlantic Ocean. The military haven was further developed by Colbert, who improved the dockyards and mooring facilities. The minister of the French navy also founded a school of gunnery, a college of marine guards, a school of hydrography, and a school for maritime engineers. Chevalier de Clerville improved the castle defenses and surrounded the city and its suburb Recouvrance, as well as the maritime arsenal and naval base, with a bastioned

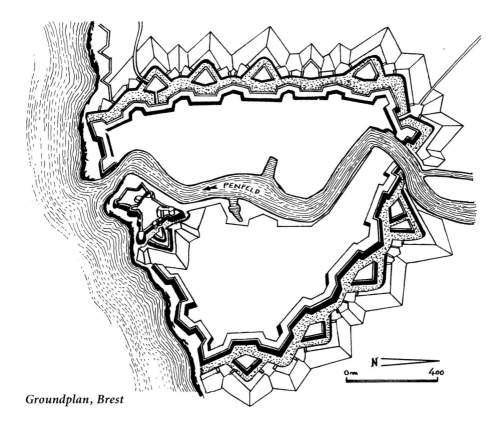

Groundplan, Brest

Brest Castle. The castle is the last reminder of the fortifications of Brest. The Penfeld gate has been fortified since Roman times. The towers and wall were built between the twelfth and the seventeenth century.

enceinte. Between 1682 and 1692, a new wall was built according to a design made by engineer Sainte-Colombe. Featuring bastions, demi-lunes, ditch, covered way and glacis, the fortifications were very large in order to put ships and harbor out of range of enemy artillery. The castle was reinforced by a huge bastion called Sourdéac. Vauban, helped by engineers Niquet, Garangeau and Robelin, completed the harbor installations and the urban lay-out. They also organized the defense of the *Goulet* (strait) of Brest on a large scale by establishing detached batteries: in the south at Camaret-sur-Mer and Cornouailles, in the north at Bertheaume and Léon. After the repulsed English invasion of 1694, Vauban reinforced the defensive network by placing new coastal batteries at Portzic, Cape des Espagnols, Île Longue and Plougastel.

Camaret-sur-Mer

Camaret is situated on the Crozon peninsula facing Brest. The site has a large beach which could be used by enemies for a landing, and Vauban decided to protect this weak point. Designed by Vauban and set up in 1689 by engineer Traverse, the Camaret tower is typical of Vauban's coastal fortlets, composed of a semi-circular low battery and a hexagonal four-story-high tower. It served as a model for other coastal strongholds such as Fort Chapus, Fort Lupin, Fort Saint-Louis and Fort Ambleteuse. The work at Camaret is called *Tour Dorée* (golden tower) because its wall is covered with shining, yellowish-red plaster-

Camaret battery with Tour Dorée

ing. The Camaret battery proved its effectiveness on June 18, 1694, when its garrison — commanded by Vauban — repulsed an English landing. The battery of the *Tour Dorée* proved very effective. Several enemy ships were put out of action, the landing troops were decimated, a charge by dragoons on horse scattered the attackers, and the coastguard militiamen completed the rout. The battle, which caused a sensation at Louis XIV's court, ended with 1,200 killed and 450 prisoners from the British side, and only 45 wounded among Vauban's force.

FORT PORTZIC

Situated on a rocky cape west of the port of Brest, Fort Portzic constituted one of the key positions defending the Bay of Brest. The fort, designed by Vauban in 1695, included

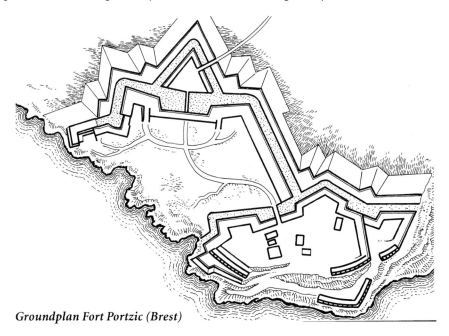

Groundplan Fort Portzic (Brest)

gun batteries facing the sea and a bastioned enceinte covering the fort on the land front. The fort was enlarged in 1793 and reinforced with two bastions, a demi-lune and a ditch with counterscarp. This large extension had a bombproof underground barracks accommodating 600 soldiers.

FORT TAUREAU

Fort Taureau (Bull's Fort) is situated on a rocky bank in the middle of the estuary of the River Dossen in Morlaix. The town was attacked and looted by British raiders in 1522, therefore the inhabitants of Morlaix built the castle Taureau at their own cost to guard against another attack. The massive fortress built in 1542 is composed of a heavy, masonry ring flanked by two heavy towers defending the entrance to the harbor. Under Louis XIV's reign, in 1661, the fortress was taken over by the crown and transformed into a royal prison. In 1680, Vauban renovated the fort, installing casemates housing a powerful artillery.

Fort Taureau (Morlaix)

SAINT-MALO

Saint-Malo is situated in the mouth of the River Rance (département Ille-et-Vilaine). The name originally comes from the Irish evangelist MacLeod (later gallicized as Maclou and Malo). In the Middle Ages, the city developed into a commercial harbor which was fortified by its bishops from 1144 onwards. In the fifteenth century, Duke Jean V of Bretagne built a huge castle, which became a citadel. External defenses of the town included Fort La Latte and the tower Solidor (set up in 1370 in the nearby village of Saint-Servan).

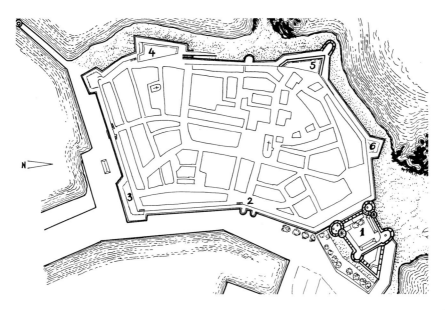

Groundplan, Saint-Malo. (1) Duchess Anne's castle; (2) Grande Porte; (3) Saint-Louis bastion; (4) Holland half-bastion; (5) Bidouanne tower; (6) Queen's half-bastion.

Fort de la Conchée (Saint-Malo). La Conchée Fort, designed by Vauban in 1693 and completed in 1695, is built on the small, rocky island Quincé, four km. northwest of Saint-Malo. Its plan completely deviates from classical bastioned principles. The fort consists of a service building placed on high and thick masonry walls, forming a wide oval gun battery with embrasures turned towards the open sea. The fort was declared obsolete in 1889. Today, it is a nature reserve for seabirds.

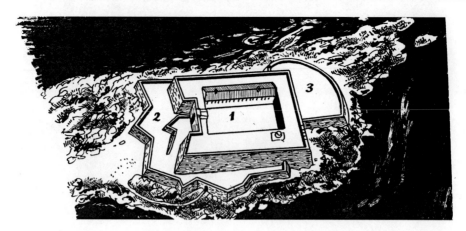

Fort Royal, Saint-Malo. Fort Royal (today called Fort National) is built close to the entrance of Saint-Malo on the islet rocks. Fort National is composed of a hornwork (1) sheltering a barrack, a low irregular fausse-braie (2) providing close range defense at the town side and a low battery (3) with guns directed towards the open sea.

Solidor Tower (Saint-Malo). Situated on a rocky cape at Saint-Servan close to Saint-Malo, the Solidor Tower was built circa 1370 by Jean IV Duke of Bretagne, on the site of an ancient Roman castrum. Originally intended to check the rebellious inhabitants of Saint-Malo, the tower became an advance work for the defense of the port. The tower is 18 meters high and divided into three stories. It is actually composed of three cylindrical towers linked together by small walls. It was redesigned in 1636 and Vauban incorporated it into the defense of Saint-Malo. The Solidor tower was reinforced in 1737, and became a prison at the time of the Revolution of 1789. Today the sturdy building houses a museum of fishing.

These fortifications were adapted to firearms at the end of the fifteenth century, at the time when Saint-Malo had declared itself an independent free republic, whence the proud device of the city: "Ni Français, ni Breton, Malouins suis!" (I am neither a Frenchman nor a Breton, but a man of Saint-Malo!) In spring 1689, Vauban designed a program of reconstruction with engineer Jean-Simeon Garangeau. The medieval city walls were reinforced with bastions and new detached works were built to deny any attack from the sea. These included Fort Royal, Fort Petit Bé and Fort Harbourg. In 1693 another defense was added by Vauban: Fort de la Conchée, placed on the small, rocky island Quincé, northwest of Saint-Malo. Well protected, Saint-Malo was a commercial haven and a privateer base. The most famous of them all was René Duguay-Trouin (1673–1736) and later Robert Surcouf (1773–1827). Vauban also had a very ambitious plan to enlarge the port, and to build dams and sluices as well as to fortify Saint-Malo and the nearby suburb Saint-Servan, but this project was dropped. Badly damaged during the Battle of Normandy in 1944, Saint-Malo has been rebuilt in its original state and the surrounding forts are well preserved.

Fort La Latte

The castle of Roche Goyon (named Fort La Latte since the sixteenth century) is situated southeast of Cape Frehel in the Côtes-d'Armor. Dominating the bay of Saint-Malo, the château is believed to have been built by a lord of Goyon, probably about 937. The existing castle was erected by the family Goyon-Matignon in the 1360s. The fortress, separated

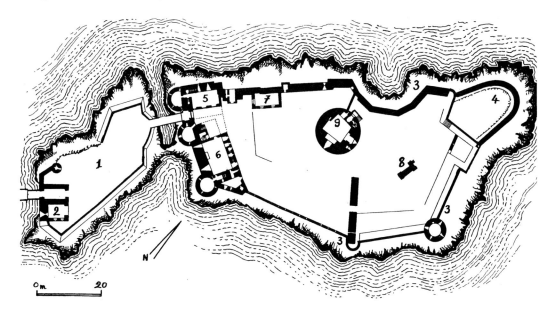

Groundplan, Fort La Latte. The castle includes an irregular and large barbican (1) defended by a first gate-house (2); a ditch is dug in the rocks and the irregular stone wall (3) follows the outline of the promontory; it is reinforced by three round towers, a gate-house with towers and drawbridge and Vauban's battery (4). The second gate-house is fitted with a guardhouse (5), a governor's residence (6) and the Saint-Michel chapel (7). On the terreplein, various service buildings are placed, notably a cannonball oven (8) constructed in 1793. On a rocky mound, a massive circular keep (9) with machicolation gives the work a typical Middle Ages feel.

View, Fort La Latte

from the mainland by two crevasses which were crossed by drawbridges, played a role during the Hundred Years' War and during the Wars of Religion. Besieged, taken and burned in 1597, the castle was abandoned until 1689. By that time Fort La Latte was restored by Vauban and engineer Simon Garengeau, who reinforced the two fortified enclosures, the inner yard, the guard room, the governor's living quarters, the cistern and the chapel. At a high cost, the fort was reshaped and fitted with a gun platform facing the waters off Saint-Malo. Fort La Latte was completed in 1694 and improved in 1713. The fort still exists today and gives a good sense of Vauban's re-use of an ancient medieval work. From the top of the keep there is a superb panorama over the Bay of La Frênaye to Cap Fréhel and Saint-Malo.

SAINT-VAAST-LA-HOUGUE AND TATIHOU

Saint-Vaast-la-Hougue is situated south of the cape of Barfleur in the Cotentin peninsula. Between 1693 and 1701, Vauban and the director of fortifications

Tower at Saint-Vaast-la-Hougue. The tower, built in 1694, could accommodate about sixty soldiers.

Fort Tatihou (Saint-Vaast-la-Hougue). Situated 1.4 km. off Saint-Vaast-la-Hougue, the island Tatihou was fortified in 1694 by Vauban, who designed an 18-meter-high cylindrical artillery tower. A bastioned enceinte was built in 1860, inside which stood barracks, stores and a chapel.

in Normandy, Benjamin Descombes, designed two towers enclosed by bastioned forts: the first one on Cape la Hougue and the second one on the small island of Tatihou, facing Saint-Vaast. Both works are good examples of Vauban's coastal forts, combining a low artillery platform and a high masonry tower acting as powder house, barrack, reduit, observatory and lighthouse. Off La Hougue, a naval battle took place in June 1692. The French fleet was defeated and that put an end to Louis XIV's naval ambition.

LE HAVRE

On a marshy site chosen by Grand Admiral of France Guillaume de Gouffier de Bonnivet, Le Havre-de-Grâce was founded in 1517 by order of King François I to replace the

Le Havre. The sketch shows the situation after 1541 with Bellarmarto's bastioned fortifications. A new citadel and new, modern, bastioned fortifications were later built under Louis XVI.

silting-up Harfleur. The ambitious project was essentially military and intended to provide the French navy with a harbor to protect navigation in the channel and to avoid invasion on the River Seine. The brand-new city and its port were fortified by the Italian engineer Jeromino Bellamarto in 1541. The entrance to the port was defended by artillery towers. The land-front was fitted with bastions with ears and a triangular citadel was erected east of the town. Under Louis XIII's reign, the citadel was enlarged and outworks were added by engineer Pierre d'Argencourt. The bombardment of Dieppe and Le Havre by the British fleet in 1694 demonstrated the weakness of the old fortifications. Vauban, aware of the harbor's importance, presented a design in October 1699; this project was refused by Louis XIV. Vauban's plan, only slightly modified, was carried out between 1786 and 1790 under Louis XVI.

DIEPPE

The port of Dieppe, situated at the mouth of the River Béthune in Normandy, originated from a small fishing village in 1030. After the conquest of England in 1066 by the duke of Normandy, William the Conqueror, Dieppe developed as one of the most important ports between Normandy and England. In the twelfth century, the port enjoyed an increasing prosperity, and a dungeon was built west of the city in 1188, later to become a powerful fortress. Claimed by both Richard the Lionheart and Philippe Auguste, the town

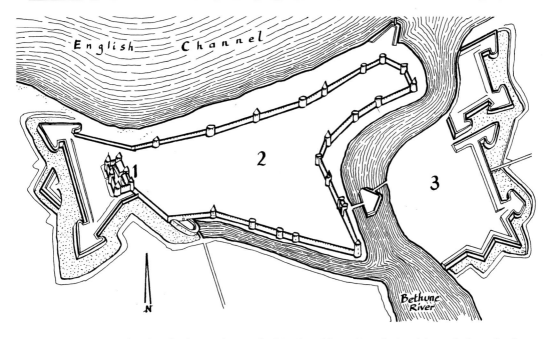

Dieppe in 1694. The sketch shows the castle (1), the old medieval city (2), and the suburb Faubourg du Pollet (3).

was devastated in 1195. Dieppe played an important role in the Hundred Years' War. Raiders and privateers launched a victorious raid on Southampton in 1399. Taken by the English in 1420, the town was retaken by the Frenchman Charles des Marets in October 1435. By that time, new fortifications were built around the port, and the castle was reinforced. During the sixteenth century, early Italian-style bastioned defenses were added to protect the eastern bridgehead/suburb of Pollet on the right side of the River Béthune, and to defend the suburb of Barc west of the castle. Dieppe was then an important harbor for French privateers such as the famous Jean Ango, and the Florentine Verrazano, who in April 1524 discovered the site that would become New York, to which he gave the name Land of Angoulême. Vauban visited Dieppe in 1681, and designed a project to reinforce the obsolete defenses. Curiously, his design was not implemented for the following odd reason: should the English capture the port, it would be difficult to retake it. The real reason was certainly disagreement and bad blood — some historians say hatred — between Louvois and Seignelay (Colbert's son) who was minister of the navy beginning in 1683. Anyway, poorly defended, Dieppe suffered huge damage when it was bombarded in July 1694 by a large Anglo-Dutch fleet. Vauban gave engineer Ventabren valuable advice about rebuilding the city, while engineer Peironet established three coastal batteries. The defenses of Dieppe were redesigned in the eighteenth century. Dieppe is also famous for the controversial "reconnaissance in force" raid (Operation Jubilee) on August 19, 1942, when the Allies made an attack to test Hitler's "Atlantic Wall." The landing attempt resulted in a bloody fiasco.

CHAPTER 6

Vauban's *Oisivetés*

Vauban regarded himself as a soldier. We have seen his competence in siege warfare and artillery, and his role as a military commander and inspector, as a fortifications builder, as an architect and as a town planner. Raised in the country, formed in military camps and living his whole life among soldiers, Vauban was, however, more than a tough man of action and an insensitive warrior. On the contrary he was a man of great cleverness, showing interest and curiosity about subjects reaching far beyond his official military occupation. But he was neither a hobbyist nor a dry thinker nor a rigid theoretician. Vauban was an open-hearted man with a strong commitment to the king's service, the public good and the common people. He was a great traveler and certainly one of those who knew France the best at the time of Louis XIV. During his long and numerous journeys, he looked at the world around him, listened and talked to ordinary people, made notes and gave thought to the numerous aspects of French society. He noted France's diversity, potential wealth and resources, but at the same time, saw the population's poverty and misery. Vauban's experiences and thoughts are revealed by numerous writings which he regrouped at the end of his life in a book ironically titled *Oisivetés de Monsieur de Vauban ou Ramas de plusieurs mémoires de sa façon sur différents sujets* (*Idle thoughts* or *Leisures by Monsieur de Vauban or a Gathering of Several Treatises about Different Matters*). The *Oisivetés*, a monument to his life's work, is an educational and practical book aiming to improve people's lives, and a remarkable overview of many, varied aspects of France under Louis XIV. It contains a dozen manuscript volumes, illustrated and carefully bound, dealing with military considerations but also giving Vauban's reflections on very eclectic issues.

Agriculture and Inland Navigation

In Louis XIV's time, between 80 and 90 percent of the French population was rural. Production was overwhelmingly rural and much of the limited industrial activity was dispersed in the countryside. Being himself an experienced landowner, Vauban was very interested in agriculture and economic activity. From his father, Albin Le Prestre, he had inherited a real love and a profound knowledge about forest management. In one of the *Oisivetés*'s chapters ("Traité de la Culture des Forêts") written in 1701, he described the ideal long-term management of forests. Vauban detailed sylviculture, studied plantations according to their locations, and recommended well-ordered exploitation, maintenance and development. Opposed to wild and unconsidered deforestation, he warned of its dramatic consequences: soil erosion, aridity and infertility. To conserve wood, Vauban suggested an alternative fuel: coal. He pleaded for systematic surveys and measures for its exploitation. For industrial development, he recommended the same attitude regarding iron, copper and lead.

In the essay, "De la Cochonnerie ou calcul estimatif pour connaître jusqu'où peut aller la production d'une truie pendant dix ans de temps," written in 1699, Vauban demonstrated the possibility of developing pig-breeding in order to feed rural populations who were consistently underfed and regularly endured famine. To increase agricultural production, he advocated improving the quality of the soil by rotating crops, by spraying and by irrigation. In "Description géographique de l'Election de Vézelay," drafted in 1696, Vauban studied the soils, rivers, resources and living conditions of people in the region around Vezelay. Out of this monographic, he deduced a statistical method of analysis which could be used at a national level to improve knowledge and achieve maximal exploitation of the resources.

Vauban was a tireless traveler who had experienced France's bad road network every day of his life. It took about two and a half days on horseback to go from Paris to Lille, five days from Paris to Strasburg, six days from Paris to Lyon, more than seven days from Paris to Brest and nine days from Paris to Bayonne. Roads were dry and dusty in summer, and muddy and impassable in winter. As a soldier, Vauban also knew how difficult it was to transport heavy guns and ammunition on land. In "La Navigation des Rivières," written in 1699, he studied inland waterways, described the possibilities of transport on French rivers and designed a vast waterways network project aiming to improve transportation and stimulate trade. He pleaded for the establishment of a canal between the rivers Meuse and Moselle and a waterway running parallel to the Rhine. Vauban participated in various civilian hydraulic projects, notably in 1691, when he worked on sluices in the Canal du Midi. This waterway, which links the Mediterranean Sea to the Atlantic Ocean, was built from 1666 to 1681 by engineer Pierre-Paul De Riquet. The canal is 241 km. long and includes 65 sluices; it begins near Toulouse and along the Garonne valley makes its junction with the River Aude valley near Carcassonne.

As already mentioned, Vauban participated in the construction of the monumental (but never completed) Maintenon aqueduct, intended to supply water for Louis XIV's Versailles castle.

Colonies

European civilization had always shown a tendency to expand, but in the sixteenth, seventeenth, and eighteenth centuries (with the exception of America, where European civilization was taking root), no European powers subjected Asia and Africa to their political control, being content with a few influential coastal trading stations. The older empires of the pre-industrial centuries were maritime and mercantile. The European traders simply purchased the wares brought to them by native merchants on a kind of cash-and-carry basis. They had no territorial ambitions beyond the protection of way stations and trading centers, and, on the whole, did not venture far in the hinterland. Before the nineteenth

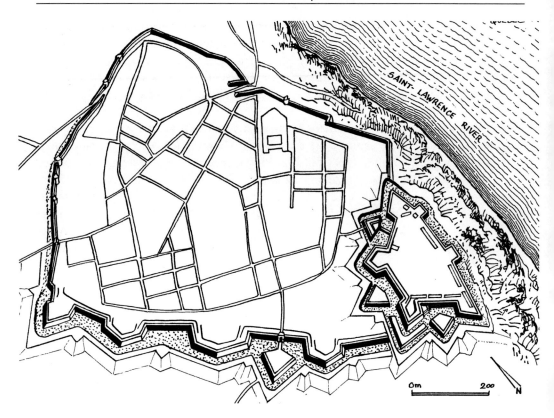

Québec (Canada). The Saint Lawrence Bay was explored in 1534 by Jacques Cartier. The territory was annexed and baptized Nouvelle-France. Samuel de Champlain developed colonization and founded Québec city in 1608. Situated on a 106-meter promontory dominating the rivers Saint Lawrence and Saint Charles, Québec was the fortified capital of the Belle Province. The early enceinte, built in the seventeenth century, was designed by Louis de Buade, lord of Frontenac. Modifications were later carried out by French military engineer Jacques Levasseur de Néré and approved by Vauban in 1701. Further works were added by engineer Gaspard-Joseph Chaussegros de Léry in 1745. The town was besieged and taken by British troops under General Wolfe's command in 1759. The fortifications were renovated, and a citadel was added by British engineer Elias Walker-Durnford between 1820 and 1831. Constructed on the highest point of Cape Diamant, the citadel today houses the famous "Van Doos," the French-speaking Royal 22nd Regiment of the Canadian Forces. It is also one of the official residences of the governor general of Canada.

century, France had possessed the following territories: Canada from 1608 to 1763; Acadia, Newfoundland and Hudson Bay until 1713; Cape Breton Island until 1758; Sainte-Lucie Island from 1650 to 1803; Louisiana (stretching from the Great Lakes to the Gulf of Mexico, thus corresponding approximately to the present states of Michigan, Wisconsin, Iowa, Illinois, Indiana, Ohio, Missouri, Arkansas, Tennessee, Mississippi, Alabama and Louisiana) from 1682 to 1803; Saint-Domingue (Haiti) from 1697 to 1804; the Malouines Islands (Falklands), temporarily held during the reign of Louis XIV; the Seychelles Islands from 1742 to 1804; and Maurice Island from 1764 to 1814.

French colonial expansion was stimulated by Colbert's commercial policy, with the goal of reducing imports from European commercial powers, namely the Dutch and the British.

Vauban spent his whole life trying to give France territorial unity and safe frontiers. He was a continental man who had never traveled across seas and oceans. Informed by reports, conversations and second-hand experiences, Vauban was, however, a convinced backer of French colonial development, particularly in North America. In his treatise "Moyen de rétablir nos colonies de l'Amérique et de les accroître en peu de temps" (*How to Re-establish Our American Colonies and Develop Them in a Short Period*), written in 1694, Vauban proposed to reduce the power of the missionaries (mainly Jesuits) and private companies, the former being too much controlled by the pope of Rome, and the latter only concerned with their own profit. According to Vauban, French colonial presence could only be secured by the creation of a royal enterprise, carried out by a military force and supported by voluntary and determined civilian colonists. After a while, durably planted and well populated, colonies would live and grow in prosperity owing to active and fruitful exchanges with France. Vauban was very evasive about native populations. It seems that no autochthonous populations existed in his theoretical and idealized scheme. In Vauban's simpleminded, distorted and incomplete vision, Europeans created efficient, ideal, new and harmonious societies in America. Far from Vauban's naïve dream, the reality was quite different. There was always a lack of would-be colonists and the French colonial effort was seriously thwarted by British and Dutch rivalry. The continental-minded Louis XIV paid little attention to colonial problems and most French capital holders and rich bourgeois prudently preferred to buy lands and purchase noble titles rather than to invest in hypothetical colonial businesses. Colonies were not a prime concern either for the crown or for the general public. This went hand in hand with the reluctance to grant both state funds and private capital for development.

Religion

Louis XIV's reign was a time of religious passions and the absolute, "Very Christian" king intended to influence the religious life of his subjects. Louis XIV was opposed to Jansenism (a theological predestination doctrine developed in 1640 by Bishop Jansenius from Ypres). The doctrine was forbidden and the monastery of Port-Royal-des-Champs, the principal jansenist center in France, was closed down in 1709. The king favored gallicanism (independence of the French church from Rome) and this attitude provoked a serious crisis with Pope Innocent XI in 1673. Louis XIV also wanted to restore the religious unity in his kingdom and manifested an increased hostility towards the Huguenots (French Protestants). Françoise d'Aubigné, marquise de Maintenon, morganatically married to Louis XIV probably in 1683, and Father François de La Chaise (Louis XIV's Jesuit confessor) strongly influenced the king to religious intransigence. As early as 1679, hard measures were taken against the French Protestant community: pressures, civil rights restriction, fines, persecutions, imprisonment and conversion by force or blackmail (dragonnades). Claiming that no more Frenchmen were Protestant, Louis XIV revoked the Edict of Nantes. The reformed religion was officially forbidden by the Edict of Fontainebleau (October 1685).

Vauban was a sincere Christian who believed in religious unity for the sake of social order. For his soldiers he built churches, and he pleaded for Sunday rest and army chaplains. But in no way was he a theologian or a fanatic zealot. Without passion, he merely considered the practical aspects of religion. For political reasons, in order to increase national coherence, Vauban backed gallicanism and did not hesitate to criticize the Catholic Church's corruption and papal doings and abuses. He was, however, deeply shocked by the forced conversions and by the revocation of the Edict of Nantes. Convinced that religion was a matter of individual conscience and not royal decision, he wrote in 1689 "Mémoire pour le rappel des Huguenots" (*Dissertation to Call Back Protestants*). Showing courage, tolerance and humanity, Vauban underlined the disastrous consequences of the revocation: indignation and hatred in northern Protestant Europe and the exile of an important part of the French élite. Religious unity was only apparent anyway, as Protestant congregations met in secrecy. Besides, the repressed Huguenots, only posing as converted, formed henceforth a threat within the country. Vauban's dissertation was completely ignored by Louis XIV, but Madame de Maintenon was seriously irritated. She discreetly but firmly let him know he should mind his own business and stop writing about religion.

Politics and Organization of the State

Vauban, considering the economy, could not avoid thinking about political issues. Clearly, Vauban was not a revolutionary, a democrat, a liberal or a reformer. He was a disciplined soldier, a privileged gentleman in a social organization based on inequality according to medieval customs. The aristocracy was supposed to fight and defend the nation, the clergymen prayed and administered sacraments and the common people worked in order to feed both privileged classes. Vauban's convictions, writings and actions never questioned the fundamental principles upon which society and state were based. However, if Vauban totally accepted the established order, he was not always "politically correct" as we would say today. He expressed criticism and proposed audacious and sometimes utopian reforms far ahead of his time. Doing so, he was convinced he was serving his king, his fatherland and the public good. Vauban, as each and every man of his century, could not imagine another sort of social organization, but, if he never contested the principle of absolute monarchy, he sometimes considered that the king was annoyingly blinded by flattering courtiers and badly informed by incompetent and obsequious ministers. Bearing this in mind, he did not hesitate to make clear what were the king's rights and duties and did not fear to say what Louis XIV should do. Vauban had a good knowledge of history and had gained a clear experience of war with its sufferings and its horrors. While Louis XIV considered war as a righteous means to achieve glory, Vauban judged it merely an inevitable evil caused by ambition and greed. He was not a pacifist, of course, but he was strongly opposed to unnecessary conquests and adventurous expeditions abroad. In previous chapters we have already pointed out his belief that France should have natural and reasonable borders defended by strongholds.

Socially, Louis XIV's reign was a period of renewal of the nobility. The upper class was opened to very rich members of the middle class, who were ennobled by purchasing functions, titles and lands. This access to the top was favored by the king himself, who ruled with ennobled bourgeois, represented by Colbert and Louvois and caricatured by Molière's play the *Bourgeois Gentilhomme*. Vauban was proud to belong to the rural nobility, and criticized the growing power of money and despised the *nouveaux riches*. In his dissertation "L'Idée d'une Excellente Noblesse et des moyens de la distinguer par les générations," Vauban expressed the idea that aristocratic status could not be bought but only obtained by birth and merit. He therefore proposed a reclassification of nobility according to military and civil service. Vauban's thoughtful reform could not come to anything: it would have cost the crown too much, it would have spoiled too many interests and would have discontented too many people. The king himself preferred to be served by competent, servile and zealous ennobled people who were nothing without his favor. As for the high nobility, Louis XIV had never forgotten the Fronde. The nobility was excluded from all political or administrative responsibilities.

Fiscal Considerations

There can be no politics without finance and no finance without taxes. Vauban therefore pondered fiscal considerations. During the Ancien Régime in France (until 1789), according to medieval privileges, men of the nobility and of the church did not pay taxes. The whole royal treasury was financed by the king's most numerous and poorest subjects: the commoners. The populations were burdened with various contributions such as *taille* (direct tax on the commoner's condition), the *dîme* (paid to the church), the *gabelle* (a tax on salt) and *aides* (taxes for war). The burden was worsened by numerous tolls, duties and levies inherited from the Middle Ages. From 1680 on, taxes were gathered by private collectors (called *Fermiers Généraux*) who had purchased the office. This system allowed the king to get funds without having to finance a collecting administration, but it also favored corruption and abuses. Manorial oppression and heavy royal spending along with bad harvests and vintages (notably between 1692 and 1694 as well as in 1709) led to wide popular misery. Vauban knew perfectly well that Louis XIV's wars ruined France and that the generous funding he was given to build his fortifications came from a deeply unjust and unfair taxation system. Numerous urban riots and peasant revolts broke out, followed by armed and bloody repression. Vauban witnessed the dramatic situation of most of the population and started to write risky tracts about taxation. In 1695, he wrote a treaty entitled "Projet de Capitation." This proposal included a temporary and exceptional tax which would be paid by *all* inhabitants of France, including noblemen and clergymen. Vauban's fair proposition was partly applied but was changed to exclude the nobility and the clergy, and appeared to be another burden on the commoners.

Vauban gave full support to Colbert, who wanted to suppress the surviving medieval tolls, which formed within the realm numerous artificial customs and obstacles to economic development. Vauban also launched the idea of a European currency. This project, inconceivable and utopian to his contemporaries, was realized three centuries later with the introduction of the Euro.

Le projet de Dîme Royale was a small book published in 1707. As already mentioned, it marked Vauban's ultimate action to serve Louis XIV and France. The marshal proposed fiscal reform consisting of a fair, equitable and efficient tax on all goods, paid by all and without unreliable collecting intermediaries. The book — to which Vauban had devoted his last energy — was distributed anonymously, secretly and illegally among friends and relatives. Published at a time when the military situation was critical, with enemies forcing the borders, Vauban's book could not have any impact. Furthermore, intolerance, inequality and conservatism were too strong and too dominant to allow such an idea to take hold. Vauban's ambitious project aroused suspicion and anger. The book was forbidden, and the old and ailing author was disturbed by the royal secret police right before his death on March 30, 1707.

List of Vauban's Written Works

The following list of Vauban's writings was established by Jacques de Gervain and André de Lafitte-Clavé in 1768.

VOLUME I

"Mémoires pour le rappel des Huguenots," written in 1689 and reviewed in 1692 (for the recall of the Protestants)

"De l'importance dont Paris est à la France," written in 1689 (dealing with citadels and fortifications to be build around Paris)

"Le Canal du Languedoc," written in 1691 (about the waterway in the southern province Languedoc)

"Plusieurs maximes sur les bâtiments" (on construction of buildings)

VOLUME II

"Idée d'une excellente noblesse" (Idea of a good nobility)

"Les Ennemis de la France" (France's enemies)

"Projet d'ordre contre les effets des bombes" (about protection against bombs)

"Projet de Capitation," written in 1695 (about tax)

"Mémoire qui prouve la nécessité de mieux fortifier les côtes du Goulet," written in 1695 (about fortifications around the harbor of Brest)

"Mémoires sur les siège que l'ennemi peut entreprendre dans la campagne de Piémont," written in 1696 (about sieges which enemies could undertake in Piemont, Italy)

"Description géographique de l'élection de Vézelay," written in 1696 (geographical description of the county of Vezelay)

"Fragment d'un mémoire pour le roi," written in 1696 (an uncompleted memoire for the king)

VOLUME III

"Places dont le roi pourrait se défaire en faveur d'un traité de paix," written in 1694 (about exchanging fortresses versus peace treaties)

"Mémoire des dépenses de guerre sur lesquelles le roi pourrait faire quelque reduction" (about reducing war costs)

VOLUME IV

"Moyen d'établir nos colonies d'Amérique et de les accroître en peu de temps," written in 1694 (how to establish and increase colonies in America)

"Etat raisonné des provisions les plus nécessaires quand il s'agit de donner commencement à des colonies étrangères" (how to begin a colonial establishment)

"Traité de la culture des forêts," written in 1701 (about forest exploitation)

"La Cochonnerie ou calcul approximatif pour connaître jusqu'où peut aller la production d'une truie pendant dix années" (about pig growing)

"Navigation des rivières," written in winter 1698–1699 (about inland navigation)

VOLUME V

"Projet de vingtième ou taille royale," written in 1707 (about tax)

VOLUME VI

"Mémoires et instructions sur les munitions des places, l'artillerie et les armements en course faits en divers temps" (about the navy and privateers)

VOLUME VII

"Moyen d'améliorer nos troupes et d'en faire une infanterie perpétuelle et très excellente" (how to improve infantry)

VOLUME VIII

"Attaques des places," written in 1704 (about siege warfare)

VOLUME IX

"Défenses des places," written in 1705 (about defense of strongholds)

VOLUME X

"Traité de la fortification de campagne, autrement des camps retranchés," written in 1705 (about field fortifications and entrenched camps)

VOLUME XI

"Instruction pour servir au règlement des transports et remuement des terres" (about digging and transport of earth by construction of fortresses)

VOLUME XII

"Projet de navigation d'une partie des places de Flandres à la mer," written in 1705 (about inland navigation between Flanders and the North Sea)
"Projet de Dîme Royale," written in 1707 (about tax)

Conclusion

Vauban's Legacy in France

Vauban's defensive system, of course, did not outlive the progress made in military techniques, but after his death in 1707 he left such an enormous legacy that his successors were forced to respect him in an almost religious way. The sheer number of fortresses he had built and the numerous projects he left behind were astonishing. It seemed to the French engineering authorities that Vauban's genius could never be surpassed, and this

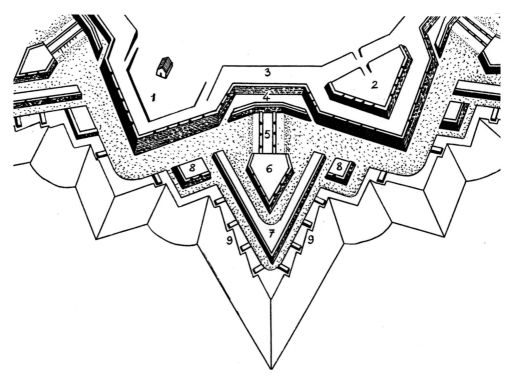

Cormontaigne's fortification. (1) Bastion; (2) bastion with cavalier; (3) curtain; (4) tenaille; (5) caponier; (6) demi lune; (7) counterguard; (8) place of arms or lunette; (9) covered way "en crémaillère."

exaggerated admiration was to have disastrous consequences. French eighteenth century fortification was characterized by ultra-conservatism, which may partly be explained by the historical context. After Louis XIV's death, a long period of peace succeeded, and France — well protected by Vauban's fortresses — was not threatened by invasion. Wars during Louis XV's reign took place abroad and military circumstances made only a few modernizations necessary. The art of fortification, disconnected from actual practice, tended to theory and ossification. Vauban had been the leading military engineer of Louis XIV's age and arguably the best known of any, whose impact on fortification and siegecraft was enormous, and somehow the bastioned system tended to take his name. Long after Vauban's death his work was studied, analyzed, codified in "three systems," commented on, continued and perpetuated by generations of French engineers, who frequently interposed their own concepts, making it somewhat difficult to see precisely what Vauban had in mind. In the eighteenth century there were a profusion of engineers who tried to improve on Vauban, if only on paper. Many treatises presenting new systems of fortification were published, particularly in France, where engineers were convinced that Vauban's fatherland was the sole fountain of knowledge on that subject. The most noteworthy of the authors was Louis de Cormontaigne (1696–1752) who became directeur-general des fortifications in 1745. Cormontaigne wrote a manual, "Architecture Militaire," in which he defined a new bastioned system directly influenced by Vauban, with a few minor modifications. In practice, Cor-

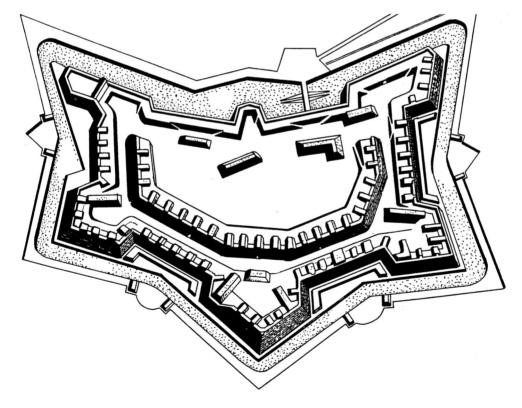

Fort Queleu, Metz Built between 1867 and 1870, Fort Queleu was still a Vauban-style stronghold, in spite of the fact that this form of fortifying had become completely obsolete due to tremendous artillery improvement by the Industrial Revolution.

montaigne redesigned the fortifications of Thionville, Metz, Verdun, Longwy and the citadel of Bitche. Known as the Modern French System, this method of fortification was to remain the accepted standard for bastioned fortifications in France until 1874, even after the great revolution caused by the introduction of rifled artillery in the mid–1860s.

Vauban's Influence Abroad

During the eighteenth century, Vauban's methods—both offensive and defensive—dominated European fortifications. Examples of European fortresses influenced by the

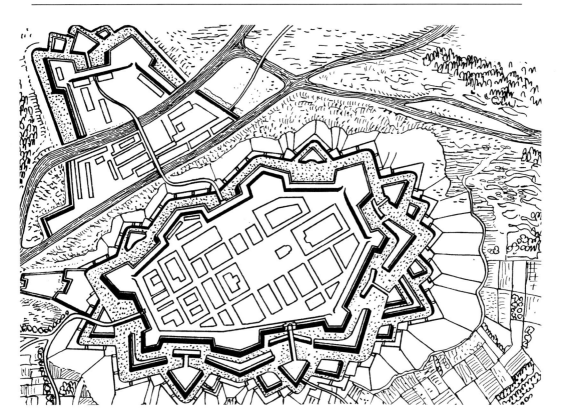

Fortress Josefov (Bohemia)

French model are numerous. The Peter and Paul Fortress in Saint Petersburg was designed in 1703 by the tsar himself and his French military engineer, Joseph Gaspard Lambert. In Finland, the city of Hamina situated east of Helsinki was constructed about 1723. In Britain, Fort George, on a promontory jutting out from the Moray Firth near Inverness, was designed by military engineer William Skinner, and built between 1747 and 1769. In Portugal, the early eighteenth-century fortifications of the towns of Elvas, Valença and Evora were influenced by Vauban. In the Czech Republic, the fortress of Josefov near Prague, built between 1780 and 1787 on order of Emperor Josef II, is yet another. The bastioned system was widely exported to fortify trading posts, forts, cities and ports in the colonies.

However, at the beginning of the nineteenth century, new concepts, developed by German engineers after Montalembert's work, gave birth to a modern "perpendicular" defensive system. Vauban's classical bastions were replaced by large, multi-story, masonry, casemated, circular gun-towers and jutting-out caponiers in England, Austria, Prussia and the Netherlands. German experimentations in the middle of the nineteenth century led to the appearance of the so-called "polygonal Prussian" system. This new style was characterized by a low profile and pentagonal outline, bomb-proof barracks, a ditch defended by massive caponiers, masonry casemates for rifled artillery and open gun emplacements

Opposite: *"Des Angriffs und der Verteidigung der Festungen." Front page of Vauban's book on attack and defense, translated and published in the German language in Berlin in 1745.*

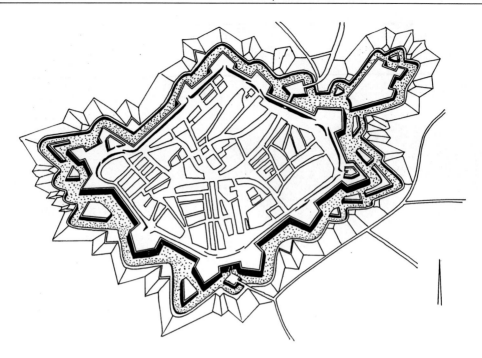

Elvas, Alentejo (Portugal)

protected by traverses. The main principles of bastioned fortification, based on flanking and protection, remained — on the whole — sound, but the scale had totally changed. Owing to a tremendous increase of fire power, range, accuracy and rate of fire, modern artillery by the end of the nineteenth century caused the appearance of new fortifications based on armor and concrete.

Bibliography

Books about the seventeenth century, Louis XIV and Vauban are numerous; to them may be added many books, brochures, leaflets and articles on Vauban's local fortifications. It is thus impossible to list all relevant publications. The list that follows includes books that were consulted during the preparation of this volume for their interest and authority, and selected for their usefulness to readers seeking additional information.

Association des amis de la Maison Vauban. *Vauban, sa vie, son œuvre.* Saint-Léger-Vauban, 1984.

Association Vauban. *Vauban et ses successeurs dans les Alpes de Hautes-Provence.* Colmars-les-Alpes, 1992.

Augoyat, A.M. *Aperçu historique sur les fortifications, les ingénieurs et le corps du génie en France.* 3 vols. Paris: Editions Tenera, 1860.

Babeau, A. *La Vie militaire sous l'Ancien Régime.* Paris: Editions Plon, 1980.

Bély, L. *Les Relations internationales en Europe XVIIe–XVIIIe siècles.* Paris: Presses Universitaires de France, 1992.

Blanchard, A. *Vauban.* Paris: Editions Fayard, 1996.

Blondel, François. *L'Art de jeter les bombes.* Paris: Editions N. Langlois, 1683.

_____. *Nouvelle Manière de fortifier.* Paris: Editions N. Langlois, 1683.

Blomfield, R. *Sébastien Le Prestre de Vauban.* London: Methuen, 1938.

Bordonove, G. *Les Rois qui ont fait la France; Tome 3, Les Bourbons: Louis XIV.* Paris: Editions Pygmalion, 1982.

Bornecque, R. *Briançon.* Ville de Briançon, 1985.

_____. *La France de Vauban.* Grenoble: Editions Arthaud, 1984.

Brisach, C. *Le Musée des plans-reliefs.* Paris: Editions Pygmalion, 1981.

Bruant, Y. *Les Traités d'architecture militaires française à la fin du XVIe et au début du XVIIe siècles.* Paris: Picard, 1988.

Bulletin de la Société des Sciences, Lettres et Arts de Bayonne. *Vauban et les fortifications des Pyrénées-Atlantiques.* Bayonne: La Bibliotheque, 1984.

Châtillon, Claude. *Topographie française ou representation de plusieurs villes, bourgs, châteaux, places, forteresses.* Paris: Editions Boissevin, 1655.

De Roux, A. *Villes neuves urbanisme classique.* Paris: Editions Rempart, 1997.

De Roy van Zuydewijn, N. *Neerlands Veste: Langs vestingsteden, forten, linies en stellingen.* Den Haag: SDU Uitgeverij, 1988.

Dogen, M. *L'Architecture militaire moderne, ou Fortification ... mise en français par H. Poirier.* Amsterdam: Uitgeverij Elzevier, 1648.

Dollar, J. *Vauban à Luxembourg.* Luxembourg: RTL Edition, 1983.

Durant, W. and A. *The Age of Louis XIV.* New York: Simon & Schuster, 1963.

Faucherre, N. *Places fortes, bastion du pouvoir.* Paris: Editions Rempart, 1986.

Goubert, P. *Louis XIV et vingt millions de Français.* Paris: Editions Fayard, 1966.

Groupements d'Etudes Rétaises. *L'Enquête de Vauban en 1681.* Saint-Martin-de-Ré, 1985.

Haettel, J.P. *Vauban aux frontières de l'Est.* Strasbourg: Editions Le Verger, 1997.

Halévy, D. *Vauban.* Paris: Editions Grasset, 1923.

Haye, T. *Het Dagelijks leven in het midden van de 17e eeuw.* Amsterdam: Pictura Uitgeverij, 1962.

Historia Thématique. *Vauban l'homme de l'année.* No. 106. Paris: Editions Tallendier, 2007.

Hogg, I. *A History of Artillery.* London: Hamlyn, 1974.

Labatut, J.P. *Louis XIV un roi de gloire.* Paris: Imprimerie Nationale, 1984.

Lazard, Pierre E. *Vauban 1633–1707.* Paris: Editions Félix Alcan, 1934.

Lebrun, F. *le XVIIème siècle.* Editions Armand Colin, 1986.

Lepage, J.D. *Vestingbouw stap for stap.* Zutphen: Uitgeverij Walburg Pers, 1992.

Méthivier, H. *Louis XIV.* Paris: Presses Universitaires de France, 1950.

Ministère de la Défense/SGA. *Sentinelles de pierre, forts et citadelles sur les frontières de France.* Paris: Editions d'Art Editions Somogy, 1996.

Mongrédien, G. *La Galerie des plans-reliefs.* Paris: Caisse Nationale des Monuments Historiques et des Sites, nd.

_____. *La Vie quotidienne sous Louis XIV.* Paris: Editions Hachette, 1948.

Musée des plans-reliefs. *Forts du littoral.* Paris, 1989.

Pagan, Blaise comte de. *Les Fortifications.* Paris: Editions Besongne, 1645.

Parent, M., and Verroust, J. *Vauban.* Editions Fréal, 1971.

Petitfils, J.C. *Louis XIV.* Paris: Perrin Editions, 1995.

Poppema, S., and Lepage, J.D. *Historische verdedigingswerken.* Amsterdam: Stichting Open Monumentendag, 1995.

Pujo, B. *Vauban.* Paris: Editions Albin Michel, 1994.

Rebelliau, A. *Vauban.* Paris: Editions Fayard, 1962.

Reinders, H.R. and De Bruin, C.A. *Nederlandse Vestingen.* Bussum: Uitgeverij Fibula van Dieshoeck, 1967.

Rorive, J.P. *La Guerre de siège sous Louis XIV en Europe et à Huy.* Bruxelles: Editions Racine, 1998.

Rowen, H. *A History of Early Modern Europe 1500–1815.* New York: Bobbs-Merrill, 1966.

Sauliol, R. *Le Maréchal de Vauban.* Paris: Editions Charles Lavauzelle, 1924.

Schukking, W.H. *De Oude Vestingwerken van Nederland.* Amsterdam: Uitgeverij Allert de Lange, 1941.

Schulten, C.M. *Het Leger in de zeventiende eeuw.* Bussum: Uitgevrij Fibula van Dieshoeck, 1969.

Severin, J. *Vauban, Ingénieur du Roi.* Paris: Editions Fayard, 1962.

Stichting, Menno van Coehoorn. *Atlas van Historische Vestingwerken in Nederland.* (Limited edition not published.)

Tapié, V.L. *The Age of Grandeur: Baroque Art and Architecture.* New York: Praeger, 1961.

Truttmann, P. *Fortification, architecture et urbanisme aux XVIIème et XVIIIème siècles.* Service Culturel de la Ville de Thionville, 1976.

Van Hoof, J. *Langs Wal en Bastion, Hoogtepunten uit de Nederlandse Vestingbouw.* Utrecht: Uitgeverij Matrijs, 1991.

Vauban, Sébastien Le Prestre de. *Abrégé des services du Maréchal de Vauban.* Ed. by A.M. Augoyat. Editions Ausselin, 1839.

Ville, Antoine de. *Les Fortifications du Chevalier de Ville.* Lyon: Editions J. Mallet, 1628.

Ville de Neuf-Brisach. *Neuf-Brisach, cité fortifiée de Vauban.* 1989.

Vincennes Castle. *French Army Archives.* Series A1, volumes 168 to 2421, covering the years 1661 to 1714.

Viollet-le-Duc, E. *Histoire d'une forteresse.* Paris: Editions Berger-Levrault, 1874.

Virol, M. *Vauban et la gloire du roi au service de l'état.* Paris: Presses Universitaires de France, 2003.

Warmoes, I. *Musée des plans reliefs.* Paris: Editions du Patrimoine, 1999.

Wenzler, C. *Architecture du bastion: l'art de Vauban.* Rennes: Editions Ouest-France 2000.

Zeller, G. *L'Organisation défensive des frontières du nord et de l'est au XVIIe siècle.* Paris: Editions Berger-Levrault, 1928.

Index

Abatis 90
Absolutism 10
Advance works 110–115
Aides (tax) 279
Aiming (artillery) 33–35
Aix Island 249, 251, 252
Alps (mountains) 194
Alsace (province) 8, 13, 27, 135, 143, 170, 180, 181, 187
Ambleteuse 148
Ammunition 34, 35, 37
Ancien and Neuf Brisach 82, 102, 185–187
Antibes 143, 207, 208
Armurerie 128
Arras 166
Arrow 113
Arsenal 127
Artillery regiments 32
Artillery tower 23, 79, 192, 213, 273
Artois (province) 9, 15, 18, 27, 143, 145, 147, 166
Ascent 87
Assault 51, 52
Ath 159, 160
Audenarde 167
Auxonne 192
Avesnes-sur-Helpe 164

Balovardo 79
Baroque (style) 1, 93, 124, 158
Barrack 124–126
Bastard musket 38
Bastia 64
Bastide 135
Bastille 78
Bastion 78–85
Bastioned front 78, 136
Bastioned tower 85, 86
Batardeau 91, 92, 98
Battery 115
Bayonet 21
Bayonne 121, 230, 231
Bazoches castle 17, 26
Béarn (province) 229
Beins, Jean de (engineer) 69, 196
Belfort 188, 189

Bellamarto, Jeromino (engineer) 242, 272
Belle-Île-en Mer 143, 257, 258
Bergues 156
Berm 90
Besançon 13, 189, 190
Billeting 124
Bishop's miter 114
Blanchard, Anne (historian) 20, 287
Blaye 93, 236, 237
Blockade 44
Bodin, Jean (philosopher) 10
Bomb 37
Bonnefons, Raymond of (engineer) 69
Bonnet 104
Bonnet de prêtre 114
Bordeaux 234–239
Bossuet, Jacques (theologist) 1, 10
Boulevard 79
Breach 50, 51
Breastwork 88
Brest 263, 264
Briançon 92, 133, 198, 199
Bridgehead 115
Brisach (scandal of) 11
Britain 22, 65, 139, 255, 285
Brouage 242, 243, 249
Bruant, Liberal (architect) 130
Bulwark 79

Calais 148, 149
Caliver 38
Camaret-sur-Mer 22, 264, 265
Camisards (protestants) 25
Canal du Midi 21
Candia (Heraklion, Crete) 45
Cannon 33, 34
Capitainerie 118, 119
Capitulation 52
Caponier 102, 103
Carcass 37
Carmignolle, Edmée de 7
Cartier, Jacques (explorer) 276
Cartography 139
Casemate 81–83

Caserne 124
Castle Fouras 249
Castle If 216, 217
Castle Queyras 200
Cavalier 84
Cavalry barrack 126
Champlain, Samuel de (explorer) 276
Charleroi 165, 166
Charles II (King of Spain) 24
Charles VIII (King of France) 31, 62, 218, 255
Château d'Oléron 252, 253, 254
Château Trompette 235, 236
Chatillon, Jean (engineer) de 45
Chicane 108
Choisy, Thomas de (engineer) 141, 145, 174
Church 133, 134
Circumvallation line 44, 56
Citadel 120–122
Citoni, Girolamo (engineer) 10
Clamping 83
Clerville, Louis-Nicolas, Chevalier de (engineer) 6, 9, 14, 18, 263
Coastal fort 117, 118
Coastal gun tower 119
Colbert, Charles (entrepreneur) 11
Colbert, Jean-Baptiste (minister) 11, 15, 16, 17, 138, 206, 212, 244, 249, 256, 257, 259, 263, 273, 276, 278, 279
Colbertism (doctrine) 16
Collioure 15, 221–223
Colmar-les-Alpes 25, 203, 204
Concarneau 24, 259
Condé-sur-l'Escaut 160
Construction of fortifications 135
Contravallation line 44
Cordon 90
Cormontaigne, Louis de (engineer) 283
Corned powder 31
Cornichon 110

Corps de guard 119, 128–130
Corsica Island 27, 64, 207
Count of Monte Cristo (fictional hero) 217
Counterfort 83
Counterguard 85, 103, 104
Counter-mine 76, 105, 106
Counterscarp 90, 105
Courtine 86, 87
Couvre-face 104
Covered way 76, 106
Crownwork 111, 112
Cunette 91
Curtain 86, 87

Dame 91, 92
D'Artagnan, Charles de Batz, count of (man of war) 167, 257
Dauphiné and Savoy 193, 195
Dead angle 83
Déblai 138
Demi-lune 101, 102
Descombes, Benjamin (engineer) 119, 153, 256, 271
Design of fortifications 134, 135
Detached works 115–117
De Ville, Antoine (engineer) 40, 69–71, 73
Dieppe 272, 273
Dîme (tax) 279
Disabled soldiers 130
Disease 130
Ditch 90–92, 137
Dormitory 125
Dos d'âne 92
Double glacis 109
Double tenaille 114
Doullens 67
Dragonnade 19, 277
Drawbridge 96, 97
Dry ditch 91
Duguay-Trouin, René (privateer) 269
Dumas, Alexandre (novelist) 167, 217
Dunkirk 14, 152, 153

Ear (or orillon) 69, 70, 80, 81, 136
Early fortification designers 60, 63
Echauguette 88–90
Ecoute 105
Edict of Fontainebleau 277
Edict of Nantes 242
Elvas 286
Embrasure 87, 88
Enfant de troupe 127
Engineer Corps 39–41, 65
Entrenched bastion 84, 85
Entrenched camp 123, 124, 246
Entrenched demi-lune 102

Entrenched hornwork 112
Entrevaux 205, 206
Enveloppe 71, 105
Errard, Jean (engineer) 40, 65–69, 147, 231
Esplanade 121

Fathom 135
Fausse-braie 99, 100
Fermiers Généraux 279
Ferré, Léo (singer and poet) 2, 122
Ferry, François (engineer) 207, 229, 230, 238, 239, 241, 242, 246
Firing angles 35, 60, 80, 116
Flank 60, 80, 81, 136
Flanking 71, 60, 80
Flèche (or freccia) 113, 115
Flooding 122, 123
Fontenelle, Bernard le Bovier de (writer) 27
Fort 84, 117
Fort Alycastre 213
Fort Barraux 196
Fort Bellegarde 229
Fort Boyard 252
Fort Carré 207, 208
Fort Chapus 254, 255
Fort de La Conchée 22
Fort de la Kénoque 155
Fort de La Pointe 250, 251
Fort de La Prée 244–245
Fort de La Rade 251
Fort des Bains 228
Fort du Montalban 61
Fort Estissac 212
Fort Exilles 63
Fort Joux 191, 192
Fort La Garde 227
Fort La Latte 269, 270
Fort Liberia 224, 225
Fort Louis du Rhin 21, 182, 183
Fort Lupin 117
Fort Médoc 239, 240
Fort Nieulay 150, 151
Fort Paté 238, 239
Fort Portzic 265
Fort Puymaure 61
Fort Queleu 283
Fort Roovere 55
Fort Saint André 190, 191
Fort Saint Elmo 222
Fort Saint Louis 211
Fort Salses 220
Fort Socoa 232, 233
Fort Tatihou 271
Fort Taureau 266, 267
Fortifications of Paris 143
Foundation 138
Fouquet, Nicolas (minister) 11, 257
Fraise 108

Franche Comté (province) 27, 188
François I (King of France) 2, 40, 65, 67, 192, 203, 206, 209, 214, 216, 218, 231, 240, 271
French colonies 276
French provinces 27
Fronde 8, 72, 143, 279
Frontenac, Louis de (explorer) 276
Fuerte del Aguila 261
Furnes 154, 155

Gabelle (tax) 279
Gabion 47, 50
Gallicanism 277
Garangeau, Jean-Simeon (engineer) 256, 264
Gardhouse 128–130
Garrison life 127
Gascogne (province) 229
Gate and gatehouse 92–95
Génie 40, 41, 135
Glacis 76, 108, 109
Governor's hotel 127
Gravelines 153, 154
Grenoble 195, 196
Grid plan 135

Half-counterguard 104
Half-moon 101
Hardouin-Mansart, Jules (architect) 131
Hendaye 234
Henri IV (King of France) 2, 19, 31, 66, 68, 69, 72, 130, 150, 195, 198, 215, 229
Herse 92
Home of Christian Charity 130
Honor of War 52
Hornwork 110–112
Hospital 130
Hot shot 35
Hôtel des Invalides (Paris) 17, 130, 131, 236
Huguenots (Protestants) 19, 20, 21, 25, 215, 238, 242, 277, 278, 280
Huningen 109, 114, 137, 187

Inundation 122, 123
Invalid 131
Invalides Church 27, 131
Italian military engineers 63, 65

Jacopolis-sur-Brouage 242
James II (King of England) 22
Jansenism 19, 277
Josefov 285

Knife edge 92
Knights of Saint John (or Hospitallers) 9, 65

La Chaise, François (confessor) 19, 277
La Hougue (naval battle) 271
La Motte-Villebert, François de (engineer) 145
Landau 181
Landrécies 163
Languedoc (province) 206, 207
Laon 69
La Rochelle 241–242
Latrine 88, 125
League of Augsburg 21, 22, 24
Le Havre 143, 271, 272
Le Palais 258, 259
Le Prestre, Albin 7, 274
Le Prestre, Emery 7
Le Prestre, Paul 17
Le Prestre, Sébastien *see* Vauban
Le Quesnoy 94, 162
Leszcinski, Stanislas (Duke of Lorraine) 10
Le Tellier, François-Michel (Louvois's son and successor) 249
Levasseur de Néré, Jacques (engineer) 276
Lighthouse 118, 216, 223, 271
Lille 12, 109, 137, 157–159
Loading (musket) 38
Logistics 56
Longwy 174
Lorient 259, 260
Lorraine (province) 10, 18, 27, 135, 142, 143, 170
Louis XIII (King of France) 2, 7, 8, 40, 69, 72, 178, 195, 198, 212, 218, 221, 234, 241, 242, 263, 272
Louis XIV (King of France): and Absolutism 10, 11; death 28, 29; and decision to build fortification 134; and fortifications 142; and France's natural frontier 12; and French colonies 25, 277; and the Fronde 8; gifts to Vauban 13, 56; patron of the arts 1, 54; refusal of fortification project 143, 258, 272; and relief maps collection 139; and religion 19, 134, 277; and siege warfare 42, 57
Louis XV (King of France) 29
Louis XVI (King of France) 271
Louisiana (American territory) 276
Louvois, François-Michel Le Tellier marquis de (minister) 2, 5, 6, 7, 11, 14, 31, 44, 73, 81, 103, 124, 130, 134, 138, 139, 142, 143, 147, 158, 187, 200, 206, 220, 223, 256, 273, 278

Lunet 104, 107, 113
Luxembourg 18, 49, 168–170

Maastricht 45, 48, 167, 168
Machiavelli, Niccolò (writer and philosopher) 10
Maginot Line 18, 123, 143, 144, 179, 200
Magistral line 87
Maintenon, Françoise d'Aubigné, Marquise de (Louis XIV's wife) 19, 275, 277, 278
Maison de la Charité Chrétienne 130
Marchi, Francesco de (engineer) 58
Maria-Theresa of Austria 9, 19
Marlborough, John Churchill, duke of (military commander) 26, 153, 160, 167
Marolois (engineer) 114
Marseille 214–216
Martigues 216
Matchlock musket 38, 39
Maubeuge 163, 164
Menin 156, 157
Mercenaries 52
Merde à Vauban! 122
Merlon 88
Metz 178, 179
Mézières 171, 172
Middle ages fortifications 59, 77, 118, 142, 199, 269
Military building 124–134
Mine 51
Monk 91, 92
Montdauphin 202, 203
Montlouis 19, 225, 226
Montmédy 173, 174
Montmélian 197, 198
Montreuil-sur-Mer 146, 147
Montroyal 179, 180
Morlaix 266
Mortar 36, 37
Musketeer 39
Muzzle loading 32, 34, 36

Nancy 10, 11, 18, 142
Navarre (province) 229
Nec Pluribus Impar 33
Nine Years' War 21–24
Noyen, Sebastien van (engineer) 165

Officers' pavilion 126, 127
Oisivetés 26, 274–280
Old Dutch fortification (style) 100
Oléron Island 14, 240, 249, 251–254
Operation Jubilee 273
Organisation Todt 150, 242, 261

Orgue 92, 93
Orleans, Philippe of (regent) 29
Orsoy 15
Osnay, Jeanne of (Vauban's wife) 11
Outworks 106–115

Paciotto, Francesco de (engineer) 62
Pagan, Blaise de (engineer) 40, 65, 71–74, 80, 288
Palisade 90, 108
Parallel 45–51
Paré, Ambroise (surgeon) 130
Parent, Michel (historian) 44
Parpaillots (Protestants) 19
Pas-de-souris stair 107
Perpendicular fortification 285
Perpignan 219, 210
Pertuis Breton 240
Pertuis of Antioche 240
Phalsburg 181, 182
Philippe V (King of Spain) 24, 25
Philippeville 164, 165
Pierrier 37
Pignerol 201, 202
Pillory 134
Place of arms 107, 121, 124
Port de Bouc 216
Port Louis 261, 262
Port Man 212
Portcullis 92, 98
Porte 92, 93
Post 115
Poste de police 132
Postern 91
Powder house 127, 128
Prats-de-Mollo 225, 226
Pré Carré 18, 25, 144, 145, 151, 154, 155, 159, 160, 163, 165, 171, 172
Priest's cap 114
Principle of command 76, 99
Prison 132
Projects of works to be made 134
Projet de Dixme Royale 26, 279, 280
Projet des ouvrages à faire 134
Protestant immigration 20
Prussia 20, 26, 175, 187
Prussian system 285

Quebec (Canada) 276
Quentovic 147
Queue d'aronde 114

Rampart 79, 82, 83, 86, 90, 106
Ravelin 101
Redan 113, 115
Redoubt 115, 116
Redoute de l'Aiguille 248

Redoute de l'Île Madame 250
Redoute de Sablanceaux 246
Redoute des Portes 246
Redoute du Martray 247
Reduit 71, 76, 84, 85, 102, 122, 154, 158, 185, 221, 233, 251, 271
Ré Island 17, 84, 244–247
Relief Map 139, 140
Remblai 138
Réunions à la Couronne 18, 21, 22, 23
Revetment 79, 82
Révocation of Nantes Edict 19–21, 209, 278
Richelieu, Armand Duplessis, Cardinal of (minister) 7, 40, 72, 150, 212, 213, 218, 242, 243, 246, 249, 254, 263
Ricochet fire 21, 35, 108
Riquet, Pierre-Paul (engineer) 21, 275
River Eure aqueduct 18
Rochefort 90, 95, 117, 127, 240, 241, 244, 246–248, 251, 252
Rocroi 7, 144, 171
Rodin, Auguste (sculptor) 150
Rojas, Cristobal de (engineer) 261
Rorive, Jean-Pierre (historian) 139, 288
Roussillon (province) 9, 14, 18, 27, 141, 218, 219, 228

Saint Denis Gate 53
Saint-Jean-Pied-de-Port 70, 71
Saint-Malo 266–269
Saint-Marguerite Island 208, 209
Saint-Martin-de-Ré 93, 114, 122, 245, 246
Saint-Omer 151, 152
Saint-Tropez 67
Saint-Vaast-La-Hougue 77, 270, 271
Sally 101, 108, 122
Sally port 91, 101
Sapper 41
Sarrelouis (Saarlouis) 175
Scarp 89, 90, 91
Shrapnel 34, 37, 38
Scons 115
Sedan 172, 173
Seignelay, Jean-Baptiste Colbert marquis of (Colbert's son and minister) 143, 256, 273
Sélestat 184, 185
Sentry-box 88, 89

Seyne-les-Alpes 203–205
Siege warfare 41, 42–58
Single tenaille 114
Sisteron 68
Solidor Tower 266, 268
Sortie 108
Spanish Succession, War of the 24–26
Speklin, Daniel (engineer) 115
Stenay 43
Stevin, Simon (engineer) 115
Strasburg 183, 184
Sully, Maximilien de Bethunes, duke of (minister) 40, 65, 66
Sun King see Louis XIV
Surcouf, Robert (privateer) 269
Swallow's tail 114

Tablette 90
Taille (tax) 279
Tarade, Jacques (engineer) 180
Tartaglia, Nicolo (engineer) 106
Tax 279
Tax collection 279
Tenaille 100, 101, 113, 114
Thionville 175, 176
Toul 177
Toulon 209–212
Tour Royale 211
Traverse 67, 84, 102, 106, 108, 125
Treaty of Aix-la-Chapelle 13, 14, 16, 142, 144, 168, 189
Treaty of Nimegue 18, 21, 142, 144, 159, 160, 163, 166, 168, 174, 180, 188, 189
Treaty of Ryswyck 23, 24, 142, 144, 168, 183, 185
Treaty of the Pyrenees 9, 143, 218, 225
Treaty of Utrecht 15, 25, 144, 153
Twelve Apostles 39

Underground warfare 105, 106
Uniform 39
United Provinces 13, 22
Urban riots 279

Valenciennes 160, 161
Valetta (capital of Malta) 72
Van Coehorn, Menno (engineer) 115
Vauban, Sébastien le Prestre marquis de: on agriculture and inland navigation 274, 275; and coastal defense 117, 118; collaborators 73, 141, 145,

170, 195 218, 229, 256; on colonies 275; in command at Camaret 22, 265; and design of fortifications 134, 135, 244; disgrace and death 26; fortresses built by 141; and Génie 41; and Huguenots 20, 21, 277; and inspection journeys 15, 16, 20, 22, 134, 274 ; last campaign 26; legacy in France and abroad 282–286 reputation 2; personal patrimony 6; personality 5; on politics and nobility 278, 279; practical manuels 51, 132, 138; predecessors 65–73 rebellious Frondeur 8; on relief maps 139; on religion 277, 278; and rivalry with Clerville 13, 14, 18, 141; as secret diplomat 11, 15, 200; sick leave 22; and siege warfare 42–58 spying at Namur 44; on taxes 279; "three Systems" 72–76; as urbanist 135; and use of entrenched camp 123, 124; and use of flooding 122, 123; and use of mortar 37; views on fortification 73, 76, 97, 100, 108, 114, 117, 123, 135, 142; youth 7
Verceil 200, 201
Verdun 68, 177, 178
Ville de garnison 126
Villefranche-de-Conflent 223–225
Villefranche-sur-Mer 62
Vitry-le-François 64, 65
Vollant, Simon (architect) 12, 158
Voltaire (writer and philosopher) 1

Walker-Durnford, Elias (engineer) 276
Wallwalk 87, 88
War of Devolution 13
Water supply 130, 131
Watergate 98, 99
Weather in siege 56
Well 131
Wet ditch 91
Wicket 92
Willem III of Orange-Nassau (stadhouder of Holland and King of England) 16, 22, 23, 167
William the Conqueror (Duke of Normandy) 272